Elect*able*

Electable

WHY AMERICA HASN'T PUT A WOMAN IN THE WHITE HOUSE . . . YET

Ali Vitali

DEY ST.
An Imprint of WILLIAM MORROW

DEY ST.

HarperCollins books may be purchased for educational, business, or sales promotional use. For information, please email the Special Markets Department at SPsales@harpercollins.com.

FIRST EDITION

Library of Congress Cataloging-in-Publication Data has been applied for.

ISBN 978-0-06-305863-7

22 23 24 25 26 LSC   10 9 8 7 6 5 4 3 2 1

For Josephine:
Who inspired every good thing about this book—and about me. I
love you. Thanks for always saving me the good chocolates.

Tomorrow, our seeds will grow.
All we need is dedication.

—LAURYN HILL, "EVERYTHING IS EVERYTHING"

The Trail Map

Introduction:
The Assignment   1

1   The "Audacity" of Joe Biden:
Chosen, but Not Elected (November 2020)   17

2   Kamala Harris and the Sparkly Jacket:
Authenticity (February 2019)   35

3   Memorial Day Weekend:
Campaigning While Female (May 2019)   49

4   Kamala Harris:
The Rules of Engagement (June 2019)   69

5   One Night in Washington Square Park:
Using History to Make Herstory (September 2019)   93

6   Who We Take Seriously:
The Qualification Question (November 2019)   119

7   Can a Woman Win?
The Electability Question (January 2020)   145

8 New Hampshire:
Reckoning with the Inevitable (February 2020)   167

9 Nevada:
Going Down Swinging (February 2020)   183

10 And Then There Were None:
Opportunity, Lost. Again. (March 2020)   207

11 "It's Just Time":
Female VP Candidates and the Mystical Gender Gap
(Spring 2020)   231

12 "Just Not That Woman":
What Hillary Learned (September 2020)   263

13 Madam Vice President:
How Kamala Navigates Being First (January 2021)   287

14 "I'd Love to See It in My Lifetime" (March 2022)   303

Acknowledgments   319
Notes   323

—————— ∧ ——————

Introduction: The Assignment

Tell me what I can tell you."

It was just after Election Day in November 2020, and I hadn't seen or spoken to Senator Elizabeth Warren in months—which was weird given I'd just spent a year following her into every union hall and candidate cattle call (and even a few McDonald's) on her quest for the presidency. A week after she dropped out in early March 2020, the pandemic hit and the lockdowns came and, well, I don't have to tell you, everything changed.

But here we were again: a woman who could've been president and her former assigned-beat reporter. Her hands curled around a mug of tea and face beaming into my living room from her DC apartment, Warren had a few questions about what I was working on now.

I'm focused on "why we haven't had a female president, after a race that saw more women run than ever before," I said. I had my book pitch down to a well-practiced art form at that point.

"So," Warren replied, ever the professor, "how are you gonna answer that question?"

"I don't know," I laughed. Shockingly, that wasn't an answer I'd been asked for yet. *I was still working on it! I hadn't done all the research yet! And hey, aren't I the one asking the questions here?!*

"I'm working on it."

"Yeah, good, good," she deadpanned slowly. "I was working on it, too."

We both laughed, but it wasn't really funny.

We knew the year that we'd just lived through—experienced from different sides of the same small-town town halls and polling places and spin rooms—was unique, until it wasn't. A primary that saw more female candidates run for president than ever before, and a primary that ended with none of them left standing as the victor. A massive, diverse Democratic field that was whittled down to . . . two (and then one) older white men who looked like almost all of the presidents America had had before.

There was some disappointment among some voters initially, but ultimately it didn't dampen Dems' determination for the fight ahead. That Joe Biden was the one chosen to take the Democratic mantle at such a do-or-die moment for the party was either a foregone conclusion or an utterly shocking finish, depending on which political watchers you talked to. Both would be right.

Biden's competitors, detractors, and allies alike chalked his nomination up to Democratic voters wanting a familiar entity, a tried-and-true politician whom they knew and trusted to go up against, and beat, President Donald Trump. Someone electable and likable, but tough and capable. Someone who carried little risk.

In these assessments of how Biden rose to the top, there were double meanings. Overt political explanations, with subtle gendered undertones. What made someone trusted or tried and true enough to go up against Trump? What had America so convinced that Biden was the "risk-averse" or "electable" choice? And could we ever confidently apply those descriptors and assumptions to a female candidate—after 2016, in 2020 or in any presidential election thereafter?

These were questions I sat with during the early months of the pandemic and into the general election. My attempts to think them over and, maybe, find some answers are the point of these pages. When friends have asked me, "Okay, why haven't we had a woman president yet?" I joke: "I don't want to shock you but, it's sexism."

The real explanation, of course, is hardly that simple. Some of the women who ran and lost were simply bad candidates or ran bad campaigns. That happens with male candidates, too. And yet. The structures that make up the tent poles of the presidential process are often tilted in favor of certain candidates but slanted against others—including, and especially, women and candidates of color. Those structures range from the political parties themselves and the kingmakers within them, to the ·complicated dynamics of presidential primaries (as opposed to general elections), to the complex biases of the electorate. From who Americans view as qualified, to who the media and party gatekeepers deem electable, to the ways candidates are given the space (in the media and on the campaign trail) to present themselves as authentic political figures and people.

At its core, the invisible scaffolding that holds up the world of presidential politics was built by straight white men, for straight white men, to maintain power for—*yep*—straight white men. The ways that media covers and gauges the successes of campaigns and candidates are also implicitly steeped in this same framework. To be non-male, non-white, or non-heterosexual means working within a system that wasn't meant for you, while also shouldering the burden of bending and redefining these structures and institutions once you establish power within them. After all, we rarely specify when talking about a "male candidate" or "male lawmaker."

These fundamental, structural inequities were finally illustrated for me in a Fiona Apple song, blaring on my car speakers during one of my many drives to Joe Biden's home base of Wilmington, Delaware, in the summer of 2020.

"I grew up in the shoes they told me I could fill. Shoes that were not made for running up that hill. And I need to run up that hill, I need to run up that hill. I will, I will, I will . . ."

Driving northbound on I-95, I'd finally, if accidentally, found what I'd been looking for: an explanation that encompassed the frustration, and the opportunity, of the last few years. One that applied not just to the women

who ran, but—as you'll see in these pages—to me and the female colleagues around me, too. That sometimes the complex, multilayered, and
multifaceted explanation I'd been looking for could be summed up simply
as not being given the right shoes that'll get you to the top of the hill.

There is plenty of literature, and data, and academic work in this space
about women pursuing higher office that a real-time cable news cycle just
isn't equipped to parse through, especially not the way news develops and
breaks so rapidly in real time. And that's also part of what I tried to infuse
here, in these pages of explorations of moments that I reported on for
viewers and readers from 2015 to 2022. I thought about these political
outcomes first as a political reporter, because that's what I am, but also
as a woman. I benefited, in the 2016 cycle but also in 2020, from being
flanked in the traveling and D.C. press corps by other brilliant female
reporters and producers and embeds. Especially in the 2020 cycle, we
were more primed than ever to spot the backhanded compliments and
brushbacks and subtle double meanings with big implications because we
ourselves lived lives of backhanded compliments, brushbacks, and subtle
double meanings with big implications. That experience, plus companies
that urged us to bring our full selves to work, allowed me and us to better
relate to—and push back on—points of frustration from the campaigns
of women and people of color throughout the primary. That there is even
discussion of identifying and disrupting these unfair narratives is key to
eradicating them and leveling the playing field from the perspective of
gender and race.

Visibility and expansion of leadership archetypes is another essential.
The year 2020 itself was paramount. Six women ran for president—the
most at one time, in any presidential cycle ever—all with the goal of doing
something that has (still) literally never been done before: becoming the
first female president of the United States.

Their bids came after a watershed midterm cycle for female candidates, where it wasn't just a case of Congress being flooded with more
female and non-white electeds than ever (though that did happen), but
it was further proof that women and people of color win at the same

rates as white male candidates do when they run and make it out of a primary, into a general election. A critical point to prove regardless, but especially in the Age of Trump when skepticism about the detrimental effect of Hillary Clinton's gender on the 2016 election results permeated political chatter.

The women of 2020 ran on Hillary's shoulders, as the first woman to ever earn the title of a major political party's nominee for president and the first woman to win the presidential popular vote. But she stood on the shoulders of the women who ran for president before her, too. A mere twenty-two of them throughout history—including the 2020 Six.

That number begins with Victoria Woodhull, the first woman to ever run for president, in 1872. At the time, women couldn't even legally vote. It includes Gracie Allen—half of the comedy duo Burns and Allen—who in 1940 ran for president as a publicity stunt. "In the entire history of the United States, there's never been a woman president," her husband and comedic partner, George Burns, pointed out when she "announced." "Yeah, isn't that exciting?" Allen quipped. "I'll be the first one!" She dropped out months later, but still earned thousands of write-in votes on Election Day.

The pack is made up of Republicans, like Elizabeth Dole in 2000, Michele Bachmann in 2012, and Carly Fiorina in 2016. It's Democrats like Shirley Chisholm, the first Black woman to seek a major party's nomination in 1972. It's Patsy Mink's largely symbolic bid that same year to draw attention to the antiwar movement that made her the first Asian American woman to run. It's Carol Moseley Braun in 2004. And of course, Hillary Clinton in 2008 and 2016.

Add in the women who have been vice-presidential nominees—Geraldine Ferraro in 1984, Sarah Palin in 2008, and Kamala Harris in 2020 among them—and you'll still fall shy of forty females who have dared to vie for America's highest political offices in more than two hundred years of American history. Thirty-two women. And the only reason the numbers are that high is because six ran just last election cycle in 2020. Over this period of *her*story, only one woman earned the title of nominee—and Hillary Clinton only just accomplished that in 2016. Just one woman has earned the title "Madam Vice President"—and that took until 2021.

It was progress that demanded celebration, but 2020 also laid bare some concerning realities: not that a woman can't be president, but that Americans may still be easily scared off from believing that women can be viable, trusted, winning options. And if these voters are not *personally* skeptical—and I've met dozens and dozens who are—they're concerned that their neighbors will be. After all, politics is ultimately about winning and losing. As with sports, no one likes to bet on the losing team; you want to pick a winner. And at this point in presidential history, the track record shows only male winners. Forty of them.

It's why when we close our eyes—go ahead, close 'em—and imagine a president of the United States, we're probably conjuring an image of a man, middle-aged, most likely white, in a suit and tie, sitting behind an imposing wooden desk or standing behind a podium adorned with the presidential seal.

It's why, in politics and political reporting, people talk about some mythical, unteachable quality of being "presidential"; of feeling, and look-ing, like a leader. It's something reporters had been trained somewhere along the way to call out as raw political talent; not mentioning that this intangible quality likely stems, subconsciously or consciously, from what we've been primed to accept as presidential. From someone's skin color, gender, and the fact that white male candidates start off by looking like what we'd always seen as politically successful. The embodiment of the Great Man Theory: leaders who are born, not made, with essential traits that make them great leaders.

The political-upstarts-we-never-saw-coming-until-they-beat-the-odds-and-won were mostly ambitious and male and the very profile of a candi-date that American politics has rewarded for political risk-taking, even if their resumés weren't quite right or they lacked foreign policy experience or they flip-flopped on policy. That diamond-in-the-rough, just-something-about-them quality? It comes from being a white man in politics—which, of course, is why it's so unteachable for everyone else. There's "just something about him" that makes us want to explore their potential further.

There's also a well-worn "just something about her," too. You've heard it before and you'll hear it again. It usually crops up around female candidates who are openly seeking power, showing their ambition, exuding the stereotypically masculine leadership qualities required to attain these offices but penalized for doing so. It sounds like, "I want to vote for a woman, just not *that* woman." Or, "I can't quite place my finger on it, but there's *just something about her* that I don't like" or "don't trust" or "can't vote for."

But as more cracks are put in the electoral glass ceiling, at the presidential level and below, the wider the cracks become and a broader swath of women and BIPOC can make their way through. There may not be a widely embraced parallel "Great Woman Theory," but that doesn't mean female candidates aren't forcing us to create one in real time with each new candidacy and electoral success. Eventually, the ripples of those electoral gains make a wave—like in 1992, a mere thirty years ago, when four women were elected to serve as senators in the "year of the woman." Small by today's standards of "waves," but still a celebrated—if tolerated—phrase, then and now.

"Calling 1992 'The Year of the Woman' makes it sound like 'The Year of the Caribou' or 'The Year of the Asparagus,' " Senator Barbara Mikulski, the first Democratic woman to win and hold a Senate seat not previously held by her husband, said at the time. "We are not a fad, a fancy, or a year."

And yet, more "years of the . . ." followed.

In 2018, for the "pink wave" of predominantly Democrats in Congress, and then again in 2020, when Republicans made their own record gains adding women to their congressional body. As their ranks grow in government, the outright novelty of female leadership fades. And more broadly, studies show that as women have joined the workforce and attained leadership positions since the 1960s, outdated and previously held gender stereotypes—like men being seen as smarter and more competent than women—have (thankfully) evaporated.

But even as those stereotypes disintegrate, others hold fast. Men are still seen as more "agentic"—decisive, independent, strong, confident, calm in emergencies—than women. Women, on the other hand, are seen as more communal—able to handle people well, compassionate, nurturing, sensitive, patient.

"We think of them as different," Madeline Heilman, a psychology professor at New York University and expert in bias and gender stereotypes, told me of how society conceptualizes leadership qualities between the genders. When women *do* act in more stereotypically male ways, they violate the way society thinks they "should" act. In this should/shouldn't structure, according to Heilman's and other work, women shouldn't self-promote or seek power or speak authoritatively or be competitive or even show anger.

"They shouldn't be leaders in a traditional way," she said. "And when they do these things, which really are necessary to be successful, to move a career along in more traditionally male domains, there are penalties for that." These stereotypes, perceptions, and impacts on women are foundational for considering how women are adjudicated in these pages as presidential candidates.

Because, of course, the United States remains far from gender parity in government, far from reflective of its population, and far behind other democratic countries that have elected female executive leaders. Many of those countries have elevated female leaders already due to their styles of government. In several cases, these "first" female prime ministers or chancellors have risen to top leadership positions within parliamentary governments that require consensus-building in order for the governments to actually form, and lend to female leaders being elevated to top positions. If the U.S. were a parliamentary system, for instance, House Speaker Nancy Pelosi could already claim the mantle of America's first female president. But of course, that's not our way. And in several of the instances where women rose to the top first, they came from the conservative ideological wings of the political spectrum—lending to the idea that a conservative or Republican woman might be primed to assume the mantle of Madam President first. It may surprise you who thinks so, too.

But in this quest, as gains have been celebrated, the failures cast long and enduring shadows. When men lose elections to other men, no one furrows their brow and contemplates whether or not any man who runs after them will have to prove his electability anew. And yet in 2020 this was a foundational, if unfair, question, given 2016's result. One that informed media and voter views of female candidates in the Democratic field before it had even formed.

I heard people talk about Hillary Clinton's loss in all kinds of ways. I met voters who were furious and voters who were thrilled. Voters who saw it as a clear result of sexism and voters who saw it as a result of Russian tampering or then–FBI director James Comey, whose last-minute decision to reopen an investigation adjacent to Clinton's emails came mere days before Election Day. (Clinton herself says it was some combination of all three.) Voters who realized voting for a third-party candidate probably was a bad idea, in retrospect. Voters who sat out and wished they hadn't. Voters who voted exactly the way they wanted—"fake news" be damned—because they agreed with "lock her up" and "Trump That Bitch." And voters who *just knew* that arguably The Most Qualified Candidate to Ever Run would, unfortunately/of course, lose to arguably The Least Prepared Man to Ever Do the Same.

Women, especially, seemed to dwell on that last part. The unfinished business of it all. One woman I met on my first trip to Iowa in 2019 wasn't sure who'd get in the race—and was very sure it was too early to talk about it—but simply told me that of the candidates who could run, "I like the women." It was far from the last time I'd hear that sentence. And it also didn't mean women would come to the electoral call of their sisters in political arms. We'll explore that here, too.

But women were mobilizing. Not just to run—though we would see Warren run alongside senators Amy Klobuchar, Kamala Harris, and Kirsten Gillibrand, as well as Congresswoman Tulsi Gabbard and author

Marianne Williamson—but to volunteer and fight. I met these women while they marched at Women's Marches, gripping hand-painted signs and pink hats, at the back of elementary school gymnasiums as they waited to greet candidates, and five days before the Iowa Caucus on a below-freezing day twenty minutes outside of Des Moines in Clive, Iowa, door-knocking for Amy Klobuchar.

Becky Visconti and Lara Horgan were here for the chance to preach the gospel of Amy. They were part of a small group of women who'd rented a van to go to their local 2017 Women's March. "We went up crying, we came home laughing and energized, and we just promised each other we're never going to let this stop."

Now, with the campaign's namesake senator stuck in D.C. for Trump's first impeachment trial, here they were. Their "turf" lists—addresses of persuadable voters assigned to them by the campaign—in hand, they curled their gloved fingers into loose fists and readied their best persuasive arguments and smiles for when the door opened to their knocks. And in case anyone had questions about who they were with, Lara's blond hair cascaded over big, green circular earrings bearing the Klobuchar campaign logo. She'd made them herself, she told me proudly.

This was democracy at—admittedly—its most tedious, but also at its finest.

"We identify with her, and we want a woman as president. And a smart woman, and one with experience like she has," Becky said of Klobuchar. "The main thing is her integrity and honesty. That's my dream for this country. That we have a leader *like that*."

Being "like that"—honest, with integrity—should've been a low bar to clear for the would-be most powerful leader in the world. But in the Age of Trump, Becky's threshold for positive leadership felt to many voters I talked to like a prayer badly in need of an answer from a Political God that might have stopped listening. To these Democratic voters, "like that" meant a return to the foundational morality and competency that Trump sorely lacked.

But it was clear talking to Becky and Lara that "like that" also meant something more personal. "Like that" meant *like me*. Hillary Clinton's 2016 run had shown them they could vote for someone *like them*. That candidates who were reflections of themselves existed—and could even, someday, win, even if Clinton didn't. The marches and midterms that followed her loss showed them how women who had never been politically engaged before could start a national movement. They were starting again here in Iowa. The question, in 2020, was what kind of fruit this movement would bear.

We walked and knocked for several more hours, each door opened and voter interacted with deepening the volunteers' resolve. Returning from one house, Becky told me, "One lady even said, 'I just needed someone to knock on our door.' "

I also needed this. I lived for it, if I'm being honest.

The 2020 cycle was, for me, a continuation of the journey I began in 2015. I was a twenty-five-year-old production assistant who left a predictable schedule in cable television, a stable (if slightly boring) relationship, and all her friends and family in New York City to chase a dream of covering a presidential campaign as one of NBC News's political embeds. I readied myself for the whirlwind that our political director, Chuck Todd, advised (and warned) was like getting a PhD in political journalism in just eighteen months.

Chuck would know, having covered multiple presidential campaigns from local dinners to the White House briefing room before landing in one of Washington's most coveted chairs as host of NBC's *Meet the Press*. For most viewers, Chuck's incisive political mind cuts through their airwaves "if it's Sunday." For me, he's been a mentor every day since I started reporting. To come up in the "school of Chuck Todd" is to know the inside baseball and the 30,000-foot view; the minutiae of Washington paired with the voter insight you can only get from going outside of D.C. and New York City. But the only way to gain entry into this exclusive school in the first place is to have a palpable passion (read: borderline obsession) for politics. In 2015, that's what he saw in me.

I prepared to shlep gear—tripod, camera, microphones, and a backpack satellite (called a LiveU) that let us make TV from anywhere. To fly ceaselessly and sleep never. I imagined *The Boys on the Bus* (though with fewer boys and more women), shuttling from diner to diner. Glimpses of candidates being themselves—their *real* selves—during off-the-record drinks or in Q&As with the reporters who they were seeing more than their own families. I dreamed of sampling fried novelties on a stick at the Iowa State Fair and pressing candidates on the ways their policy platforms would reshape life for Americans

What I got was Donald Trump. I seethed to my then-boyfriend after my boss told me my assignment, frustrated not for political reasons but because the goal was to get a candidate who could go the long haul; who could win. *Now what?* I asked, defeated. Nevertheless, I deferred law school—the usual backup plan for anyone with ambitions that they don't quite know what to do with—and took my chance at the campaign trail, assuming I'd be without a candidate, and a job, by the convention in the summer of 2016 and bogged down in law books soon after. A week before Trump clinched the GOP nomination, I officially shelved my law school plan. And, well, you know how the rest of this story goes . . .

Trump won. I moved to Washington to cover his White House, trading history-imbued white everything for tacky, gold everything. I was catapulted into the most esteemed press corps in Washington, far faster than I would've gotten there otherwise. I was also burnt out, depressed, and struggling. My therapist eventually told me she thought I had PTSD from my eighteen months on the Trump trail. *Ridiculous,* I told her, *I'm a campaign reporter, not a war correspondent.* She was, of course, right.

I thought about leaving journalism, and took meetings with lobbying firms and friends in consulting. My LSAT scores were still good; I could even try law school, for real this time. I emailed Chuck, asking to talk. He agreed, but we never did. It was like he almost instinctively knew what I needed: a way out of Trump World in order to stay in political journalism. A new campaign experience to learn that not all candidates incite crowds against their press corps, that not all operatives will—figuratively and literally—try to screw you, and that not all politics comes from a place of fear. A few short weeks after my email, I was asked if I'd be up for getting back out on the road and covering the 2018 midterms. *Yes!*

Without thinking twice, I was off again. A shark swimming forward, because what else was I supposed to do? I traveled across the country covering marquee contests from Florida to North Dakota to Missouri to Texas and launching headlong into an uphill battle for a career in television.

Being on television is one of those bizarre jobs where to do it, you have to be good at it, but to get good at it, you have to start doing it. I was still shaky on camera, having done TV only sporadically since 2016, and usually only when no one else was available. I pitched myself for live shots on weekends and to work holidays, always coming ready with a new nugget of reporting from my sources to try to show that even though my "look" was off and my eyes got too wide when I was nervous (which was often), I could bring the goods: I could report. The 2018 midterms were my chance to prove I could play big.

"If you pitch stories that are too good," one manager warned me at the outset, "we'll probably just give them to *real* correspondents." Apparently, my stories were never "too good," because I ended up doing them all myself.

Then, after that was done, I went back on the road immediately for Decision 2020.

As I'm writing this book, Joe Biden is the president of the United States at one of the most tumultuous times in this country's history—with the COVID-19 pandemic still spreading throughout the country, albeit in less deadly fashion because of vaccines and boosters that hopefully more Americans will continue to take. It comes after covering a 2020 election that saw more women compete for the POTUS title than ever before, and with the memory of the 2016 election still fresh in the country's mind as chatter continues to grow about another Donald Trump bid for the nation's highest office. The more things change, the more they stay the same.

But that's not to say we've seen no change at all.

Kamala Harris is the first female, Black, and Asian American vice president of the United States. And multiple diverse colleagues are serving alongside her in Biden's cabinet. Republicans made record gains in 2020 as well, adding more than thirty women to their female congressional ranks, though Democrats still outpace them nearly three to one in the House and two to one in the Senate. Nevertheless, female GOP operatives say they feel the party has finally realized the political benefit of bolstering female candidacies. Better late than never. And as the 2024 presidential cycle kicks into gear, we will see women run again—although their political fates will largely be dictated by and tied to prominent men in both parties.

For Republicans, Trump remains the party's dominant figure, with male and female contenders alike hanging their future plans on what he decides to do. For Democrats, President Biden, at least as of this writing, says he plans to run for a second term. And should Trump tower over 2024 in the way he did in 2020, it's likely he'll stay the standard bearer for another Biden vs. Trump rematch. But should these men opt out—or not inspire the kind of fear that clears the field—we could see multiple women enter the presidential contest on both sides. And now, just before the peak of the 2022 midterms, seeing who comes out on the trail to help bolster their respective party in swing and marquee races will give us an early road map to their presidential aspirations.

These pages are steeped in my time on the road and my experiences reporting. My bosses happened to assign me the women of the race in 2020, first asking that I focus on Elizabeth Warren and Amy Klobuchar, then that I cover whoever Biden named as his VP pick. I'll admit that once we knew he'd pick a woman, I volunteered to be the one to follow her. My coverage of the day Warren dropped out—and the realization that history was lost again—was what inspired this larger exploration of *why*. That journey then evolved with Harris's elevation.

I've been lucky to talk to many of these change-maker candidates and lawmakers—past, present, and future—for this project. I embarked upon and researched this book with bipartisan vigor. Republicans, Democrats, former candidates, and potential future candidates were willing to share their candid assessments of their own bids with me, as well as the ways gender permeated those runs and their careers. My goal was to use their words and reflections to better illustrate the experience of running for president while female from the women who did it—and to bring you along for the ride of what it's been like to watch their journeys unfold.

Though I asked, some declined to speak to me, including Vice President Kamala Harris, despite her frequent eloquence on what it means to be the first but not last woman in the vice presidency. Talking with me for this book was—in the words of her team—"a No Go." I can only speculate about why they felt that dedicating time to talking about women's path to the presidency was not a good use of the vice president's time, but this was their decision, undoubtedly complicated by the dynamics of serving in the White House with Biden, a man Harris both lost to and could likely try to succeed. Thankfully, many others were willing to detail and analyze her past, present, and future role in the national political landscape.

Because that's what this book is about: the presidency and the woman who—whoever she is!—will eventually hold the title Madam President and occupy the Oval Office.

It's about the road that female candidates have traveled with the goal of getting there. It's a story about me—a woman who got to see, up close, more of them strive for the Oval Office at one time than ever before and who innately understood the invisible forces that, oftentimes, worked against them. It's that experience of covering all the women leaving the race that forced our collective reckoning with gender anew—and spurred conversations about, well, the need for a book like this one. And, because we're talking about something that's yet to happen, it's about what went wrong for past female candidates—politically and otherwise.

Some of it was bad politics—but some of it wasn't. Some of it was sexism within a political and media structure that still isn't quite sure how to handle female ambition in spaces that aren't traditionally female—but some of it wasn't. It's on the operatives and candidates to control the politics, but when it comes to the genderism and racism that we've seen permeate and impact the process, it's incumbent on everyone to disrupt it. Once you see it, it's hard to stop.

Eventually, it'll make you mad enough to do something about it.

You'll leave warm California with a fluffy jacket to canvass for the candidate you believe in. You'll don a pink pussy hat or hand-paint a giant sign and protest for the first time because you're just so mad you don't know what else to do. You'll urge your friends to vote for the person they believe in, because if they do then that candidate *can* win, regardless of whether anyone who looks like them has ever won before. Maybe you'll run for office yourself, joining the ranks of "moms in tennis shoes" and dynamic, young organizers from the Bronx who were moved to action against all odds. You'll see that the next women who run—for any office, but for our purposes here, for president—are electable. And that all the women who come after them can continue to run up the nation's steepest, slipperiest, rockiest hill, because we'll have put them in the right shoes. Finally.

My hope, then, is they'll be able to fill the biggest shoes of all—and any other shoes they want—after too many decades of being forced to run backwards and in heels.

—Ali Vitali, March 2022

1

The "Audacity" of Joe Biden

Chosen, but Not Elected

NOVEMBER 2020

My shift was over, but I wasn't ready to go home. I was wide awake, pacing America's Most Famous Parking Lot, despite not having slept more than a few hours a night the last few weeks. Caffeine and adrenaline make one helluva cocktail.

But how could I sleep now? This was the moment I'd worked toward for the last five years—from covering the first weeks of America under Donald Trump's influence as a candidate in 2015 to now, in November 2020, covering the first moments after a majority of Americans decided they wanted someone different. For me, the 2020 election was a continuation of 2016. These last five years were one long chain of political controversies and eroded norms, a film reel of democracy stretched to its breaking point set to the bizarre soundtrack of a Trump rally: "Nessun Dorma" and "You Can't Always Get What You Want" playing out our country's collective foundational principles as they foundered under Donald Trump.

On Saturday—four days after the polls had closed—Americans were learning the news about who had won the presidential election. Many spent the afternoon dancing, waving Biden-Harris signs, salty tears soak-

ing into the cloth of their masks. Exultant Biden-backers were spontaneously gathering everywhere you'd expect them to be. New York City.
Los Angeles. Washington, D.C. Chicago. Philadelphia. Atlanta . . .
Wilmington, Delaware. Far from a place that most Americans could easily point to on a map, it had become the center of the political universe
in the latter months of 2020, thanks to the pandemic that kept Joe Biden
close to home. As soon as the networks called the race, a crowd began
gathering here too, outside The Parking Lot, in anticipation of the victory
rally that Biden's campaign had been planning, then holding off on, then
re-planning all week.

The Biden team had set up a media row outside the Chase Convention Center here in Wilmington. A massive flag had been hoisted on a
crane above the area, waving to the Secret Service stationed at check-
points around the cement and greeting the steady stream of sleepless reporters who rolled in with the changing tides of their shifts. Our changing
of the MSNBC guard came daily, just before 3 a.m. My producer, Molly
Roecker, and I shuffled from our hotel across the street and into the lot to
relieve our colleague Mike Memoli from his post in front of the camera.
Mike and I had been splitting twelve-hour shifts on MSNBC, NBC News
NOW, and any other NBC-family platform that we were asked to join to
give the latest on Biden's waiting game.

Behind us, the stage had been half set since Election Day five days ago.
SUVs and trucks in Americana red, white, and blue were driven in from
a dealership nearby for the anticipated drive-in rally. Lights cast over the
stage, then went dark; mics tested "one, two three," then cut; candidate
speeches were prepared, then scrapped in favor of different remarks that
would keep Joe Biden and Kamala Harris visible on the airwaves, coming
right up to the line of declaring victory *eventually* but not declaring victory
right now while votes were still being counted.

That careful, purposeful, cautious approach was a far cry from what
the White House was doing. Trump falsely claimed he won on Election
Night, even with millions of votes still to be counted. "Stop the count,"
he said, as if that was how this worked. It's what he'd always promised

he would do if he lost: say the election was rigged, scream that he won anyway, gaslight about the results. Back in 2016 when he first crafted this built-in excuse, he didn't have to use it. Now, it was all he had.

Saturday morning on November 7th was the start of another Groundhog Day. Sources had been telling us for days that they expected to see Biden win Pennsylvania "tomorrow"; no, "tomorrow"; no, "tomorrow, it has to be." If they won PA, they'd win it all. Some of my sources were frustrated: *what were the networks waiting for?* The campaign was waiting on us to make it official, despite knowing they had the win based on the way mailed-in ballots were breaking for them, especially in historically Dem-heavy areas of the map.

The networks, for their part, all wanted to be careful. But they're always careful. The folks on our Decision Desk want to be accurate and err on the side of caution. They want to be right, and they really never (ever, ever) want to be wrong or have to retract a call. So, we all waited for victory's "i" to be dotted and her "t" to be crossed.

I stood in the same place I'd been standing for the last five days: on a two-foot-tall riser with my back turned to the parking lot, attention focused on the camera in front of me and the monitor displaying MSNBC's live air just underneath it. Molly stationed herself to my left with both ears listening to separate conversations: one on MSNBC—which matched what I was hearing in my earpiece—the other on the producer bridge, which was Molly's way to communicate with the control room if I had news to report or something to say on the air. While on standby for a hit that would never come, I took notes on the new vote totals MSNBC data guru Steve Kornacki was reporting from his famous Big Board in a studio at 30 Rockefeller Plaza. The key to "tap dancing," or filling time, on television is amassing as many facts as possible and organizing them into an overarching theme, creating lots of different steps that can be danced to the same music. But as I was scribbling ideas for my next steps, the music stopped.

"Okay, we have an announcement to make: Joe Biden is president-elect of the United States."

"They're saying it," I said, looking up at the return monitor flashing our election graphics: PRESIDENT-ELECT, JOE BIDEN. The former VP's smiling face in the corner of the screen, a big yellow check mark animated next to his new title. Literally checking Democrats' top agenda item off the list, four long years later.

You could almost hear the collective exhale of relief from Biden's staff. Now-at-ease campaign flaks and Democrats flooded my phone with messages as I stepped off the riser and delved into fresh reporting. They careened between euphoric highs—winning Wisconsin! massive turnout!—and manic lows—white women came out for Trump in bigger numbers than last time! Trump did better with Black Americans than any Republican since 2012! He upped his margins with Hispanic voters in the critical battleground states of Texas and Florida!

"Democrats have to acknowledge we do not fully understand a good chunk of this country," one Democratic strategist told me early in the week, at a point where Biden's prospects did not look nearly as rosy as they did now. Another operative, at one of the bleaker points in the Election Week waiting period, texted: "Put me in a coma and wake me up in 4 years."

Trump lost, yes, but he wasn't the only one. Democrats lost ground in the House. They would ultimately flip four Senate seats, half of them in Georgia due to years of grassroots organizing by Black women as well as good, strategic policy focus on providing Americans badly needed COVID relief in the form of direct stimulus checks, which Republicans had positioned themselves against. But broadly speaking, Biden's coattails didn't really usher in a wave of fellow Democrats with him, despite his campaign's strategy that sought to re-create the blue wave that washed over Congress in 2018. And while Barack Obama's former veep won a record-breaking number of votes, so did Trump. More than 74 million Americans believed that another four years of the forty-fifth president was preferable to the alternative. That couldn't be ignored. There were warnings in the data; signs that had to be heeded by the party going forward, Biden or not.

Still, all the sources who said "today would be the day" for Pennsylvania to deliver Biden the presidency were ecstatic about finally being right. But within the collective exhale of relief and jubilation from Biden-Harris voters, there was also some shrugging. Because to get to his electoral trouncing of Trump and become the forty-sixth president of the United States meant that Biden dashed directly through the hopes and historic prospects of six women running in the same Democratic primary cycle—more women running at one time than ever before.

We can't take that for granted. We'd seen women run before, alone in a pack of men. We'd seen women—one woman—win the Democratic nomination for president before. And that, weirdly and unfortunately, was all we'd seen. You had to specifically attend a Hillary Clinton event in 2016 if you wanted to see a Democratic woman run for president, or a Carly Fiorina event if you wanted to see a Republican woman do so. By contrast, in 2020, you could—and I did—spend a full day doing campaign trail coverage and not even realize until you packed it in that you'd just spent it with three different candidates . . . all of whom were women. The six women of 2020 ran on what Hillary Clinton had already built, while also showing how many different ways there were to run as a female leader in America. Most of these women, specifically the four senators, were not just running—but running viably and credibly. They were qualified, competent lawmakers with heavy policy portfolios. They attracted top staff and notched key endorsements. They all fell short of the ultimate prize.

This is not to say that the women stumbled solely because of their gender. It was a factor, and this book will detail how much of one and in what ways, but the usual political forces were also very much in play. All of these women lacked the national name recognition of a former two-term vice president. None of them had run for president before, meaning they needed to build out a massive national campaign infrastructure and a national donor base to pay for it. Their lists to solicit grassroots donations needed to be grown, in some cases from near-scratch.

The field's most formidably positioned female candidates were senators

Elizabeth Warren and Kamala Harris, each with her own established national brand, albeit for a very niche audience of cable news faithful and dedicated political observers. That's to say: even they had work to do to grow their public persona so Americans could get to know them. Comparatively, Senator Bernie Sanders had run for president just three years before and his campaign operation never really shut down after the 2016 primary. And Joe Biden . . . was former vice president Joe Biden. Of the Obama-Biden administration. Of eight years in the office adjacent to the one he wanted now. Of an historic and optimistic 2008 election that Democrats badly wanted to relive after the last four years. Biden's nomination closed the door to a female president in 2020. That failure is why this book exists in the first place. But his nomination also presents the promise of progress to come.

Once in the position of president-elect, Biden once again found himself on the verge of history—or at least, adjacent to it and having played a critical role in creating it. The parallel between serving under Barack Obama—America's first Black president—and serving with Kamala Harris—America's first Black, South Asian, and female vice president—wasn't lost on Biden.

On his final day in Wilmington as president-elect, he spoke from Delaware before coming to Washington for his own inauguration. There had been plans for him to take the train—one final Amtrak trip for the man colloquially known as "Amtrak Joe"—but it was scrapped due to security concerns. The train station, named in Biden's honor, stood decorated with bunting and flags for the arrival of the city's VIP who would never come to enjoy it.

Still, the terms Biden spent as VP and the term he'd soon start as president were inextricably linked. And they were on his mind that day. "Twelve years ago, I was waiting at the train station in Wilmington for a Black man to pick me up on our way to Washington, where we were sworn in as president and vice president of the United States of America. And here we are today, my family and I about to return to Washington to meet a Black woman of South Asian descent, to be sworn in as president and vice president of the United States," Biden said.

Biden's being Biden—an affable member of Washington's boys' club for decades—made him the consummate insider, but also the ideal candidate for heralding change from the inside out. While Obama and his team knew their presidential chances would not rise or fall solely on Joe Biden—running mates don't have that kind of electoral power—they knew he would bring a certain familiarity and comfort level to the ticket. Because while vice-presidential running mates don't win elections, they do have an indirect impact on the way voters think about the man at the top of the ticket. For anyone concerned with gaps in Obama's resumé, Biden's decades in D.C. provided reassurance—and a few gray hairs. But he also embodied the status quo, for anyone unsure of the change Obama was pitching, both in policy and in persona.

"He's not going to be saddled with the burden of racism that Obama was saddled with," the thinking went, according to a person close to Obama. "[Biden] can say things about police who are engaged in racist misconduct. He can talk in a language that's more direct" and not get as much backlash. "And he knows that. He knows he can push the envelope in ways others would have to tread more carefully."

Biden's stable and steeped-in-history leadership style allowed him to meet the moment—in 2008 and again in 2020. "In the wake of a tumultuous year and racial unrest, this older, working-class, white guy might be just what our country needs to make progress," the same person said of 2020.

Similarly, as Biden searched for his own Biden, his white maleness—an embodiment of what had always been—allowed him to reach for history again, this time by selecting a female running mate. The VP selection process, for all its sexist tropes about "ambitious women," brought not just history, but tangible proof that politics was no longer a game that could be played successfully by men alone. Biden saw it firsthand in 2018 from Iowa to Florida to California, talking with aides about the energy and excitement around female candidates he stumped for and using that information gleaned from the front lines to inform his own mindset in 2019 and 2020. He raised the prospect of putting a woman on the ticket hypothetically throughout the campaign, making the decision an easy one when the time came.

Even with that sentiment, though, the truth was that it would've been political malpractice not to run with a woman—especially after knocking six of them out of the primary at a time when Democrats knew women had been critical to their success in 2018 and would be even more so in 2020. There were some, including me, who thought the fresh memories of that borne-out female electoral success—combined with Clinton's unfinished business with history in 2016—would have buoyed the women of the 2020 Democratic field in their presidential bids. Studies and polls lent to this, too. Instead, they were consistently tagged with an air of risk and that elusive specter of "electability": *Can they win?* That's a foundational skepticism about one's leadership profile that Biden didn't necessarily have to confront. Though a good amount of ink was spilled over questions about his age and acuity, he was mostly seen as the man whose nomination it was *to lose.* At times, it seemed like he would do just that. But in the end, Democratic voters chose the seventy-seven-year-old former VP out of the most diverse Democratic field ever to represent them against Trump. Which made Biden's veep choice even more significant.

"It appealed to him to be positioned as a transitional figure," someone close to the Biden team recalled. "Someone who would bridge old and new," but also someone who would allow Biden to be remembered as a change-maker throughout the latter years of his political career; someone who, ultimately, "passed the torch" even as he held on to it. Slamming a door shut, to open a window later. Or, to put it plainly, female progress on a man's timeline. Selecting a woman would not just solidify his legacy as president, but also allow him to lean into actualizing a phrase he had long told members of his inner circle: "It's time" for a woman.

Biden didn't even consider any men during his VP selection process, a choice that led to mixed reviews among Democratic women and political watchers. Some found that empowering—the idea that Biden was telling the men of his party to "sit down"; that *this* time wasn't *their* time. Others, meanwhile, felt it would have been better if Biden picked a woman after a public vetting process that considered both genders, leaving overt identity politics aside. Picking the best *person* for the job, as opposed to the best *woman* for the job. Even though the former is who he and his team believe he chose, process aside.

"He could have just waited until he chose a running mate," a longtime campaign aide allowed, detailing the deliberations around Biden's March 2020 promise to run alongside a woman. "But he wanted people to understand that this was important to him, and he wanted to do it from a position of strength," having just all-but-clinched the nomination.

"This was like, 'I'm going to be the nominee and so I want to make this commitment that I'm going to elevate a woman, that I want people to see my partner in governing,' " the aide recalled. "It was important for people to know that it's going to be a woman."

The woman he finally chose was a former prosecutor with a resumé full of firsts. In nearly every role she attained, she was denoted as "the first woman" or "the first African American and South Asian American woman"—or both—to hold it. District attorney to California attorney general to senator from California to Democratic candidate for president. First, first, first, and only. On her political journey, Kamala Devi Harris— KDH as her aides abbreviated over text—often quoted her mother, who told her "you may be the first to do many things, but make sure you're not the last."

The Biden-Harris ticket showed what had always been, as well as what could be. And while it remains difficult to singularly find the impact of a running mate, one survey released after the election showed that 68 percent of female Biden voters said Kamala Harris was a factor in their voting decision. "Factor" could mean many things, including adding enthusiasm where there was little. The same poll showed more than 60 percent of women excited about having a female VP—including one in four Republicans.

The government Americans saw Biden assemble in 2021 was yet another sign that systems can change, but members of the oppressive class of patriarchal society can, and must, be forced toward hastening progress. Those with privilege must be part of leveling the playing field. What it came down to for Biden was a lived allyship. Not necessarily for fully altruistic reasons—this was good politics above all else—but for decisions made by a male leader with an eye toward changing structures that had been built to protect and enshrine male power. Biden blew up the status quo of who holds power in Washington when he chose a woman, and woman of color.

"He was the president who chose the first African American and Asian woman as vice president," historian Michael Beschloss told me, a sentence so simple, and yet it would have been almost unbelievable even ten years earlier. "That required some boldness, since it had not happened before."

I've wondered often—and asked many—if we could ever have seen these steps toward progress from anyone other than an older, white, male politician of Joe Biden's generation. Whether any other archetype of a politician would've offered the same reassurance and moderating public presence while changing the very makeup of what government looks like and who has a seat at the policy-crafting table. In the end, it comes down to an answer someone close to Biden gave me: "I don't know if anyone else could have, but the reality is: he's the one who did."

It's not clear whether Kamala Harris will be the one to clear the threshold of that final "first": first female president of the United States. But because of what she called the "audacity" of Joe Biden to put someone who looked like her on the ticket, she's closer than anyone else has ever been.

Experts and sources on both sides of the political spectrum insist that having her there—in the most presidential non-presidential role there is—makes it a little easier for any woman who comes next. But all these women—Republicans, Democrats, and even Harris herself—will have to contend with the reality that while a woman has been *elevated* to the closest presidential point, she has never been *elected* to the presidency, outright and on her own. That's where things get tricky. The question is how that happens. And why it's (still) taking so long. These are not easy questions to answer, but we must try.

Make no mistake, though: 2020 and the things that have changed in leadership because of it have literally changed the face of the political world. That is due to voters' deciding to back Joe Biden, yes. But it's also very much about Biden's deliberate decisions to create the most reflective government in U.S. history: The first female vice president, Kamala Harris, who he chose. A cabinet made up of ten women and eleven people of color, whom he nominated. Seven of them—eight including Harris—broke barriers with their confirmations and elevations. The numbers were similar for under and deputy secretaries throughout agencies. Representation that touches all parts of policy and governing practice.

Some of these still struggled under the weight of Capitol Hill politics. Neera Tanden's nomination for Office of Management and Budget director, for instance, was felled by a slew of "mean tweets" against progressive Democrats, like Bernie Sanders, and Republicans alike. During her confirmation hearings, Republican Louisiana senator John Kennedy—who himself regularly riffs about the story of the day with colorful quotes to the Hill press corps—described the Twitter dust-up: "It wasn't just about Republicans. And I don't mind disagreements on policy. I think that's great, I love the dialectic, but the comments were personal. I mean, you called Senator Sanders everything but an ignorant slut."

The wave of criticism of her words, and then the administration's pulling her nomination, was followed by questions about whether Washington would've demanded the same penance from a man for the same actions—especially in a time when sassy tweets are par for the course in an increasingly hyper-partisan D.C. echo chamber.

Still, Biden exemplifies a lifelong politician heralding forth the kind of systematic change that can only happen when someone trusted and on the inside of a system decides it needs to happen. Public pressures help, too, of course. Sustained polling from after 2018 bolstered enthusiasm about female leadership. So, too, did research and data that speaks to the increased financial productivity and intellectual innovation that comes from inclusivity and an overarching goal of diversity in team structures within business, and in this case, government.

President Biden elevated women to positions of leadership, branded their diverse lived experiences as strengths, and allowed them to thrive as leaders in their own right across cabinet-level positions. Janet Yellen: the first woman to lead the Treasury Department, during an economic recession that decimated the female workforce and rolled back a decade's worth of gains for working women. Deb Haaland: the first Native American to lead the Interior Department, with responsibilities over millions of Native people, as well as the steward of hundreds of millions of acres of public land and federal waters. Avril Haines: first female director of National Intelligence after sustained erosion of public confidence in U.S. intelligence apparatuses by President Trump.

And women were not the only ones breaking barriers. Lloyd Austin is the first Black man to head the Pentagon. Alejandro Mayorkas is the first Latino to lead the Department of Homeland Security, at a time when the immigration crisis is at a continued fever pitch. The first Latino to lead the Health and Human Services Department, Xavier Becerra, is serving during a years-long COVID pandemic that has killed in greater numbers along racial lines.

In that parking lot in Wilmington, we had no idea of the cabinet Biden would create. The doors he would open and the diversity of demographics and lived experiences he would usher into powerful positions in Washington. But we did know we were experiencing history.

The sun was setting, my shift was long over, but I was still on TV. It was Biden's moment, to be sure, but the historic nature of Kamala Harris's elevation needed its due. Videos of her in gray athleisure against a rustic backdrop were everywhere as she announced the long-awaited results on the phone with Biden. "We did it!" she crooned. "We did it, Joe. You're gonna be the next President of the United States." It was internet gold and perfect cable news fodder in an instant.

The clip played right before MSNBC's Joy Reid brought me into the discussion, the sun setting in Wilmington behind me. As with all of my TV hits, there are the questions the show wants me to answer, the points they ask me to highlight from my reporting, and then the points that I am personally passionate about bringing into the conversation. I laid out what to expect from Biden's anticipated remarks—"healing the nation"— and how he found out he'd won—from his grandchildren, who had all gathered with him for this moment after quarantining and testing. Then, finally, I came to the reporting I really wanted to talk about: this moment for Kamala Harris and women across the country who shared in it.

This moment, I said, is "not just Joe Biden getting the job that he's been questing for since he first ran for president in 1988. But historic in that Kamala Harris is the first female vice president. You and I talked about this on your podcast, Joy, a lot of little girls out there, for Halloween dressing in their blazers and Chuck Taylors [sneakers], now, tonight, seeing themselves in the next vice president–elect of the United States, Kamala Harris."

After Joy Reid's thanks and Molly's praise of my last hit, I was off the clock—brain totally fried from forming sentences on too little sleep, at all hours, for weeks—but my heart was still in it. The impact of Harris was more than Chucks and pearl necklaces on Halloween. It was women and girls across the U.S. seeing themselves reflected and respected. It was the Black and South Asian women who would see Harris on stages across the country and say, "I feel seen."

During Kamala's own run for president, a teenager holding a KAMALA banner at the San Francisco Pride parade in June 2019 told the California senator, "I'm Jamaican and Indian too. I've never met someone else who's Jamaican and Indian before."

"Well, now you have," Harris said back.

And now America sees someone with that lived experience and demographic profile as vice president—even as speculation about what Harris will do next heats up in real time. Given that she is the rare politician who literally re-molds history every day she shows up for work, and that she ran for president before, the speculation is unsurprising. It also complicates an already complex role. Every success and every screw-up are historic because no one like her has ever done them. Every mundane vice-presidential task takes on an aura of newness. Each cabinet secretary who she swears in, every small business she elevates, every policy specialty she adds to her portfolio—new, in that everyone who's done them before has never done them looking like, living as, and knowing what Kamala Harris does.

Now, there is no filter and no degrees of separation between the female experience and one of the top people advising the president. There's a lot of power in that, evidenced by the ways in which women were prioritized in the initial Build Back Better Biden-Harris agenda and the deliberateness with which this administration has sought to implement policy that dismantles systemic racism. That's not to say it's all because of her, but her perspective at that table helps keep those issues at the fore.

What Harris embodies and normalizes, though, also *other-izes* her. It puts her successes and failures through a second lens, layering and contextualizing her vice presidency "as a woman" or "as a person of color" over the political frame of the moment. That requires extra strategizing, more time dedicated to avoiding pitfalls, and an immeasurable, if often unseen, emotional toll. In Harris's role there is both power and risk; signs of progress, but also constraints. In her unique perspective there is opportunity—expanding the breadth of policy championed by the White House on maternal mortality or voting rights, for example, from the viewpoint of a woman of color. But it also means the leeway given to failures or mistakes is often less; each stumble imbued with the potential to be a massive trip-up.

It's a reminder that the progress Harris represents comes at a price, one that she will uniquely bear. It's true of all barrier-breaking women. Her moves will be scrutinized more keenly—sometimes fairly, sometimes not. Her mistakes will be bigger; her successes, shared; her ambition mistaken and manipulated as something sinister or to be mistrusted.

Breaking through glass ceilings means you get cut. It was true for Hillary Clinton, and it's true for Harris. Some who've spent time around her see the scars from the glass she's already shattered manifesting in reticence and second-guessing that make it harder for her to follow her instincts.

"The battle scars of her career experience and the [Democratic] primary have left her a little bit unsure," one person who worked closely with Harris during the 2020 campaign told me. "It is hard to articulate that knowing that whatever you say, some people are gonna cut you down. And it is hard to articulate that when you know, as a Black woman, you're not gonna be given benefit of the doubt."

More than a year into her time as VP, America is still learning the answer to the question "Who is Kamala Harris?" And it's incumbent on her to define that—"battle scars" and all. In Wilmington, on the night the race was called and Harris skyrocketed into the history books, she began that self-definitional process.

Before Election Night's festivities began, Molly and I popped into the lobby of the nearby Westin Wilmington Hotel to buy ourselves tiny mini-bar bottles of wine. We'd earned it, after all. Sitting in plastic folding chairs at the foot of the media riser on which I'd done dozens of live shots, we poured the bottles into to-go coffee cups and smushed our Styrofoam together in solemn cheers.

That night meant the beginning of the end of our year together, one that started in Atlanta, Georgia, just before a Democratic debate and would go through Inauguration Day in Washington. We began as two strangers who both operated on the energy frequencies of people who were either drinking coffees, holding coffees, or looking for their next coffees. We were also both young women who had advanced quickly on our career tracks by being perpetually prepared, rarely asking questions without first trying to find the answer ourselves, and rising through the ranks by asking for what we wanted—in a typically "no worries, if not" way that was neither too brash nor too ambitious nor too offensive. After a year of nonstop work, nonstop travel, and nonstop stress, we walked away dear friends who shared a deep understanding of how having a true partner who makes you better can make even the hardest work joyful and fulfilling. Some of the best work I've done I did with Molly, in large part because she saw the political world of 2020 through the same intersectional-feminist lens that I did. She also felt it was an essential frame to impose on our coverage because it was a perspective that percolated through the voters we met in states across the country, to the female candidates we covered on the road. To explain this moment in politics, you had to showcase the female experience across geographic and demographic spectrums.

Molly and I had encountered women in America who told us a woman couldn't, or shouldn't, be president because it wasn't a woman's place. There were also women who wanted so desperately to see one elevated: "someday, in my lifetime," they'd say wistfully. There was the woman and her two daughters whom I met in Montana in 2018 at the peak of the Kavanaugh confirmation hearings who were enraged by the allegation of sexual misconduct against him. "Groping [a woman]? What is that?!" the woman exclaimed. "I mean how many guys do you know that think that's no big deal?" She turned toward her nodding daughters. "It's not a big deal. It doesn't take away from his character." Thankfully, there were thousands of other women motivated to scream, march, protest, and organize because they felt the normalcy of that kind of status quo was very much a "big deal." There were the women buoyed by Biden's choice of Harris, and also women who would never be swayed from Trump and Pence and party politics. We refused to let these conversations with, and about, women fall too far out of our daily political, and then pandemic, coverage, constantly pushing to elevate women's stories out of the niche and into the mainstream.

Tonight, though, there was no push needed. No one could deny the power of women in this moment, embodied by one woman who took the stage just as dusk fell, decked in white—a nod to the suffragettes, imperfect in their work because as they fought for women's right to vote, Black women were not largely included. Here, Harris was not, as vice presidents can be, a political decoration or a sideshow. It was Joe Biden's night and Joe Biden's win, of course, but it was Kamala's chance to begin her place in history.

Soaking in it, she greeted the crowd with several "good evenings" as she began her remarks. "You chose Joe Biden as the next president of the

United States of America!" she told the crowd, who responded with honks and waving flags. But they also chose Kamala Harris.

In the aftermath of that choice, Harris was thinking of her mother: "I am thinking about her, and about the generations of women, Black women, Asian, white, Latina, Native American women who throughout our nation's history have paved the way for this moment, tonight. Women who fought and sacrificed so much for equality and liberty and justice for all. Including the Black women who are often—too often—overlooked but so often prove they are the backbone of our democracy."

Kamala's speech harkened back to a conversation I'd just had with a Black woman I met in the celebratory crowd in Wilmington. I interviewed her live on MSNBC. I talk to everyone, but today I wanted to center women, specifically Black women, in our reporting because they were a big reason why we were here. Black women turned out—big—in the primaries for Biden in South Carolina, and then again nationally on General Election Day. Their reactions were critical to understanding how America reached this milestone.

"I wanna introduce you to one of the women I met out here," I told Ali Velshi, who was anchoring our broadcast in New York. "What comes next?" I asked her. "What are you hoping to see from this ticket?"

"Well, I hope it'll be a progressive ticket. I hope he'll be able to pass progressive legislation that supports the people who put him here, especially the Black women, the Black people who voted for Biden-Harris; we need to see progressive legislation that will directly impact our lives," she told me.

Tonight, Harris was talking to her. To "all the women who have worked to secure and protect that right to vote for over a century. One hundred years ago, with the Nineteenth Amendment. Fifty-five years ago, with the Voting Rights Act. And now in 2020 with a new generation of women in our country who cast their ballots and continued the fight for their fundamental right to vote and be heard.

"Tonight, I reflect on their struggle, their determination, and the strength of their vision to see what can be, unburdened by what has been. And I stand on their shoulders," Harris intoned, her voice washing through speakers and over the cement parking lot. "And what a testament it is to Joe's character, that he had the audacity to break one of the most substantial barriers that exists in our country and select a woman as his vice president."

History can be the dry words of textbooks. The stuff you have to cram into your brain for tests and then forget as soon as it's over. But *this history*—living it, front row from a plastic folding chair in a crowded parking lot with cheap wine and dear friends—was emotional, raw, real, and unforgettable. As Harris spoke, women around us silently cried, tears dripping over the smiles on their lips. Their hearts were full. And so was mine.

Not because of the politics, but because of the personal. I'm a journalist at work, assigned beats or candidates to become an expert on, but I'm a human being the rest of the time. I'm also a feminist—which doesn't make me partisan or biased, it just makes me a believer in equal treatment, pay, and opportunity for both *men and women*. I believe in parity and the elevation of women to every space where important decisions are being made. So, for just a few minutes, I let myself take in the moment devoid of the policy and politicking and sources sniping on background of the last five years. Progress was still progress, even if it wasn't as all-encompassing as many had hoped.

"While I may be the first woman in this office, I will not be the last," the new vice president–elect said. She addressed "the children of our country" who could see tonight that "regardless of your gender, our country has sent you a clear message: dream with ambition. Lead with conviction. And see yourselves in a way that others may not, simply because they've never seen it before."

Now we'll see if she's right.

2

Kamala Harris and the Sparkly Jacket

Authenticity

FEBRUARY 2019

I heard Kamala Harris coming before I saw her. It often happens this way, with the *click . . . click . . . clickclickCLICKCLICKCLICKclick* of the photographers' camera shutters announcing a candidate's arrival to the rest of the press corps.

"Hiiii!" Harris said as she walked through the front door of Styled by Naida, a thrift store in Columbia, South Carolina, on Lady Street—which was exactly what it sounded like: a street of predominantly lady-owned small businesses, most of the owners women of color.

"I'm so glad to see you," Kamala said as she greeted Naida Rutherford like an old friend with a hug that made the room feel warm.

"Come on in!" Naida, the owner, said, matching her enthusiasm.

I was enthusiastic, too, being in the best/worst primary state. I say "best" because South Carolina is home to great weather and a fantastic food scene. I say "worst" because *somehow,* for reasons that still escape me, my jeans are always a little tighter when I leave the state. Go figure.

But I was also enthusiastic about getting to see Harris—not at a press conference like the one I attended on the day she announced at her alma

mater, Howard University in Washington, D.C., less than five weeks earlier, but in a true campaigning environment. A day before driving north
here to Columbia I had hovered, salivating in the corner, as Harris dined
out on barbeque in Charleston at the ever-scrumptious Rodney Scott's
BBQ. When she finished, she made the rounds to other tables, people wip-
ing the sticky sweet sauce off their hands in order to shake hers properly.
Harris seemed at ease in the one-on-one conversations, some with people
who knew her, most with people who didn't, all with folks she hoped to
turn into part of her budding voter coalition.

After all, the conventional thinking went, South Carolina should be
prime territory for Harris. The Democratic electorate was majority-Black
and Harris's historic potential as the first Black female president could
carry her with them. For many reasons, this never *actually* translated into
a real groundswell of support from Black voters here, but the expectation
still persisted for the first months of Harris's candidacy.

The premium put on these voters as important electoral decision-
makers was well-known from the start of the primary. It was one of the
few takes of the presidential cycle that was neither too oversimplified nor
overblown. To win, candidates needed South Carolina's majority-Black
electorate. The game-changing power of this state, and this electorate,
went on full display in late February 2020 when they single-handedly
saved Joe Biden's candidacy. And in the first year of his presidency, he
would be reminded more than once that he resided in the White House,
in large part, because Black voters, in the Palmetto State and beyond,
put him there.

But all of that was months away when Harris went to the heart of Lady
Street.

"I can campaign *and* shop?!" she said, laughing loudly and liberally—
something that critics would deem both inauthentic and grating over the
course of the campaign. She headed straight to the racks of clothes, taking
in the bright colors and touching the loud patterns that didn't have much
of a place in her campaign wardrobe of neutral tones and tailored suits.

Still, she remarked on the flamboyant hats in yellow, white, and green—"I don't know when I'll wear it, but . . ."—and the belts—"let's do that, too." Naida, ever the saleswoman, suggested a turquoise, wide-brimmed hat and black suede belt, pulling them down and passing them off to Harris's sister, Maya, who was standing nearby, but just out of view of the cameras. Maya was rarely visible in the press, but she was influential in her sister's campaign, carrying the scars of having worked for Hillary Clinton in 2016 and now channeling the unfinished business of that race into this one. She was small in stature but exuded bigness, both for the power she wielded on this campaign full of high expectations and for the connection she had with her sister at the center of it. Some people close to her likened theirs to a Bill-and-Hillary-style connection that similarly cut both ways: the involvement of a family member who has all the political acumen and experience to have been hired into the inner orbit even if they weren't blood, and the inevitable tension that comes because, despite those skills, they still are.

"Would anyone else like to shop?" Harris turned and teased the reporters clustered around her, more than a dozen of us with some form of camera—video, still, or iPhone—pointing in her direction.

On this particular day of touring female-owned places of business, Kamala Harris was followed by a predominantly female national press corps and surrounded by a coterie of mostly female aides. I stood next to women I admired—people like Maeve Reston of CNN, Caitlin Huey-Burns of CBS, and Juana Summers, then of the Associated Press—all of whom had covered previous elections and were known as fair-minded, smart reporters. They were also fun people, which matters when you aren't just covering campaign events but also trying to feel some semblance of normalcy by having dinners and commiserating about travel.

"Tell me about your business," Harris told Naida, her tone more serious now. This was, after all, why she was here.

"Styled by Naida started as garage sales," Naida said, explaining her life journey from the foster care system to homelessness. When she got to Benedict College in Columbia, she "literally didn't have sheets to go on my bed," but she did have people who "poured into" her during that time. Now, Naida wasn't just an entrepreneur, she was an inspiration: running her own business, mothering her kids, giving back to her community through a program that gave clothes to people who needed them, and explaining it all to a California senator who was trying to become The Most Powerful Person in the World.

Harris used to talk about campaigning as getting to meet "the angels among us," a nice sentiment, and mostly true—but not always. At least not in my experience. I thought, for instance, of the dozens of times I was called "a traitor" to my country or told to "fuck off" for doing my job, or tear-gassed as pro- and anti-Trump protesters clashed outside campaign events. Hardly moments that call to our nation's better angels.

But here, there were.

Americans innovate constantly. For a wannabe president, meeting them, knowing them, and learning from them can build a road map for Washington lawmakers to solve problems. And maybe that's the story that would've been written about this Saturday on Lady Street. But then someone brought a sequined, rainbow-colored jacket to Kamala Harris's attention.

I'm still not quite sure how it happened. Some of us were told to head outside to pre-set for Kamala moving to the shop next door. When the transition took longer than usual, I reentered the shop just as the jacket became the focus of conversation. As Harris was checking out, a reporter asked Naida about the sparkly jacket hanging nearby. Naida (of course!) urged Harris to try it on. To me, a graduate of New Orleans's Tulane University, the coat screamed "Mardi Gras," with its boxes of colorful sequins and retro, structured shoulder pads. To Harris, it was perfect for the upcoming season of LGBTQ+ Pride parades. The reporters laughed and *oooh*'ed at the item. It wasn't fashionable, but it was a fashion statement.

Harris reluctantly yet playfully pulled it on over her blazer, adjusting the too-big shoulder pads as she walked toward the mirror. There was a chorus of "oh yeahhh"'s.

"Oh my God. It's amaaaazing," a voice intoned.

"That's it," someone mocked gently. Giggles abounded. Hell, I laughed! Harris, of course, did, too.

"No pictures!" she fake-yelled at us.

She started to take the jacket off, but then pulled it back and turned toward the full-length mirror on the shop's back wall. Her hands fully covered by the sequin-laden sleeves, Harris declared, "I think it's too big."

The sleeves could be taken up, Naida offered. "You *need* something this fun in your life," she said.

CNN's Maeve Reston posted a video of the try-on to Twitter, crediting me with the Mardi Gras moniker and adding her usual hashtag: #CampaignFashionReport. She had popularized this niche space on social media over several election cycles, filing photos and videos to it that ranged from the bizarre to the inane from events that spanned both sides of the aisle. Other trail reporters contributed, too—a way of capturing voter color and playing with your colleagues online, while also letting followers in on the joke. This sparkly jacket was a definite campaign fashion moment.

I re-tweeted Maeve and Caitlin Huey-Burns, while tweeting my own: "@KamalaHarris trying this amazing rainbow coat (to me this screams Mardi Gras coat!), inspired by an inquiry from @MaeveReston of #campaignfashionreport fame."

I followed up with tweets that "she bought the jacket" but also the important context that while "These Harris stops have had a lot of levity (as you can tell from photos) . . . there's also a strong component of community activism & female business owners overcoming hardship to succeed."

It wasn't hard-hitting news, but then, my Twitter feed regularly boomeranged between informed political reporting and live-tweeting episodes of ABC's *The Bachelor/ette*. Twitter was, for most reporters, a stream-of-consciousness platform where scoops and nuggets were posted but so, too, were self-important takes about the woes of incessant travel and pictures of our pets for a bit of humanity. For a platform that I regularly call "the hell site," I had to find some upside to staying on it. We all did.

Press and candidate alike left Naida's shop in good spirits—and Harris's staff left with a few more bags than they'd entered with. In one of them lay said sparkly jacket, the prize find of the day, made for whimsy and celebration. And also, apparently, made for controversy.

While we continued our coverage into the T-shirt shop next door, some White Men of Political Media tuned in to the women covering the woman. They, I imagine, clutched their ties and patted their furrowed brows with kerchiefs. Brit Hume of Fox News fame was among those first offended. "This is just embarrassing," he tweeted. "So now journalists are going shopping with Harris, helping pick out clothes and then putting out glowing tweets about it."

The "outrage" ballooned from there. James Taranto of *The Wall Street Journal* chided Caitlin: "This is a CBS reporter noting, without evident disapproval, that a CNN colleague is helping dress a Democratic candidate she's supposed to be covering." *The Daily Mail*'s David Martosko tweeted: "If this is what the 2020 campaign is going to be like, President Trump's complaints about the media could have even more staying power with his base than the last time around."

Conservative radio hosts, Trump staffers, and random users alike sent similar tweets, swelling the chorus to the point where conservative news blogs and FoxNews.com wrote up the story, embedding our tweets and seeking to legitimize the outcry. "Reporters have historically interacted with candidates on the campaign trail," FoxNews.com wrote, "but picking out clothing pushes boundaries in the eyes of many critics."

There were two things happening here: a criticism of the female-led coverage that seemed overly chummy and a second, and more veiled, discomfort that stemmed from the nature of the campaign event itself.

Harris was hardly the first candidate to make a stop that involved frequenting local businesses and buying something local. In fact, "retail stops"—which this, quite literally, was—are as much the bread and butter of presidential campaigns as the classic, booming rally. Most candidates stump in coffee shops, burger joints, and diners before reaching the level of notoriety that earns them the ability to do the classic big rallies and town halls. No mom-and-pop shop left unfrequented; no local delicacy left untasted.

The difference this time was *who* was doing the retail politicking. In the same way that the small number of female presidential candidates has left a pitifully small set of leadership archetypes, it's also meant creating and normalizing the playbook of campaigning while female somewhat in real time. The male playbook for that has been settled for, well, ever. And it includes, allows, and even rewards a wide range of events that help to humanize the candidate. From breweries—a frequent stop for now–Colorado senator, once–Colorado governor John Hickenlooper during his brief 2020 presidential bid that earned him good local coverage and called to his business background—to skeet-shooting, which reporters tagged along for with Senator Lindsey Graham in July 2015 as he was running for president. "I actually stood directly to the South Carolina Republican's left at one point, calling out 'Pull'—the required command, apparently, to launch a clay pigeon into the air—and popping off a few (wildly off the mark) rounds," Ashley Parker wrote then in the *New York Times* of the outing.

Shopping, it turns out, was also an option.

In March 2014, President Barack Obama went shopping at The Gap during a trip to New York City, considering sweatshirts and stripes, ultimately buying sweaters for his daughters and a workout top for Michelle. While he shopped, photographers maneuvered with reporters in tow. "It never hurts to bring something back when you've been on a road trip. You get points when you go home," he quipped to the press. "I think the ladies will be impressed by my style sense," Obama bantered, telling one of the cashiers to repeat herself for the cameras when she said, "He's better looking in person!" and faking surprise that you can "sign on the screen" after swiping his credit card. "I'm just kidding, everybody," he said, facing the press and laughing.

The stop was, like Harris's years later, literal retail with a relevant policy connection. The White House later explained the visit as a show of support for Gap's wage increase for U.S.-based employees, the need for which Obama had spoken about in his State of the Union that year. The *New York Post* snarkily dubbed the president "the Shopper in Chief," but neither the event nor its coverage caused journalistic alarm.

During the 2012 cycle, then–GOP presidential candidate Mitt Romney shopped for local memorabilia for his grandkids in Iowa and for a new coat for his wife at a shop in New Hampshire, bringing his press corps along for the ride on both occasions. Media types were not offended or outraged that the press followed the candidates, or that items of clothing were considered and purchased. One colleague of mine who covered Romney remembers some even thinking it was thoughtful of him to shop for his family. Maybe Harris's sequins were just a step too fashion forward?

Point is: these are all typical retail politics stops for politicians. They can sometimes relate back to policy and they can sometimes just be made-for-TV moments meant to highlight how "real" or "down to Earth" or "authentic" politicians are—even ones who have already spent several years in the White House. They're low-calorie political fodder, light on substance and big on humanizing sugar high. The casual setting can make it easier to connect one-on-one with voters and provides a chance for the press to get to know the candidates a little bit beyond their policy platforms. When done right, these stops are big on upside for local media coverage, which translates into the chance to get their message—or even just their name!—in front of more primary-state voters.

"The woman who owns that business, and patronizes that business, or gets her coffee down the street, and sees a candidate where they spend time is meaningful," Harris's then–communications director Lily Adams told me. "That's just good strategy."

The male candidate moments I laid out are unremarkable. There are dozens like them. Retail stops that mostly served their intended purposes. Some, like Parker's "freewheeling" outing with Senator Graham, were described as "revealing—not to mention refreshing and fun." But then, they would be, wouldn't they? Barring any gaffes or awkward photos of eating phallic-shaped foods on a stick, they're made not to be breaking news events. Certainly, there was little outcry from conservative men in the media—or media broadly—about those events or about the way reporters covered them. We're used to seeing male politicians visit breweries or go shooting or shop for the women in their lives. We're less used to seeing a female politician do those things. And we're certainly less used to seeing a female politician do a stereotypically female task, in a female-owned place of business, surrounded almost exclusively by female reporters.

Or, as my colleague Chris Jansing wryly described it a few days later when I joined her on MSNBC: "Suddenly, Twitter blows up, Ali, because Kamala Harris tries on a sparkly jacket. You were there. Explain, sort of, the context of that."

The camera turned to me, twenty-four hours post–"Sequin Gate," now stationed far from South Carolina on a snowy New Hampshire front lawn. "Well, Chris, as you well know, on the campaign trail you do retail politics stops. You meet with store owners, you go into communities, and you try to get a sense of what makes these communities tick. While she was in Columbia, South Carolina, Senator Kamala Harris stopped into several Black female-owned businesses. One of these was a thrift shop . . . The rest is Twitter history," I explained, my voice tired and a little gravelly, worn from days of travel and little sleep.

I loved that we did the segment. I loved the opportunity to highlight how asinine it all was, in real time, in hopes of avoiding more sexist news cycles like this going forward. But I also couldn't help but shake my head at the chicken-and-egg nature of the news cycle. We were calling it out, but were we also amplifying the very issue in the first place?

Months after the shopping trip, Caitlin Huey-Burns would still get an occasional Google Alert about it. More than a year later, when Harris was announced as Biden's VP pick, the stories resurfaced once again, revived on Twitter and social media. Maeve, Caitlin, and I joked about it over text, laughing to keep from crying over the unfortunate reality that sometimes (oftentimes) there are extra potholes in the path of female reporters, even as we're covering a political landscape becoming more and more crowded with female politicians. And if there are extra objects in *our* path? There are definitely extra objects in the paths of the candidates.

"I say she revives the sequined jacket for her debut tomorrow," Caitlin joked in our group text on the day that Harris was announced as Biden's running mate.

The sequin jacket was a reminder: just because candidates had shopped on the campaign trail before, none of them had shopped while Black and female and running for president in the modern political age. It was a reminder for me that the old male guard of political reporting was very much still present, and some were seemingly unwilling to expand their view of what it looks like to campaign for president and cover that endeavor. We were shifting the window of "what's allowed" for both women campaigning, and women covering them, in real time. And while we shifted it, female candidates risked that those moments that should be slam dunks carried higher potential for negative fallout.

The whole thing was also a lesson in how non-stories could become real stories within hours: fringe tweets from biased actors picked up by sympathetic outlets, which then inject the story into the mainstream. Maybe that story is then covered extensively, maybe it's briefly mentioned or questioned; either way, it's brought to the attention of the audience. Stories like Sequin Gate can balloon into something that needs to be dealt with and prepared for, even if it deflates into nothing quickly. What makes it tougher is the unpredictability.

Unpredictable for how some could react to women covering women doing stereotypically female tasks (like shopping), even after decades of men doing the exact same thing. But it also spoke to how we allowed female politicians to present different sides of themselves. In Harris's case, her longtime spokeswoman Lily told me she saw it as a lack of respect being paid to Harris "as a three-dimensional person," while instead trying to put her in boxes (Black, female, progressive, etc.).

"Do we even let female politicians be three-dimensional?" I asked, while also thinking about it myself. "Like, if she *does* go shopping and is *also* a tough prosecutor, if one of those things doesn't jell with the other, is there this recoiling?'"

"Mhm," Lily said. "I think the answer to your question is we don't do it enough. We don't *let them* do it enough."

And when that space is given, the questions come quickly. Is she being genuine? Is the authenticity authentic—like *actually*, or is it politically calculated in some way? If it doesn't match our initial perception of who this person is as a politician, if it reads as fake, it's immediately treated with skepticism or mocked. That's not just a line to walk for women—male candidates can read as inauthentic or stiff or inaccessible, too—but it takes less for women to be viewed this way. In 2020, we'd continue to see it with Harris, Warren, and other women in the field. Be it over sequin jackets or drinking beers in the privacy of their own kitchen on Instagram Live. And we'd certainly seen it before with Hillary Clinton.

Specifically in April 2016, when Clinton appeared on the popular urban radio show *The Breakfast Club*—a well-trod stop on the campaign circuit due to its mostly Black listening audience—and said she always carries hot sauce with her. "Really?!" the hosts exclaimed.

"Are you getting in formation right now?" co-host Charlamagne Tha God asked, referencing Beyoncé's smash single "Formation" and its iconic "I got hot sauce in my bag, swag" lyric.

"Hot sauce! Yes! Yes," Clinton said.

Charlamagne warned her people would say she was pandering to Black people with that line. "Okay!" she said facing him. "Is it workin'?"

Clinton had long been a hot sauce aficionado, her campaign flacks reminded, but the skepticism and cringe were swift. Even half a decade later, Clinton aides still remember this day as a clear example of being dinged and mocked for inauthenticity and pandering when really, she just answered a throwaway question in the moment. The public expected the worst of her motives. It *felt* inauthentic. A pander, a fake.

"Even when they are themselves," a former Clinton aide who was staffing the candidate on Hot Sauce Day told me, "there's always this perception that it's a Machiavellian thing. That was the moment for me personally. 'Oh, holy shit, she's just treated differently.' "

He thought about it, then, in reference to the women he'd worked for since Clinton.

"If a female politician ran into the middle of the road and saved a dozen puppies from being run over, someone on Twitter would say, 'What a fucking bitch.' "

The third thing that the sequin jacket unpredictably underscored is how long the Twitter outrage will last and what forms it will take. Let me tell you the bizarre nature, and emotional toll, of being caught in a Twitter maelstrom. Twitter is not real life, but when your entire timeline is flooded with, at best, people telling you *you fucking suck* and, at worst, people telling you *you should die*, it feels very real. Those emotions are very real—for the people sending them, sure, but definitely for the person receiving them. The anxiety, the stress, the concern about both your reputation and your safety is *very* real.

The Sequin Jacket wasn't even close to the worst of the social media storms I'd ever been caught in. That prize goes to the days and weeks after I asked President Donald Trump if he'd consider "extreme vetting" for people trying to buy firearms in the same way he advocated for Muslims to be screened before immigrating to America. We were in Seoul, South Korea, in 2017, on Trump's first big swing through Asia, and back in the U.S. yet another mass shooting was unfolding, this time at a church in Sutherland Springs, Texas, where a gunman took twenty-six lives. Press Secretary Sarah Huckabee Sanders unexpectedly called my name—"Ali Vitali, NBC News"—and I stood to ask Trump my question. The president seemingly didn't appreciate my query. Nor did his backers. Most commenters attacked my looks: my eyes were wide, or "crazy." Others were more specific, saying I would "look good in a body bag." There were even a few conspiracy theories. The death and rape threats came on all platforms. My anxiety spiked. My then-boyfriend, who was on the trip for another outlet, took my phone from me and started deleting the most explicit comments so I wouldn't have to see them. The few that seemed like real threats were passed on to NBC's cybersecurity teams. I expected the onslaught—there's no bigger platform than a televised presidential news conference—but I didn't prepare myself enough for how it would feel doing that part of my job.

The Twitter storm with Kamala was tame by comparison but special in that I didn't expect it. As I was sitting at the airport waiting to board a flight home, Richard Hudock from NBC's always-on PR team called me and asked if I'd seen the tweets. "Nope," I answered, now scrolling Twitter. I tuned in in the middle of a Twitter-amplified moment that I found baffling, if frankly kind of hilarious. *These Very Important Men are wasting their time talking about *us*? On a Saturday?!*

But the jacket was, at its core, a silly yet stark metaphor for the rest of the campaign to come. A warning that the women running would be held to a different standard. That unscripted moments were more potentially dangerous. That the women running could be more easily thrown off course by seemingly innocuous happenings seen and amplified by the wrong detractor. That they were playing by different rules in a game that had been played for decades. Reporters and voters, alike, demanded to know their candidates—truly *know* them—but there were invisible boundary lines drawn around how authentic these female candidates could be. It was impossible to know where the lines were and too late to tell until they'd already been overstepped.

3

∧

Memorial Day Weekend
Campaigning While Female

MAY 2019

Wind gusts whipped up the water on the Hawkeye State side of the Mississippi, hurling it into the windows of the Port of Burlington's North Bay Event Space. Tornado sirens were blaring, drowning out Dolly Parton's "9 to 5," which was playing on loop, as ever, at this campaign event for Senator Elizabeth Warren.

Like the movie that inspired the song, this weekend was about following three women on their quest to topple the patriarchy.

Senators Amy Klobuchar, Kirsten Gillibrand, and Elizabeth Warren spending their holiday weekends barnstorming through Iowa. And though my assignment over these four days was to track these presidential aspirants on the trail, what I really got was a new opportunity to watch three distinctly different female candidates showcase the range of ways a woman could run for this elusive highest office.

No strangers to the stump, but new to the presidential arena, they were expanding the mold of what presidential candidates looked like in real time, giving Americans more mental touchstones for female presidential candidate models beyond just Hillary Clinton. That the 2020 race started with all these women being, some way somehow, compared to and tagged with the baggage of the former Secretary of State, made it clear that Clinton being the only female presidential paradigm in most voters' recent memories presented a barrier for the women who were trying to pick up where she'd left off.

A lack of imagination, or, more likely, a very limited exposure to women being on the ballot meant an extra mental hurdle in the minds of the electorate. Not that it's totally their fault.

From 1992 to 2008, voters did not even get the chance to consider voting for a woman to be the presidential nominee of either major party. That meant years of dormant American imaginations that could have further normalized women in the presidential space. And in the years when women did run, they were singular figures in fields of men. In 2000, Republican Elizabeth Dole ran—and was considered a top candidate— but dropped out before votes were cast. In 2004, it was Carol Moseley Braun, but she, too, dropped her bid before ballots were counted. In 2008, voters at least got their chances to consider women on the ballot for this role when then–New York senator Hillary Clinton ran as the lone female candidate in her field. That same election cycle saw Alaska governor Sarah Palin elevated as Senator John McCain's running mate—only the second woman ever to be tapped as a major-party VP pick. It was only progress from there. Then–GOP representative Michele Bachmann ran for president in 2012, followed by Republican businesswoman Carly Fiorina and Clinton again on the Democratic side in 2016. And on, and on. A positive, albeit relatively newly formed, habit of voters being forced to actually consider voting for female candidates on their primary and general election ballots.

Here, though, Elizabeth Warren was campaigning to get there—the focus of a dozen Iowans lined up, waiting patiently for their chance at a selfie. She enthusiastically greeted and posed her way through the line, seemingly unfazed by the quick turn of weather events. This was confusing to me, a girl from Westchester County, New York, who hadn't contended with many (read: any) tornados in my lifetime. The only person in freak-out mode was my then-producer, Olivia Santini, who was urging me and our camera crew to *please* find somewhere in the window-filled space that would be safe should the twister materialize.

We decided that our Alamo would be a brick-walled room just outside of the event hall that had been designated as the Warren campaign's holding area: a no-frills "greenroom" with folding chairs where the candidate and her staff could store their belongings and hang out, unbothered, before and after getting on stage. This hold room featured a large, tiled bathroom and several shower stalls that gave it a high school locker room vibe. Typically, this was a campaign's space, not to be intruded upon by reporters unless invited. But today, in the name of safety and tornados, this space was ours, too.

I grabbed veteran journalist Joan Walsh—whom I'd just met that weekend and who also seemed out of her depth with this kind of weather—and told her we were heading to the back. She snatched her laptop and moved to join us, along with several other television and print reporters, most of whom would become the dedicated traveling press corps following the Senator from Massachusetts Who Wanted to Be President.

As Warren selfie'd toward the end of the line, our ranks in the greenroom grew to about a dozen reporters, producers, embeds—and one Random Iowa Man who made it his mission to follow candidates throughout the state, asking them about bridging the country's political divides and gifting them with personalized yarmulkes (small, circle-shaped caps usually worn by Jewish men during prayer). I'd seen him at events for Senator Kirsten Gillibrand and Senator Amy Klobuchar that same weekend.

Warren's arrival in our storm zone now marked the end of a jam-packed long weekend—for her and for me. Over the last three days she'd charted a path east and south of Des Moines, speaking in hotel ballrooms, from convention halls, and on farmhouse porches. Each event packed a crowd that matched the polling: Warren was gaining traction.

For me, the weekend was a blur of towns, candidates, and interstates. This Memorial Day weekend Olivia and I logged more than five hundred miles in three days, jumping from Des Moines to a coffee shop in Iowa

Falls for events with Gillibrand and Klobuchar and then to larger town halls with Warren. We prioritized coffee over food (almond or oat milk lattes, when I wanted a treat), and with the rare free minutes between candidate events and MSNBC live shots we trolled vintage shops for political paraphernalia. Our cameraman, Steve Azzato, was particularly adept at finding the old campaign buttons I collected and gifted me a large, round Jimmy Carter/Walter Mondale 1980 campaign pin at the end of that weekend. As Dolly says: *"What a way to make a livin' . . ."*

Warren, too, was working overtime. The Massachusetts Democrat churned out a consistent stream of policy proposals from the moment she officially jumped into the presidential race in February 2019, in-depth plans ranging from leveraging public lands in the fight against climate change to student loan debt forgiveness. Now that was fueling her polling rise. While other candidates worked to increase their name recognition, Warren pushed to make her name synonymous with having "a plan for that," hoping it would differentiate her from the Democratic field that boasted, at the time, more than twenty contenders.

"I talk about plans because it's got to be not just that we go to Washington in order to talk about change, but we go to Washington to make change. That's the idea here," she told a crowd gathered before her at East Grove Farms in Salem, Iowa, on the Sunday night before Memorial Day. The sun was setting, the almost-summer air was brisk, the campaign was in a good mood, and everything felt possible.

The Warren campaign's consistent flurry of policy papers put meat on the bone for reporters, as well as added pressure on her fellow opponents to keep up, but it was also translating where it truly mattered: with voters in all-important Iowa, the nation's political trendsetter because of its first-on-the-calendar caucus date. For Warren, this state was the critical springboard from which she hoped to catapult herself through the rest of the primary states and to the Democratic nomination. It was the center of her campaign's primary plan.

"She's the plan girl right now, isn't she?" Keith Kuper of Ackley, Iowa, told me of Warren that weekend. I was at an event for Senator Kirsten

Gillibrand in Iowa Falls when I met him. Iowans were candidate shoppers, often meeting lots of contenders multiple times before coming close to making up their minds. "She really has specifics, plans on almost everything." He was leaning toward supporting Warren, even as he attended this event for Gillibrand, and wanted other candidates to be more specific if they hoped to peel off his support.

"I think America is ready for more than a personality," another Iowa voter, Carolyn Jones, told me that same weekend. I met Carolyn in Oskaloosa while she waited in line for a selfie with Warren. "We need policy . . . over what we've got right now, which is a personality and a character." Carolyn was leaning toward supporting Warren, too. But it was still early. Iowans could (and would) fall in, then out of, love with dozens of candidates between now and Caucus Night. Everyone from reporters to candidates knew that this time was very much the peak of Iowans' Candidate Dating Phase.

But just because Iowans weren't ready to settle down yet didn't mean candidates could stop wooing them. Which may have been why Warren waited until all the selfies had been snapped in Burlington before she came back to join us in the makeshift tornado shelter, offering a roughly thirty-minute period that is any campaign flak's worst nightmare: the candidate trapped with the press and unable to leave.

Alternatively, this situation is the dream for any campaign reporter. And so it was for me, as I huddled with Warren and listened to her talk. First, about growing up in Oklahoma with its frequent tornado warnings, then regaling us with other weather-related stories. Like when, she told us, a freak rainstorm forced her to abruptly abandon a family picnic, throwing everything into her car and then driving away—almost setting her young son (and their family car) on fire while driving, due to unwittingly leaving a hot plate on in the backseat. That story, taken in tandem with a regular stump-speech riff about the dangers of toaster ovens before consumer regulations were put in place to make them safer, made me wonder about Warren's propensity toward fire-starting, however accidentally.

There were no rolling video cameras or spinning tape recorders here.

It was one of many conversations Warren and I would have like this. Rarely, they'd be off the record—making it, for the viewing or reading public anyway, as if the conversation never happened—but still valuable, yielding snippets of information that would eventually become reportable once the dust of this election cleared. Others, like this day in Burlington, Iowa, were casual, but very much reportable. And while waiting out this impending tornado, the idea of "OTR" was never mentioned—not by us, not by the campaign, and not by the candidate.

Warren's traveling press secretary, a Black, Boston-bred twenty-something named Gabrielle Farrell, orbited around the group like a satellite, snapping a photo of us clustered around her candidate and texting it to us while we talked. I tweeted it, despite my hair being in the kind of half-up ninja warrior bun that drives my mother crazy.

Gabrielle had worked for key political players in Boston before hopping on Warren's presidential campaign. It was her first time in the national political arena, and while she led with toughness, she could also be vulnerable. Over the course of the campaign, she shared stories with me of the regular microaggressions that she'd experienced as a Black woman trailing a powerhouse presidential candidate. Like being stopped as she tried to walk backstage with Warren at events, or how some mostly white, mostly male reporters dismissed her as nonessential when they first met her . . . only to realize she was one of the ways they could try to get some one-on-one time with the candidate.

On this whirlwind adventure Gabrielle was under the tutelage of Kristen Orthman, Warren's communications director, who ascended to the Massachusetts senator's tight inner circle from the office of former Nevada senator and Democratic power broker Harry Reid. Her colleagues called her "KO." The nickname was cool, but it also fit. KO could pack a punch when she needed to. Quiet by nature and fiercely loyal to Warren, she ran a tight ship on the communications front for a campaign determined to let the candidate and her policy—not anonymous leaks—create the narrative.

Because of KO's comms shop's discipline, this campaign had few "sources with knowledge"—a term often used when reporters talk to in-the-know people but agree not to use their name—giving sassy quotes (or any quotes at all!) to reporters. No talking about process or how the campaign was "feeling." None of the kinds of fleeting nuggets that most other campaigns traded in and that I'd gotten increasingly habituated to during my years covering Trump, where staffers would double-cross each other with colorful quotes regularly in the press for fun. Admittedly, this was just as fun for the reporters, trust me.

But the campaign trail with Warren was a cleaner kind of fun, if that exists in politics. Most campaign-generated news cycles revolved around childcare policy or healthcare reform. And the campaign orbited around a boss who evinced a deep loyalty from her staffers and who, as a candidate, was (at least publicly) humbled by her missteps, such as when she and her campaign royally messed up the strategy around Warren's Native American heritage, and a DNA test she took to prove it—a move that angered some tribes, who called taking the test "a mockery."

That's not to say Warren didn't have an edge. She could be exacting and sometimes frustrated by the pettiness and pace of the political process— both here on the trail and on the Hill, where she'd spent the last several years. But after spending more than two years enmeshed in Trump World, where a good day felt like being hit in the face with a fresh wave at the beach before you'd even coughed up the sand from the last smackdown, this setting took some getting used to for me. Standing around a candidate asking her press corps questions about their upbringings, sharing her own personal (and bizarre) experiences with extreme weather and asking us to share our own. A pretty . . . normal conversation. A far cry from the unvetted conspiracy theories seen on Fox News or name-calling political opponents.

So, too, was the scene that played out at The Coffee Attic in Iowa Falls, where on the Saturday of this long weekend Kirsten Gillibrand took over the basement—a book-lined room that felt more like a library reading corner than a coffee shop—and Amy Klobuchar later rallied in the larger, upstairs space.

Seated at a long rectangular table, Gillibrand shared the spotlight with local leaders and medical professionals discussing rural communities' needs for access to health care. Imagine the angst of a mother in labor, Gillibrand explained, knowing she had a forty-five-minute drive ahead of her before she could deliver her child, not to mention how dangerous it could be for a pregnancy with complications. The New York senator also freely shared her own experiences with motherhood—think of that: a presidential candidate talking about her own pregnancy and parenting experiences—before tying them to the policy theory she was there to talk about: a bundle of ideas aimed at alleviating the financial struggles of parents and families, aptly titled the "Family Bill of Rights."

"These are things women know. But again, if our legislators are all men, and if our governors haven't experienced this . . . Just getting us to have a little more diversity will help us solve more problems. Because the combination of those life experiences, male and female, is fabulous. It's much more powerful and effective," Gillibrand said.

"I'm the first presidential candidate ever to have this comprehensive approach to wellness and families because I've lived it. I've seen it. I've seen it up close."

Hers was a policy conversation that sounded different from what we usually get in Washington, which is policy from a white, male perspective—at least as a starting point. Here, it was all through the lens of women. And for Gillibrand, that was the point. The New York senator centered her candidacy on womanhood: framing policy proposals around how they'd impact families, promising that "as a mom, I'll fight for your family as hard as I fight for my own," and even, as she reminded everyone in attendance, putting pink in her logo. She wasn't hiding womanhood; she was using it as an explicit selling point.

"I've never been afraid to run as a woman because I am a woman," she told me later over Zoom, looking back at her candidacy months after it had ended. But she and her staff also believed that the successes of 2018—female candidates powering Democrats' take-back of the House, and female voters powering those candidates—could be replicated successfully on a national, and presidential, scale.

"Either there was something there to tap into, you build on top of, or you don't, and the experiment doesn't work," one of Gillibrand's senior campaign aides told me of their foundational thinking. From the Women's March to #MeToo to 2018, "women in this country had taken their democracy back. And that's a space Kirsten was in. In all these fights. Politically, legislatively. That's just who she *is* and was. So if you're not that [as a candidate], you're what?"

There is an inherent risk in this approach, though. Family-related issues like health care and maternal health, specifically, were among the top polled issues of importance to voters, making them politically savvy issues to run on. But they could also be pegged as "women's issues" and considered niche. Especially with a white female messenger, framing her policies "as a mom" and an elected official.

It wasn't that voters wouldn't accept, or even embrace, "calling card" policies from non-white, non-male candidates on issues that reflexively align with their communities. Female candidates talking about reproductive rights, Black candidates focusing on civil rights, Hispanic candidates on immigration. It's expected, fairly or unfairly, that those issues will be brought to the fore by candidates who physically embody those communities. And candidates were able to generate buzz talking about those issues in 2020. Warren talking about universal child care, for instance, or Senator Cory Booker's personal story, and policy work, on the discriminatory housing practice of "redlining."

But the expectation that these candidates would prioritize these issues did sometimes make it harder for voters to see them *beyond* those policies, too. As presidents lead on all issues, so, too, must presidential candidates. And if they are stuck in feedback loops around one policy item that they're expected to speak to, that can derail an all-encompassing candidacy. That's a feedback loop that must be thought about, and strategized around, more often by BIPOC and female candidates. They must push harder to be seen outside of overly niche policy spaces. As candidates who can speak to anything because, as president, they will be required to.

For Gillibrand, her focus on the family served as her calling card but also offered one potential explanation for why it was harder for her to gain broader, national appeal. And she was hardly the only one forced to grapple with the double bind.

"I don't think that people will metabolize a candidate with a marginalized identity—a candidate of color, a woman candidate—taking the issue that we most associate with their community and making that their calling card," Maya Rupert, who ran Julián Castro's presidential campaign until he left the race, then joining the Warren campaign as a senior advisor, told me, talking about the experience of non-white, non-male candidates running for president.

Maya's words were informed by years in politics. In the same way that Gillibrand led with family, motherhood, and women, Julián Castro's first policy was immigration, and the first trip he made after announcing his candidacy was to Puerto Rico. When I asked him to look back on the race, he talked about the "built-in assumptions" that were present toward candidates of color, like him, and women. An April 2019 interview he did with Bill Maher came to his mind.

"Your first stop was Puerto Rico, right?" Maher asked, kicking off the interview.

"That's right, I went to San Juan right after I announced," Castro replied.

"So, and then, you announced your first policy. It was about immigration. My question is: why'd you pick that policy? Because it would be like if Obama, when he first came out, his first issue was reparations or affirmative action, when he was trying to say 'I'm gonna be the president of everybody.' It seems like that's the obvious issue for you, is immigration. You got those people. You got that issue."

"Well, you know," Castro interjected, his voice heavy with skepticism. "But I think people also wanna know what's close to your heart and that's close to my heart . . . My family has lived an immigrant's American dream story. And it also is the issue that this president is hell bent on using as a political ploy every time he wants to score some points with his base."

Maher's question was met with pushback on social media, especially from Latinos, some calling it a "trap" that Castro avoided and "yet another example of what is wrong with white liberals."

On the phone with me more than a year later, Castro picked the moment apart as both fair and unfair. "In some sense, that's an honest question, you know?" he said. "Maybe better to honestly ask the question. People were thinking it, I'm sure . . . Here you have a Hispanic candidate rolling out, as their first policy, immigration . . . because you're Hispanic. And that you're kind of biased. That you can't just take a look at the issue and sort of say what's best for the country, but that you kind of have skin in the game on one side of it. I did feel there were shades of that."

Castro's former campaign manager, Rupert, called it "a very, very frustrating double bind. People are already immediately going to think of you first in terms of your race, so you need to show people that you can appeal to broader audiences and broader means white. But if you aren't prioritizing issues relevant to your community, who would?"

While immigration did not get the consistent attention of, say, health care during candidate debates, it made political, as well as personal, sense for Castro to prioritize it, given it was Trump's central issue—"Build the Wall"—from the moment he announced his own candidacy. Yet Trump was never tagged as solely "the immigration candidate," whereas Castro was quickly pigeonholed.

There is also a potential difference evidenced here between Republicans and Democrats, one that we'll explore later regarding how conservative voters tend to eschew the gender identity lens more than their liberal counterparts, but that is also valid in regard to racial identity. Senators Marco Rubio and Ted Cruz spoke often about immigration and foreign policy during their 2016 races, both doing so as Hispanic candidates whose backgrounds were often noted in written coverage of their campaigns.

Rubio's demographic and lived background as a Cuban, for instance, was and continues to be regularly cited when he talks about foreign policy that deals with both Cuba explicitly and combating the creep of socialism, broadly. But he'd also worked on these issues in Congress, bringing an actual policy portfolio into the race while also leveraging his geographic ties in Florida to bolster his bona fides on Cuba commentary. Cruz, as a Texas lawmaker, acted similarly.

But they rarely explicitly tied their heritage to their policy prescriptions—allowing identity to take a backseat to policy, even as that identity bolstered their credentials and made them among the first candidates sought for comment on big news in these areas. Rubio, for his part, regularly recounted his parents' tale of leaving Cuba in 1956, his father working as a bartender and his mother as a maid in search of the American Dream. He launched his campaign in the shadow of that decision, from Miami's Freedom Tower, where Cuban exiles seeking asylum were processed for decades. While former secretary Castro wondered if people thought his background made him biased on the issue, Cruz and Rubio were not impacted in the same way and were seemingly unbothered by the demographic and policy overlap.

And while some Democratic candidates in 2020 were given ample coverage and attention as "single issue" candidates—Washington governor Jay Inslee was The Climate Change Guy, for instance, or even to some (early on) Bernie Sanders fashioned his candidacy around the idea of Medicare for All—most marginalized candidates either fell into the trap or had to strategize out of it.

"If you are a part of that one community, I do think that it just gets people thinking 'oh so then you're the brown candidate talking about brown things, you're the Black candidate talking about Black things, you're the female candidate talking about women's things,'" Rupert said of her experience with Warren's and Castro's bids.

Climate change and health care? These issues don't just impact small swaths of voters; they're issues that impact everyone—just like immigration and family issues do. Yet each issue spurred different expectations and feedback loops for the candidates who chose to center them. It created and creates a tricky path for how marginalized candidates can run national campaigns that speak to their communities while still making *all* voters feel seen and represented.

But it's also the bias Rupert told me she sees as "baked in" to the process but rarely, if ever, discussed. "There's an objectivity that's given to white men to take any issue and to make it broad. And there is a built-in concept that everybody else's lens is already shaded," she said.

Months after Gillibrand's bid had been boxed away in voters' memories, but before Joe Biden had won the election, she shared with me the lessons this first presidential run taught her. "Not that my issues weren't good," she said. "My issues are great, and I'm always gonna run on these issues, and the first female president will probably run on many of these issues—but it wasn't the issues. It was what the country was ready for. And I think Trump has stoked so much fear, *so much fear*," she emphasized, "about the future, about which direction the country's going in, that most voters wanted something they knew, something that was familiar, something that was certain. And that's why Biden is the best candidate for the moment."

Gillibrand sensed the skittishness of the electorate when she ran. And while her faith in the issues she brought to the fore—both in the 2020 campaign and during her years in the Senate—never wavered, her assessment made clear that even if she hadn't run on things typically designated as "women's issues," 2020 still wouldn't have been her time. Or, in her view, any *her*'s time.

"I just think it wasn't my time. It wasn't the right time for a woman to run," she told me bluntly, speaking in her typical hurried cadence but making an admission that momentarily stunned me. "And not even on the agenda I ran on. I just feel like we, ultimately, had two white men— older white men . . . And I think what the country was looking for [in the Democratic primary] was not change so much as just a different kind of certainty. And I think electing the first woman candidate *is* change. It's significant in and of itself and people aren't used to it."

It seems obvious now that there was only one person who could have had a sort of placating effect on the electorate post-Trump. "It's a certainty that Biden could offer," Gillibrand said. "Whereas they didn't even get a chance to know who I am."

True, Gillibrand—and Castro, too—lacked the name ID that is so critical in national, presidential elections. It's a large part of what made Donald Trump so formidable from the second he got into 2016's similarly crowded Republican primary: Americans knew his name from his years in reality TV. Kirsten Gillibrand certainly did not have that national notoriety or brand—and certainly not in the way that the popular, two-term former vice president, Joe Biden, who'd been in politics for decades, did.

But Biden had something else that Gillibrand didn't: the benefit of the doubt, both that he could do the job and that he could win. It was a reputation he'd earned through years of service, but something that few female politicians get without having to bring the receipts to show for it. There was usually more doubt than benefit applied to female politicians.

That 2020 would end with Biden seemed inevitable once the dust settled. But in Iowa in May 2019, dust was everywhere, and the field was massive.

A few hours—and a few almond milk lattes—after Gillibrand said her goodbyes to voters and press, Olivia and I transitioned from the coffee shop's bookish basement to its main level. Behind the barista's counter, a carpeted area was being decorated with green "Amy for America" signs ahead of the senator from Minnesota's arrival.

Where Gillibrand pitched to a two-to-one female audience with a women-and-family-centric policy pitch, Klobuchar focused on bread-and-butter basics: a trillion-dollar infrastructure plan, an understanding of Iowans' issues as a neighbor in Minnesota, and, of course, her ability to win. "Every race, every place, every time," she'd say.

Klobuchar was a prosecutor before going to the Senate, becoming the first woman from Minnesota elected to the body in 2006. As a statewide politician, she won by bridging what some have likened to five "states" crammed into Minnesota's state lines: from the diverse urban centers in

Minneapolis–St. Paul to the Iron Range counties up north that almost helped Trump tip the scales in 2016. "We came *this close*," Trump used to say. In presidential contests, Minnesota tips blue, but county-by-county races earn the state its purple reputation. It's the same state that elected Congresswoman Ilhan Omar of "the Squad" and, just a few years earlier, one-time presidential candidate and Tea Party firebrand, Congresswoman Michele Bachmann. The perfect state from which to launch a campaign built on electability at a time when Democrats wanted to rebuild the crumbled bricks of the heartland's Blue Wall. "Heartland Amy," the senator once nicknamed herself. That was the brand she hoped to take national.

Standing before a crowd of forty-some-odd Iowans, Klobuchar, somewhat haltingly, made her pitch, weaving policy with her past of legislating and her working-class roots.

"My background is a little different than Donald Trump's," Klobuchar joked. "And different from a lot of the people running for this office." She was armed here today with a new plan for rural agriculture, bringing her years of knowledge on the issue in her own state to this one.

Klobuchar stood before them, not just a seasoned legislator and proven winner, she said, but "as the granddaughter of an iron ore miner, as the daughter of a teacher and a newspaperman, as the first woman elected to the United States Senate from the state of Minnesota, and a candidate for president of the United States." That's what America is about, Klobuchar said. "I'm someone that's blunt, I tell people what I think, and I've been devoting my time when we talk about issues here to talking about the challenges that are in front of us today." Worker training, comprehensive immigration reform, taking on Trump. A moderate Democratic voice speaking to the issues of the day, competing for the center-progressive lane. Then handshakes and photos and conversation, a quick gaggle with the press about her new rural agriculture policy release, then a stop at the barista before several more events to round out the day. I lingered by the coffee counter as she waited for her order.

If you love talking politics, you wanna do it with Amy Klobuchar.

She's quick with a good story and known among reporters in both the campaign and Hill press corps as a lawmaker who's dialed in and loves to talk politics. It's not just a well-tuned political barometer, but a biting wit and—frankly—edge that allows her to cut to the core of the latest Washington debate or gossip cycle.

In another life, Klobuchar might've also been a stand-up comic. Or she was using her political career in this life to hone her act, sprinkling every town hall and roundtable with practiced one-liners. The same woman who could talk rural farm policy also regularly bragged about her hotplate skills, or that she raised $17,000 from ex-boyfriends for her first Senate run. "I'd like to point out, it's not an expanding base," she'd quip and, though I hate myself for this, I would laugh as if it was new every time.

For an entire weekend I covered three candidates. I talked on the air about who showed up for them, what their pitch was to voters, whether they were surging or trying to gain traction. I didn't even realize until it was over that I'd spent the weekend covering three legitimate candidates for president . . . who were all women. Their gender wasn't the lede, nor was it a disclaimer. "Candidate" didn't require the usual "female" qualifier. It was just "candidate." Was this the progress Hillary Clinton promised in 2008 on the day she departed that Democratic primary and endorsed then-senator Barack Obama for president?

"You can be so proud that, from now on, it will be unremarkable for a woman to win primary state victories, unremarkable to have a woman in a close race to be our nominee, unremarkable to think that a woman can be the president of the United States," she'd said then. *The New York Times* report from that day noted that after she said it, "the cheers, mostly from women, swelled so loud that Mrs. Clinton's remaining words could not be heard."

Women were cheering—in 2008, in 2016, and now—but despite the progress of the intervening years since that speech, I wasn't naive enough to think we were post-gender. If anything, Americans in 2020 were even more aware of our nation's past when it came to sexism and racism. We're only just starting the uncomfortable process of confronting this past, and its relevance to the present, in our daily lives and conversations, let alone in implementing policy that will begin to dismantle it. And I wasn't optimistic enough to think that just because covering three female presidential candidates in one day didn't jump out *to me* as remarkable, it wouldn't still be notable to voters or my colleagues in the media.

But this weekend in May was still *something*, right?

A field of six women were building, in real time, their own archetypes of what running for the nation's highest office looked like. They brought a range of knowledge and lived experience—prosecutors, professors, military veterans, thought leaders—and fell into different lanes on the ideological spectrum.

Some led with policies that were previously considered niche: "women's issues" or "Black issues" or "mom issues," mainstreaming them by centering them in their candidacies and espousing policy prescriptions that didn't just look through the standard white, male lens that's the automatic viewfinder in politics. Eventually, credit was given within the party and in media circles for candidates with policies that were deliberate about closing racial and gender gaps, dismantling systemic racism, or identifying ways to bring *all* Americans into the middle class. Once-niche conversations deemed essential to national progress. There was greater policy conversation around maternal mortality and its higher impact on women of color, thanks to candidates like Harris. Universal pre-kindergarten, championed by the likes of Warren and Gillibrand, as well as a renewed focus on reproductive rights. These women bringing these issues to the fore with their credible candidacies forced the men in the field to also prioritize them. That's not to say they wouldn't have, but it amplified the chorus.

And while some in the media still talked about how female candidates were tackling "women's issues"—which they were—Kamala Harris said it best: "When people say they want to talk about women's issues, my response is always, 'I'm so glad you want to talk about the economy!' "

Over the course of the campaign, women like Gillibrand *did* lead the charge on reproductive rights, even helping to push the eventual nominee, Biden, into reversing an outdated position on the Hyde Amendment, which blocks federal dollars from funding access to abortion and heavily impacts lower-income women. But it was, of course, beyond "women's issues." Warren, for instance, led the field by being the first presidential candidate to call on Congress to initiate impeachment proceedings against President Trump, putting pressure on Democrats both in Congress and on the campaign trail, and contributing, in part, to her rise in the polls in the summer of 2019.

These were mile markers. Tangible moments of leadership from female candidates that impacted the course of the Democratic primary. They were all undertaken differently and messaged authentically—which is the point. The women weren't reminiscent of men in history who'd done similar things before them. They weren't Beto O'Rourke, who called to mind the Kennedys, or Pete Buttigieg giving voters flashbacks to Barack Obama or Gary Hart, or Bernie Sanders in the mold of George McGovern. And they weren't running as the next Hillary Clinton, either, though we know that didn't mean they escaped the comparisons. They were new candidates, in their own individual rights.

Months after her own bid had ended, Klobuchar predicted what the impact of 2020 would be: "You aren't just going to have one woman. You're going to have different kinds of women that serve in office. You have role models for so many people. And that's going to matter."

It did matter. It was, in many ways, groundbreaking, even as it was mostly routine to see women leading. But as Julián Castro concluded, "I feared that to be groundbreaking is usually to lose."

He paused briefly as his words sank in through my phone speaker. "Unfortunately. Jesse Jackson was groundbreaking. Shirley Chisholm was groundbreaking. It turns out Hillary Clinton was groundbreaking in securing the Democratic nomination. And yet those were not successful presidential campaigns from the standpoint of winning the whole thing . . . And so, what I thought was," he sighed, "am I in a position where I'm the one beating down the door, helping to beat down the door, and then really somebody else is gonna take it in the future."

He paused again. "There are a lot of different factors that go into how one is received and what happened and whether you win or lose. Not just your race or ethnicity, not just your gender. But that is a factor. Plus," he added, "most candidates who are women, most candidates of color, are not coming with the same network of big-money supporters and longtime standing. You just layer these disadvantages on and—it's not an excuse— it's just to describe where you start off and what you have to overcome."

In 2020, the barriers—paired with the skittishness of the electorate— were insurmountable.

4

Kamala Harris
The Rules of Engagement

JUNE 2019

S outh Bend, Indiana, mayor Pete Buttigieg was halfway through a well-worn, un-newsy answer to the moderator's question on race when Senator Kamala Harris saw the makings of a moment on the first Democratic debate stage in Miami in June of 2019.

"As the only Black person on stage, I would like to speak on the issue of race," she said. Conversations about systemic racism were not new in the Democratic primary, even at this early point. But those conversations had never put Joe Biden in the crosshairs before. "I'm gonna now direct this at Vice President Biden."

Biden looked up, expectant, and wholly unprepared for what came next.

"I do not believe you are a racist." She trained her eyes on him and softened her voice slightly for this disclaimer. "And I agree with you when you commit yourself to the importance of finding common ground. But I also believe—and it's personal." Her tone hardened. "It was hurtful to hear you talk about the reputations of two United States senators who built their reputations and career on the segregation of race in this country."

She was referring to comments that already had Biden in hot water. At a recent fundraiser he'd talked about working with two segregationist senators during his early years as a lawmaker, making a point about a foregone time where progress could be made even in the face of fundamentally opposing viewpoints. "At least there was some civility," Biden reminisced during the gathering at a swanky New York City hotel. "We got things done. We didn't agree on much of anything. We got things done, we got it finished. But today, you look at the other side and you're the enemy. Not the opposition; the enemy. We don't talk to each other anymore."

The comments were classically Biden, espousing an abiding belief in bipartisanship, but also a deep commitment to the institution of the Senate. Ignoring, of course, that this institution, certainly in the 1970s and '80s, was not just a boys' club but a predominantly white boys' club whose members either embraced the segregationists in their ranks or at the very least tolerated them. Even as a member of the latter camp, Biden's comments were meant to show he valued progress and pragmatism—even if it meant working with contemptible partners.

In retrospect, this might have been the clearest path of attack on Biden. His reverence of institutionalism over the morality of the moment was also an issue in the matter of the Anita Hill hearings, which he chaired as head of the Senate Judiciary Committee during the process of confirming Justice Clarence Thomas. Congressman Jamie Raskin distilled this piece of it well in April of 2019, when Biden entered the presidential race, stating: "Biden's chairmanship of the Judiciary Committee during the Thomas nomination reflected his sense of institutionalism a lot more than any sense of feminism. None of this would be disqualifying, but it does not stand up well to the feminist sensibilities of the #MeToo era." Attacks along these lines could paint Biden as out of step with the party's current mainstream, an elder statesman of a bygone time.

New Jersey senator and presidential hopeful Cory Booker was using a similar frame. "Vice President Biden's relationships with proud segregationists are not the model for how we make America a safer and more inclusive place for Black people, and for everyone," Booker said. "I have to tell Vice President Biden, as someone I respect, that he is wrong for using his relationships with [senators] Eastland and Talmadge as examples of how to bring our country together."

Instead of apologizing, as Booker urged him to, Biden doubled down. "Apologize for what?" he told reporters when they asked him. "Cory should apologize. He knows better. There's not a racist bone in my body. I've been involved in civil rights my whole career. Period. Period. Period."

It sounded like Harris was going in Booker's direction, too. Until she wasn't.

"And it was not only that," Harris said on the debate stage, "but you also worked with them to oppose busing." A split-screen shot showed Biden's blue eyes looking straight ahead, a forlorn look affixed to his face while Harris leveled her full, practiced-prosecutor's power at him. "There was a little girl in California who was part of the second class to integrate the public school and she was bussed to school every day. And that little girl was me. So, I will tell you that on this subject it cannot be an intellectual debate among Democrats."

While the crowd cheered, the moderator offered Biden the chance to respond. His lips were pressed together, a thin line between them sloping downward from left to right. As the moment unfolded on the debate stage—Biden calling Harris's comments "a mischaracterization of my position across the board"—her campaign's digital arm mobilized, seeking to capture the moment's virality online, as all digital teams set out to do on nights like these. They attached a picture of an elementary-school-aged Kamala and quoted their boss: "There was a little girl in California who was bussed to school. That little girl was me. #DemDebate." A similar meme was posted to Instagram. T-shirts with a young Harris's face on them retailed for $29.99 on the campaign's website, spurring conspiracy theories about whether this was all some elaborate plot to cash in at the expense of the front-runner (which even years later, Harris aides vow it was not).

In the spin room in Miami, most of our NBC News political coverage team had their eyes on twenty-four-year-old Deepa Shivaram. The former *Meet the Press* associate producer had the job as the Harris embed, chronicling every word, attending every event, and effectively becoming a walking encyclopedia of Kamala Harris knowledge. *Where the hell did that come from?* our prying eyes seemed to ask her as if she had access to the candidate's inner monologue. When the debate was over and the damage done, a colleague went up to Deepa and half-joked, half-informed her: "You're covering the next president of the United States."

And in that moment—based on what she'd just watched and what everyone around her was now saying—Deepa may have thought so, too. Pundits picked apart Harris's performance as strong, while footnoting that it was also filled with potential problems, including coming at Biden in a way that risked seeming more personal than political. Overall, though, a strong showing.

This was the start of a surge, one that made good on the promise that many believed: that Harris was a top-tier contender. On the stage, she'd begun to fulfill the excited expectations about her candidacy that sprouted from her profile in the Senate, access to donor networks, and relatively high national name recognition (compared to most others in the field). Expectations that were bolstered by the reception to her presidential announcement: a thousands-strong kickoff rally in Oakland, California, and $1.5 million raised in the twenty-four hours after announcing her campaign.

But Harris's bid was also imbued with history. The possibility of not just the first woman president, but the first woman of color. In Harris's bid was the embodiment of bending the expectations of what a president looks like and how they lead. It took decades for these permission structures to be built and to develop. And while any candidate from a marginalized group is a still trailblazer, the path they're walking is more illuminated now due to those that went before them.

Where there is now Kamala Harris, there was first Shirley Chisholm—an historic and iconic touchstone rarely far from the Harris campaign's mind and nodded to in their initial rollout. "Unbought and Unbossed" was the slogan under which the congresswoman from Brooklyn, New York, ran then. Entering the 1972 presidential fray for what everyone, including her, knew would be a long shot's long-shot bid, these were some of the first words she spoke: "I stand before you today as a candidate for the President of the United States of America. I am not the candidate of Black America, although I am Black and proud. I am not the candidate of the women's movement of this country, although I am a woman, and am equally proud of that. I am not the candidate of any political parties or fat cats or special interests. I stand here now, without endorsements from many big-name politicians or celebrities or any other kind of prop. I do not intend to offer to you the tired and flip clichés which for too long have been a septic part of our political life. I am the candidate of the people of America."

She hoped, in these remarks, that voters would "make independent judgments on the merits of a particular candidate based on that candidate's intelligence, character, physical ability, competence, integrity, and honesty." Assess her, in other words, as they would any other (white or male) candidate.

Her candidacy, and initial years in Congress, coincided with the national and still-stalled push for the Equal Rights Amendment, an idea steeped in the belief that equality would come only when women were equally represented in America's governing and policy-making bodies. Yet it was also a time of persistent attitudes that women and Black people should not be rising into these spaces of power. The impediments were many, including the ability to raise sufficient money and convince donors to invest, but Chisholm had to also clear social barriers of bias and skepticism that were higher than at any point since. As she put it, "If they don't give you a seat at the table, bring a folding chair."

She wasn't just dragging a folding chair into the presidential political space, either. Her election to the U.S. House made her the first Black woman elected to the body, where she also laid groundwork that would usher more women and Black people into these halls of power. She helped to found the Congressional Black Caucus and the National Women's Political Caucus, both powerful apparatuses that helped (then, and now) to leverage the power of Black lawmakers in Congress and bolster female candidates who hope to join them there.

Here, and throughout history, it's striking that women—while forging their own individual paths forward—are almost always looking ahead, too: constantly aware that as we travel less-trodden paths we must also clear brambles for those who will, and must, come after us; and cognizant that any mistakes we make along the way will most certainly have to be answered for by those following behind us. And for the women who follow in the footsteps of their predecessors, there is always that gratitude, but also that weight, of being good enough to make their sacrifices worth it. Chisholm's portrait—my favorite of the hundreds hanging in the halls of Congress—stands in the U.S. Capitol, passed by reporters as we patrol the halls under the House Speaker's office, an ever-watching reminder of the work she did, and that still must be done.

In a press conference at the same podium from which she'd just announced her bid, Chisholm was asked by a female reporter if she represented a trend for more women to run for office. "Yes," she said. "Do I recommend a trend for more women, and specifically Black women, to enter into politics? Elected office? Yes. I definitely am feeling and recognizing that as a result of over twenty years in political life, only emerging eight years ago publicly, that there is a great need for more women in the political arena. I happen to believe that there's certain aspects of legislation that probably would be given much more attention if we had more women's voices in the halls of the legislatures on the city, state, and national level . . . Legislation that pertains to daycare centers, education, social services, mental services. The kind of legislation that has to do with the conservation and preservation of the most important resources that any nation has and that is its human resource."

No sooner did she finish than a male reporter asked if she felt her bid would "hurt" fellow New Yorker and New York City mayor John Lindsay's own presidential run. The subtext was that she was both too unconventional to be taken seriously and also risked being an impediment to a man's aspirations. "I dare say that my candidacy might not only hurt Mayor Lindsay, it might hurt a few others . . ."

It was an historical frame I couldn't help but apply to Harris's own run, especially as press and public alike digested that tense debate-stage moment. She was a woman standing directly in front of one of her party's most veteran and respected public servants, asserting her ambitions ahead of his own—just as any presidential candidate would and must. "Unbossed and Unbought" now Undeterred and Unencumbered in her pursuit of the Oval Office.

That the moment was initially celebrated as a sign of Harris's strength was yet another marker of the progress her bid represented. Where Chisholm's entry into presidential space was largely met with laughter in 1972, Harris's announcement was met with cheers and crowds and high expectation for success. She was an embodiment of progress, but also a reminder of its wrenchingly slow pace. Almost fifty years later, Harris was still notching "firsts," just as Chisholm had before her. When she served in the U.S. Senate, she was one of three Black members and the only Black woman. After she left to become vice president, there were no Black women left in the Senate—and as of this writing, that's still the case. But in 2021, the 117th Congress overall boasted a record number of Black women—twenty-six between both parties. She was rising now in Miami to meet the potential that media and political onlookers saw in her—and she was doing it by taking a big, confident swing at the front-runner.

But it was about more than dinging Biden. Democrats, if they allowed themselves to dream this dream, didn't just want to pick a candidate who could beat Trump; they sort of wanted someone who would pulverize him in the process. *If Harris could do this to a Democrat*, the thinking went after the first debate, *imagine what she'd do to the president!*

And so, Harris went from one to watch in a massive field of could-be presidents to the one to watch out for. Three polls—two national and one in Iowa—of likely Democratic voters done right after the debate showed her gaining steam and cutting into Biden's lead, although one in five polled still said the former VP was their first choice to be the party's nominee come November.

Back on the campaign trail, Harris was riding that post-debate polling surge. The crowds were big and the enthusiasm was real—but so were the questions. Because while Harris's performance packed a big punch on the stage, everything seemed to fall apart when it came to the details.

Biden's answer during the debate, while at times meandering, laid out an important distinction: he backed busing as a remedy to curtail so-called *de jure* segregation of schools, where segregation results from state and local laws. But on *de facto* segregation, which happens more organically and stems from biases at play within the community, Biden said the federal government should not impose busing as mandatory.

During an appearance a few days after the debate at an LGBTQ+ Pride parade in San Francisco, a reporter asked Harris her position on busing and the role of the federal government. She supported busing, she said, "and we need to put every effort, including busing, into play to desegregate the schools." But when it came to whether she would support federally mandated busing in areas with *de facto*—or, organically developed—segregation, she fell short of a clear position. A few days later in Iowa, she was pressed to clarify. "I think of busing as being in the toolbox of what is available and what can be used for the goal of desegregating America's schools," Harris said. A position, it turned out, that sounded pretty much like Biden's.

With the pointed attack now blunted, the bad blood between the campaigns set in. In Biden World, the candidate himself was still grappling with what felt like a gut punch from a perceived friend—not just of his, but of his late son, Beau, who served as attorney general of Delaware when Harris did in California. While Biden presented a somber front about the debate attack, his staff took up an aggressive defense of their boss on cable news and social media. Some of these staffers would hold, if not a full-blown grudge, then a deep skepticism of Harris throughout the vice-presidential coronation and into the administration.

On the one hand, it's expected that staffers get their backs up to defend their bosses. Campaigns are personal exercises, and slights can sting most keenly even after the heat of battle simmers down. But Harris was hardly the first candidate to go for the knockout punch on the debate stage or over the course of the primary against a member of her own party. And there had certainly been harsher attacks than these that had been forgiven even just one cycle prior.

Who could forget when Donald Trump accused then-rival Ted Cruz's father of being with John F. Kennedy's assassin, Lee Harvey Oswald, prior to Kennedy being shot? "I mean, what was he doing—what was he doing with Lee Harvey Oswald shortly before the death? Before the shooting?" Trump said. "It's horrible." (Never mind that it wasn't true.) Or Trump going after Cruz's wife's appearance and threatening to "spill the beans" about her. Responding to that, Cruz angrily called Trump a "sniveling coward" and warned him to "leave Heidi the hell alone." Cruz would go on to be one of Trump's most steadfast allies on the Hill during his presidency. It was just one of many intense moments that, even as the at-tacks themselves were called out of bounds, were not seen as permanently disqualifying of Trump in the eyes of the voters. And in some cases, it even brought voters into the fold, attracted by Trump's strength and willingness to say what he was really thinking.

But when it came to Harris, Biden's political allies weren't the only ones chafed by the attack. It had also offended voters, creating a backlash from Democrats who felt she'd crossed a line attacking the field's Man to Beat so ruthlessly and on a seemingly random issue that had been outside the main-stream of national elections since the 1980s. What at first manifested as a show of strength then seemed overly personal and opportunistic. Deepa was seeing minds change in real time in her text chains with voters due to both Harris's waffling and the dust settling around the moment itself.

"In the moment, I thought Kamala's interaction with Biden was on point," Heather, a woman Deepa met during a campaign swing through California, said in a text. "But then I started to think about it and realized it kind of felt like a setup, a bit planned possibly." Which, of course, most attacks on the debate stage are.

But data was also showing problematic fallout, specifically in the state that was the strategic focal point for both Biden and Harris. Two weeks after the busing comments, and the ensuing back-and-forth, Mayor Buttigieg's campaign commissioned a survey of Black voters ages twenty-five to sixty-five years old in South Carolina—a key group that every candidate needed to attract in that state's primary. The survey's findings spelled problems for any candidate not named Biden.

The "Obama halo," as the pollsters dubbed it in the memo to Buttigieg's senior campaign staff, explained Black voters' ability to forgive Biden's transgressions—on working with segregationist senators, on allegations of inappropriate touching, on views that were out of step with the mainstream—because since "their guy Barack chose him as VP, they feel like Biden has already been vetted." Further, "They recognize that Biden is a product of his time and that he probably held views in the past that were in keeping with that time," the memo analyzing focus group results read. "But he's changed as the culture has." In short: they'd seen enough to know he deserved the benefit of the doubt.

It was a sentiment also voiced by House minority whip James Clyburn ahead of the South Carolina primary more than six months later, when he endorsed Biden, saying, "I know Joe. We know Joe. But most importantly, Joe knows us. I know his heart. I know who he is. I know what he is. I know where this country is: We are at an inflection point."

There was a great, perhaps initially undervalued, store of trust and street cred for Biden. For Harris, that abiding affection—especially among this critical Black voting bloc—made her debate-stage barb a big problem. While some of the women surveyed gave "plaudits for her passion" and some men recognized it as a potentially smart political strategy, many of the South Carolina voters felt it was "below the belt" on an issue that, especially to younger members of the electorate, was obscure. That was the bad news. The other bad news was that pollsters described the group's reaction to Kamala's own presidential candidacy as "muted." And those who *could* see her in the White House pictured her sitting in another office than the Oval.

"She will make an absolutely great VP," one woman in the focus group said. A lovely sentiment, except that right now she was running to be the president, not the vice.

Around this time, on the road in Toledo, Ohio, I heard similar themes from voters who may not have picked a favorite candidate yet, but certainly were unhappy with what they'd seen so far. "People have a right to change their opinions," Pamela Hutcherson, a Black woman, told me, alluding to the busing exchange. "And some of the things that have been done in the past or said in the past . . . you know maybe their outlook has changed. And you need to consider what they've done the last five years or the last ten years . . . I think you need to look at what they've done *recently*."

It wasn't just Harris, though. When I asked Pamela, and her husband, Keith, about Booker taking Biden to task for talking about working with segregationist senators in the past and if that was a productive argument to have, she said, "No. I think they need to be talking about what's important to the people *now* . . . We've got somebody there right now that isn't doing what I feel is the correct things to be doing, so they need to be focused, together, in some frame of trying to convince us that they're going to do the things that the people need and I don't think attacking one another is the way to do it."

The Harris team's social media steps to amplify the "that little girl was me" moment had also taken on a narrative of its own in the weeks after the first debate. That they had the photo of Harris as a young girl at the ready somehow became proof of just how far Harris would go to win. It was painted as a highly coordinated assault—by debate stage, then by social media—to take Biden down while elevating the California senator. The resulting picture was one where Harris seemed politically *opportunistic*.

In that assessment there is both the possibility that that's true—good politicians rise by making the most of political opportunities to get ahead—but also something innately unfair, in that it pretends Harris was the only one doing it. Politics tends to swat back, instead of reward, women who openly politick and make power plays. That's what this was, at its core: a power play to knock the front-runner and show that Harris was a legitimate force to be reckoned with. There is a tendency from media and voters alike to recoil from, or paint as somehow sinister, those kinds of moves from female politicians more than male ones. That these women are impatient and unwilling to wait their turn. That they are too confident or too willing to be aggressive. That's part of what happened here. Harris never walked back her decision to go after Biden in this way, simply telling people who brought it up that "it was a debate." Debate stages are made for contrasting, differentiating, and, well, debating.

But even though everyone is trying to make and take their opportunities, there is also a difference between scoring political points that are well researched, well prepared, and well orchestrated versus those that fall apart in the details and flare temperatures in such a stark way. And for veteran political watchers and operatives—ones who I know are quick to cite gender's imbalance for female candidates when it flares—this moment did feel like the latter.

"It was way too obvious and assembled," a veteran Democratic operative not affiliated with any primary campaign, told me in retrospect. It felt like "opposition research"—often shorthanded in political circles as "oppo"—that is done by campaigns and party apparatuses on their opponents' dirty secrets or problematic past policy positions. And the "oppo" that Harris focused on—Biden's federal busing policy in the 1970s—was too wonky for most Americans to grasp as relevant to their own lives or to this present moment. "Forget that she's a woman," this operative said to me. "Anyone who would bring up Joe Biden's position from nearly forty years ago, people see through that. They don't think it's appealing."

What it all amounted to was a swift fall from grace. The same cable news panels that only days earlier had been considering Kamala Harris as an ascendant potential Democratic nominee were now focused on the inconsistencies that emerged in her position and how she would weather the weeks between now and the next debate in Detroit. Instead of keeping Biden in the hot seat, Harris's need to clarify and explain eclipsed the initial controversy and put her in hot water instead. The news cycle turned squarely to Kamala and her need to answer both for the attack itself and for why she'd gone there at all, when her own position seemed close to Biden's.

Her debate surge turned out to be more of a sugar rush than a sustained high. A national audience witnessed the prosecutor's steely gaze and prepared attacks, the same type they'd seen and largely celebrated during her time in the Senate grilling Trump's first attorney general, Jeff Sessions, and later, Supreme Court nominee Brett Kavanaugh. Some people wanted more. Some grappled with a new skepticism creeping in. A narrative lingered that the Harris team wished had not: that Kamala Harris wanted to be president so badly that she'd do anything, even target her friends, to win.

Whether it was a function of her gender, her race, or both, "consciously or not, on Twitter and in the press, [many] would suspect her motives more than they did with others," one former Harris aide told me. "Just dodging a question, as every politician does every day of their lives. If Mayor Pete does it, he's still on message, he's sticking to his talking points, he's a genius. If she does it, it's 'what is she hiding?' "

It led the Kamala team to feel as if the media, and some voters, regularly assumed the worst about her motives, where they either gave others the benefit of the doubt or chalked it up to the cost of doing political business. It's a feeling many staffers for female politicians, and even female politicians themselves, have expressed to me. But also one that bias expert Madeline Heilman explained is a data-backed outcome of women actively competing in male-dominated work spaces.

"Women shouldn't promote themselves, they shouldn't seek power, they shouldn't speak authoritatively, they shouldn't be competitive, they shouldn't even show anger," she told me of the permission structures at play, borne out in multiple studies. "And when they do these things—which really are necessary to be successful, to move your career along in more traditionally male domains—there are penalties for that . . . The penalties are social. [The women] are really disliked. And this kind of cluster of adjectives that are really 'the bitchy cluster.' You know, 'they're cold, they're abrasive, they're shrill, they're cunning,' there's a whole cluster of these awful things that are associated with them and they're not liked."

These dynamics were at play, both in this moment for Harris and throughout the primary for the other female candidates—especially after big nights of candidates trading barbs face-to-face on the debate stage. But there were more Harris-specific problems evidenced in these moments, as well as later in the primary. Ones that were infused with the biases of gender and race, yes, but also ones that have political explanations and that aides have since admitted to me were valid nails in the coffin of Harris's first presidential run.

Harris did, for instance, stumble during her candidacy when it came to simple questions about her policies. The lack of clarity around the details of the busing attack was a symptom of a more chronic problem during her campaign: it was often unclear what her positions were, which begged questions about whether she was effectively messaging them. And some who worked in Harris's orbit in 2020 admitted, however grudgingly, that her reputation for confusing her policy positions, especially when it came to health care, was not entirely overblown.

It was as simple as raising her hand at another moment during that same first debate, indicating she supported abolishing a role for private healthcare insurance markets along with New York City mayor Bill de Blasio and senators Warren and Sanders. A big statement and a clear dividing point for the field on one of the primary's central policy debates. But Harris would walk it back mere hours later on MSNBC's *Morning Joe*. She misunderstood the question asked of her on stage, she said, believing that the moderator, NBC's Lester Holt, was asking the candidates about whether *they personally* would give up their private plan, not whether her overall policy would get rid of private insurance (which it would not).

The questions would persist. Harris's communications director, Lily Adams, faced them a few hours after her boss did. Again on MSNBC, Lily was asked if Harris was "looking a little bit slippery on this issue" and "trying to have it both ways."

"No, I don't think so at all," Lily said, her face momentarily betraying bewilderment at the suggestion that her candidate was "slippery" on any issue, let alone one so highly scrutinized and important as health care. "She's been very clear: she co-sponsored the Medicare for All bill back in 2017 when it was introduced, she was very clear—she put her name on the bill . . . What she wants people to know is that if they need something that's not covered in the system, they of course will be able to get that. That's no question." But it was.

Forbes summed it up best: "In a few short months during 2019, Harris co-sponsored the Sanders' single-payer plan that would have completely eliminated private insurance, enthusiastically raised her hand in support of single-payer during a debate, the next day walked that back in a difficult to understand explanation of why she wouldn't entirely eliminate private insurance, and then proposed her own hybrid Medicare plan that would have eventually offered today's insurance company run Medicare Advantage plans to everyone."

It left reporters across the campaign trail confused about the details of her plan—and lent to a well-worn impression that Harris had many questions left to answer here.

She's hardly the first candidate to face this problem. Flip-flopping can be used as code for dishonesty or obstructionism, neither of which comes with good assumptions about motive. Voters want to trust their president. They want to feel the candidates are shooting them straight. Candidates, male and female, must pass this metric or be punished for it by voters and questioned about it by reporters. All of that is valid and important.

But for women, there is, as Heilman laid out for us, the added weight of *how* voters assess them through the lens of honesty and transparency. It's a view that's impacted, as bell hooks wrote, by both "the mask of patriarchal 'femininity' [which] often renders women's deceptions acceptable" and "age-old sexist stereotypes that suggest women are, by virtue of being female, less capable of truth telling. The origins of this sexist stereotype extend back to ancient stories of Adam and Eve, of Eve's willingness to lie even to God." These biases, in addition to the overt politics, were at play when we talked about how Harris didn't know or didn't have a consistent stance on an important issue like health care even more of an albatross. It made policy mix-ups into larger questions about if she were lying about a contentious policy in order to get ahead in the primary, only to flip her stance to a more politically expedient one later.

"She has a very firm moral compass and a strong sense of right and wrong," a former staffer explained to me. "So, what came across as dodgy around policy was more her legal mind not wanting to screw up any details, trying to state something in a way that didn't get anything wrong."

In addition, Kamala was relatively new to the national political scene. Unlike others in the field, like Warren or Sanders, or even Biden, who had been living these federal policy issues for decades, Harris had only come to Washington in 2017, with prior experience that had been solely steeped in California politics. That meant there was a lot of getting up to speed for her in the Senate—and fast—in part because of her presidential aspirations, but also because of the high expectations placed upon her by the national media and honchos in the Democratic Party as the only Black woman in the Senate; a woman who had already accomplished so much in California state politics and who could go on to great things.

Someone who worked for her in the Senate described those early months to me this way: "Imagine being one of the ten most well-known reporters, but you've never reported a story and you have no idea how to do it." Hyperbole, sure, but it's also true that it takes time to adjust to the pace and flow of Capitol Hill. Even acclimating to it as a beat reporter took me some time in 2021. But Harris didn't have the benefit of a long runway—especially given the stakes of the first year of the Trump administration. She was coming into her own as a senator as the entire institution in which she now served was under a barrage of verbal and tweeted attacks from the other end of Pennsylvania Avenue. Those early days in the Senate showed how little learning curve Harris would be allowed; how "astronomical," in the words of another then-staffer, were the expectations, and how slim the margin for error. It's something that lodged itself in the minds of Harris's staff ahead of the presidential campaign. Missteps couldn't be afforded, and biases had to be strategized for. What manifested, however, was what staffers described as an at-times cautious approach from the candidate on policy—one that read as inauthentic and dodgy in the press and to voters. And it's hard not to question if that would've stuck in the same way if Kamala wasn't a woman.

But the political metrics—high turnover in her Senate office, high turnover on her presidential campaign, and a lack of cohesive internal strategy—led to the Harris campaign being looked back on by many in Washington, both those who were a part of it and onlookers to it, as a mess.

"They were chasing shiny objects and there wasn't a cohesive North Star," one former Obama administration official who did not work for a candidate in the primary summed it up. The lack of cohesion manifested publicly in that Harris never cleanly adhered to a "lane"—progressive or moderate—in the primary, making it hard for voters to quickly know what political stripes they should assign her, but also privately in the blurred lines of the campaign's leadership. Another source described it to me as an "air of indecisiveness" among the campaign's top brass. It led to rank-and-file staff feeling disconnected and mistrustful of senior leadership. The candidate's messaging on the stump changed regularly, in hopes of recapturing energy and momentum, but failing to do so. The polls dipped after that post-first-debate spike and never really bounced back. The state that was priority number one—South Carolina—trended more consistently toward Joe Biden, with the state's powerful Black congressman James Clyburn expressing "amazement" to me during the summer of 2019 at how poorly Harris, and fellow Black presidential contender Cory Booker, were doing with the state's predominantly African American voting base.

"I thought for sure that there would be much more of a surge and I can't quite figure that out yet," Clyburn said to me in June of 2019, referring to polls in South Carolina that continued to show Biden with a healthy lead. Harris, he offered, "hasn't spelled out the policy stuff with her vision"—though he was careful to praise her vision itself as "tremendous." When we sat together at his campaign office in Washington, D.C., the third-ranking House Democrat told me, "I just thought 'Kamala' because this just seemed to be the year of the Black woman. I thought she would be surging a little more than she is."

That surge would never come. After slogging through the summer, the campaign was deemed in "free-fall" by reporters. To stop the bleeding, they shifted their focus from South Carolina to Iowa, a strategic move emphasized by Harris being overheard telling fellow senator Mazie Hirono, "I'm fucking moving to Iowa." Once the comments leaked publicly, *those* T-shirts pretty much made themselves.

But it was in the doldrums of her presidential campaign that Harris seemed to publicly embrace more of herself. Thus far on the trail she'd seemed unwilling to, or was uncomfortable with, the idea of talking about herself beyond her basic bio and policy portfolio.

Even on the day she announced her candidacy, as I stood among fellow reporters at Harris's alma mater, Howard University, for a press conference, she dodged on a key question that could have been an easily prepared slam dunk about being biracial and female and now vying for the presidency. Asked by a reporter there about her heritage—"you're an African American woman but you're also Indian American"—and how she would describe herself, she immediately burst into laughter and asked, "Did you read my book?" before finally responding curtly: "I describe myself as a proud American. That's how I describe myself."

The thing is, there was much more to Harris beyond the politics and the prosecutor's persona. She was "Momala" to her two stepchildren and a loving partner to a successful lawyer, Doug Emhoff, who couldn't hide his adoration for her if he tried (and he never did). She was an enthusiastic cook who would share recipes and cooking tips with at least one reporter during commercial breaks before cable news hits or snip fresh herbs from her garden in California and bring them back to her Senate staff, handing out bags of basil and oregano. She listened to old-school hip-hop and was quick to laugh from her belly. It took months for these authentic signals of who she was to permeate her presidential campaign and, as Lily and I talked about, they were not always initially embraced as truly authentic by media or voters.

She also eventually, and perhaps too late in the game, began taking on the issue of electability and the sexism and racism that were inherent in informing who could be electable and who couldn't. "I have also started to, perhaps, be more candid," she said in an October 2019 interview with *Axios*, "talking about what I describe and believe to be the elephant in the room of my campaign—electability. Essentially is America ready for a woman and a woman of color to be president of the United States?"

She went on: "There is a lack of ability, or difficulty in imagining that someone who we have never seen can do a job that has been done forty-five times by someone who is not that person . . . I'm aware of the challenges, but I know who the people are. And I know that we have an ability to see what can be."

Ultimately, that would be true—just not in the way Harris initially imagined it.

In November, days before she dropped out of the race, Harris's team released a video of Kamala at Mindy Kaling's house in Los Angeles making dosas—a popular Indian food, similar to a crepe. It was one in a string of videos that Harris did with female celebrities of color, talking about issues that impacted their communities. It's not that she hadn't highlighted these issues before—she had. She was just now showing more of herself in the process.

But the factionalism that plagued her campaign was getting worse, with aides departing and leaving letters behind detailing poor treatment of staff and no plan to win with three months left until the Iowa Caucus. The rancor within the campaign eventually spilled onto the pages of *The New York Times* with a jaw-dropping story that cited more than fifty current and former staff members and allies. In reporting circles, looking for lines like this one—that declare the number of sources outright—is something of a parlor game. A sign of just how many people were willing to gripe, or outright shit-talk their boss. But to see fifty-plus sources tell the story of how the Harris campaign had "unraveled" was stunning; a nail in the coffin of a campaign that was already gasping for its final breaths.

I was home in D.C. the day after the *Times* piece ran, making the mistake of booking an exercise session billed as "the hardest workout class you've never heard of." As I hobbled out of the studio around 11 a.m., I saw a series of texts on my phone from a donor source of mine: *Keep an eye on Harris today*, they said. She'd just cancelled a noon fundraiser scheduled at a top Manhattan law firm. Something major was up. Maybe a shake-up, maybe something more definitive; my source wasn't sure. I put the tip in an email to a small group of colleagues dedicated to the 2020 campaign beat and we all started hunting for more sources and more information. Meanwhile, my colleagues specifically covering the Harris campaign were waved off the fundraiser's cancellation as nothing more than a shifting schedule. *Leave the race? Us? No . . .*

Shortly after 1 p.m., Harris made the announcement herself: she was dropping out. In an email to campaign staff, she wrote that her campaign "simply doesn't have the financial resources we need to continue. I'm not a billionaire," she wrote. "I can't fund my own campaign." With "deep regret—but also with deep gratitude," Harris was out.

Her departure from the race spurred a brief discussion on the barriers faced by women and women of color on the fundraising circuit, given that Harris cited lack of funds as a key reason to drop out. Ability to raise money is a critical metric—considered a predictor for electoral success, especially in presidential races that require millions to even get a viable campaign infrastructure off the ground. Raising cash is a barrier that women have long faced to becoming successful candidates, in part because the donor class tends to be male, and biases of viability could stem from never having seen a woman, or woman of color, consistently succeed in the presidential space before. In an arena that's all about return on investment and backing a winning horse, it can take extra convincing for candidates that don't automatically conjure the image of POTUS.

But 2018's congressional races showed female energy manifest in cash flow to campaigns. Female donors got in the game in a big way during that cycle, buoyed by news events like the hearings around sexual misconduct allegations against Justice Brett Kavanaugh and Donald Trump's administration, helping to reverse the trend of female candidates being outraised by their male counterparts. The Center for Responsive Politics found that in the 2018 midterms, women raised more money than men across the board, regardless of whether they were running as challengers in competitive seats or in open races.

They also found that white candidates raised more than candidates of color, with Black women raising the least amount of money in 2018—half as much as AAPI or white candidates. The difference also exists among male candidates, CRP found, but was not as pronounced. They importantly note that how competitive a race is directly impacts how much money a candidate can raise. The more competitive the race, the more cash flows in from both conventional donors and PACs, but also from grassroots, small-dollar donors. Black women, they write, tend to run in "safer"—easier to win—and "poorer" districts, where less cash is poured into winning the seat. However, even with competitiveness accounted for, CRP found Black women raised less from large donors than any other candidate group.

"Given that large donors are typically the most significant contributors to a political campaign, Black women need to work much harder to raise money," their post-election report states. And certainly, in presidential races, those traditional big-dollar donors are the quickest way for most campaigns to grow their bank accounts—and fast. This donor pool itself, as you may have guessed, is largely male and white. In fact, Hillary Clinton's 2016 campaign was the first to get more than half of its large donations from women, and in 2018 the trend continued, with Democratic female donors coming up big for female candidates of the same party.

In 2020, there was an explosion of small-dollar donations, with two of the major candidates in the race, Bernie Sanders and Elizabeth Warren, only pursuing grassroots donations and eschewing the more traditional big-dollar-donor route that the rest of the field used and needed. The year also saw a big spike in female donors, making up $1.4 billion given to candidates at the federal level (including the presidential race). Studies of the 2020 cycle showed that female candidates relied heavily on female donors. In state-level contests, 46 percent of donations by women were for female candidates.

Nevertheless, in the case of Kamala Harris, she was a career California pol who was known to be a prolific and well-connected fundraiser. During her campaign, she spent lots of time in front of donors—a strategic choice that literally paid off but also kept her off the trail for weeks on end, with some members of her campaign press corps home in Washington and itching to attend any campaign event, anywhere, with the candidate at all. Nevertheless, Harris pulled a $12 million fundraising haul in 2019's first quarter, just shy of that in Q2, and $11.6 million in Q3. For a primary that promised to be long and bruising, cash was key. At the start, she was near the top of the pack in dollars raised, but she lagged in Q2 and Q3 compared to her rivals. It wasn't a question of raising funds; it was a question of how they were being used and how money was translating (or not) in polls. Which, in Harris's case as a presidential candidate, it wasn't.

Still, when she joined the Biden ticket in the summer of 2020, gone was any worry about Kamala's fundraising ability. In fact, as one *Politico* headline crooned after she'd been tapped as VP: "Harris sets off Democratic donor stampede." And in August, the Biden-Harris ticket got more than $33.4 million from women—double what the campaign had raised from female donors the month before, CNN and the Center for Responsive Politics found. While it's hard to quantify the specific impact of running mates, Harris's presence on the ticket made dollars and cents. Her power was felt in 2020—but mostly when she was elevated, as opposed to seeking an election in her own right.

Meanwhile, of the assessments that she shared too little of herself too late, some former campaign advisors still balk. "We require women, and women of color, to explain themselves more to us—which is on us, not on them," one told me. "She'd be asked all the time, 'What is it like being a Black woman running for president? What would you say about that?' But when they don't neatly define themselves, the conclusion is *they* should do a better job explaining themselves to *us*."

There's something to that. In a political reporting corps that's become more diverse, but still has a long way to go, the people tasked with telling the stories of these candidates may not be able to access the nuances of their authentic and diverse personalities. For instance, most of the D.C. press corps didn't know what the "Divine Nine" was, let alone understand the power of these historically Black sororities that Harris prides herself on being a part of. Without that access point, stories about how sisterhood can shape a candidate are less likely to be pitched or reported on. And while Harris's embedded press corps was predominantly made up of journalists of color, many of them women, some Harris staffers still saw an air of hostility toward, or innate skepticism of, their candidate from the start from legacy newsrooms. It was a feeling that would persist even after she got to the White House.

But to others in the Democratic apparatus, race and gender told only part of the story. "It was an unbelievably bad campaign," an operative who sat out the primaries told me plainly, echoing the analysis of most Democrats who closely watched Harris in 2020.

The silver lining, though, for those with hopes for Harris in the future is that many of the things that felled her in '20 could also be chalked up to her being a first-time candidate, new to the national stage. "Kamala will learn from this," this person said, citing the more clear-eyed campaign Hillary Clinton ran in 2016 after losing in the primaries in 2008. "There's no better way to learn than actually to get your feet wet and go through the process."

Ultimately, though, Harris would leave the race and then reemerge. When she did, the biggest question her campaign left behind—who is Kamala Harris?—would be answered clearly for voters. Not necessarily by her, but by the man who chose her to run alongside him.

5

One Night in Washington Square Park

Using History to Make Herstory

SEPTEMBER 2019

Joe Rospars didn't have "Personally Pick Up Wood from a Labor Icon's Homestead" on his Bingo card. It also wasn't the way he thought he and his wife would spend their five-year wedding anniversary. But there they were, on a more than ten-hour round-trip journey from Brooklyn to a farm near Portland, Maine, to pick up historically significant wooden panels for a podium that would be tailor-made for his boss. Apparently, road trips fit Rospar's job description as "senior Warren campaign strategist."

The wood once belonged, in a sense, to Frances Perkins, a trailblazing labor activist and glass-ceiling breaker in the Roosevelt administration in the 1930s. She was an icon in both feminist and labor circles. But she would also play a key role in a speech Warren was set to give from Manhattan's Washington Square Park. The campaign found out Perkins's grandson was a Warren fan, and he offered up the wood. Once Rospars had it in hand, he and his wife grabbed a lobster roll—when in Maine, after all—and then headed right back to Brooklyn, where, through the campaign's grassroots donor network, the all-female woodworking team from Peg Woodworking stood ready to craft the panels into a podium. They opted for a style like the one used by the suffragettes.

"Simple and spare, yet strong and presidential" was the vibe they aimed for, according to hand-sketched blueprints. Andrea Sun, who headed up setup and "advance" operations for the Warren campaign, suggested that the podium for the woman who aspired to be America's forty-sixth president clock in at . . . forty-six inches tall.

On the morning of September 16, 2019, a cluster of female woodworkers carried the freshly buffed homage to a female trailblazer into the shadow of the Washington Square Arch. Inside the boxy podium base, they scrawled messages of support: "You are the candidate I believe in with my whole heart. Good luck!" read one, in big looping cursive letters. "The future is female," signed a woman named Kate, with hearts. "Great leaders look inward and tell their story with authenticity and passion," someone else signed in black marker. "You are her."

Supporters started showing up in Washington Square Park hours before Warren was set to get on stage. Campaign staff were still preparing: rolling production crates, spreading out bike racks to cordon off an area near the stage for chairs, and hoisting banners up the archways. Other staff dispersed volunteers throughout the park, tasking them with playing a sort of zone defense that would yield an unofficial crowd count, while signing up supporters to receive campaign outreach, and also keeping an eye out for any would-be disrupters. Warren would be telling her story here, to the biggest crowd we'd seen for her—and most of the 2020 field—yet.

I got to the park early, too, with live shot requests for MSNBC about the latest policy proposal on rooting out corruption that was rolled out in advance of Warren's remarks. Once we finished them, my producer and I jetted off to a coffee shop in search of caffeine to keep us energized for the night ahead, but also for the refuge of air-conditioning to salvage the work of the NBC Hair and Makeup Department from the on-again, off-again showers that were now dousing the park.

This was partly a move of vanity, but it also wasn't. Frizzed hair or too-shiny cheeks were examples of very specific traps that exist for women in television, where not taking care of the basics that come off as superficial to an outside observer can distract from the smart thing you're saying or earn you demerits with bosses and viewers. TV, as I've often been reminded, is a visual medium. I'd earned my fair share of finger wags over the years for not wearing sufficient bronzer, or eyeliner, and even once for deigning to wear flannel on the air. Enough reminders and chastisements left me resigned not to let a lack of vanity be the thing that distracted people from my reporting and analysis. It wasn't lost on me that my male colleagues had less to worry about in this department.

I returned for a few more live shots as more press carted in gear and started claiming table space behind tall rows of risers. The weighty drops of afternoon rain over Washington Square Park didn't shoo away any waiting supporters. Instead, it left them waiting with the smell of water fresh on concrete, mixed with that faint aroma of pot that usually floats through this part of lower Manhattan.

I pinned on my press pass—thick paper with a blue-green hue that Team Warren called "Liberty Green." It sort of said everything about the Warren campaign that they'd planned everything down to the specific color that represented them. There were feather boas, sweatshirts, Twitter avatars, even Statue of Liberty outfits to hammer home the point that they were organized—and behind an iconic woman, no less. Staffers at all levels—and even Warren herself—adopted heavy usage of the Statue of Liberty emoji in texts.

Clouds thickened overhead as I ventured into the crowd to talk politics. "Man on the street"—or MOS—interviews are the meat and potatoes of campaign coverage. I always started the same way, regardless of whose rally I was covering: "Hey, I'm Ali with NBC News and I'm just out talking to people about why they're here. Can I talk to you?" By then, the camera was already likely hovering over us anyway, making the question more of a formality than one in need of an answer.

With those I approached, we talked about crowd size in an attempt to answer the age-old campaign question for a news story: What does a big crowd really mean (if anything)? The goal was also to take the pulse of the crowd, to more fully flesh out our coverage of this event. Were they all decided Warren supporters? Were they just Warren-curious? What were the issues that were motivating them to show up?

While I worked, two of my oldest friends—who were decidedly *not* members of the press but who were moonlighting as reporters to join me on this occasion—arrived on the scene. Molly Kadish and Shelby Coon proudly clipped on their "Liberty Green" press badges and dumped their bags next to mine in the fenced-off press area. It felt so good to see people who knew me "Before." Before I spent more time talking to strangers about politics than I did talking to friends over drinks about their dating lives or work promotions. Before I left New York City in 2015 to travel the country for years on end, vowing to return but never doing so. Before I planned my life around "in cycle" years and "off cycle" years. These two women knew me before college, before I knew what a dream job was, and well before I started doing it at NBC.

I felt lucky to be able to show them what I do now; why I am so absent from weekly brunches and hungover Sundays. They're both politically inclined, so they had reason to want to come, but selfishly I wanted them there to see that my absence was rooted in something real. *Don't you see how all-consuming this is?* I wanted to absolve myself of the guilt I felt for leaning so hard into my Road Life that my former life felt like a relic, something I would never find again. Here, I could merge those two lives—even for just a few hours.

Turning my attention from my friends to my assigned candidate, I felt surrounded yet safe, even in a sea of mostly strangers. Because at rallies like this, there was an electricity in the crowd. A spark, something magnetic that comes when people gather with thousands of strangers to hear a politician's *ideas* for the future. There's a lot that's hopeful, even romantic, about that. Truth be told, it's the reason I love covering campaigns: standing in rooms of dozens or thousands of people guided by the abiding belief that our country can do and be *better.* Crowds steered by the hope of what the country could aspire to and become. It's the foundation of potential and aspiration upon which a symbiotic relationship between candidate and supporter grows. And New York City's Washington Square Park was well-trod territory for political dreamers and American optimists such as these.

Three years earlier, the cheers of more than twenty thousand people reverberated off the trees and concrete here as they applauded Vermont senator Bernie Sanders's ideas for "revolution." Nine years before that, tens of thousands flocked below Eighth Street for a glimpse of then-candidate Barack Obama positioned under the park's famed marble archway proclaiming "yes we can." Now, on this Monday night in September 2019: same park, same 20,000-plus crowd, new candidate matching soaring rhetoric to "dream big, fight hard" with supporters' soaring hopes for change.

"We're not gaggling tonight," my childhood friend, Molly, told me while we waited for Warren to get on stage. She tried to sound matter-of-fact about it, but the smirk gave away that she had no idea what a "gaggle" was or why a campaign staffer had told her, of all people, it wouldn't be happening after the rally.

"No gaggle!" Shelby emphasized, giddy with the power of information and drunk on her temporary journalism powers. "Gabrielle told us."

I laughed at the notion of Warren's press secretary giving my oldest friends the professional courtesy of a heads-up that they shouldn't be ready to pepper the senator with questions after the speech. Given the sheer number of media present, our usual Q&A clusters, or "gaggles," around Warren after such events would be next to impossible that night. It was just one more sign—taken in tandem with the crowd being one hundred times bigger than at a typical event, as well as the attendance of Sarah Jessica Parker of *Sex and the City* fame—that this wasn't your usual Warren rally. This speech was special, meant to articulate the focus and scope of Warren's presidential campaign.

The location, in addition to the podium, was a key part of that message. Because not only was Washington Square Park a breeding ground for political hope and change, but it was also the site of tragedy that launched everyday Americans—most of them women—into action for the greater good. And, in addition to her own, that was the story Warren came to tell.

She strode on stage wearing the formal version of her usual campaign trail uniform—a deep purple blazer over black pants and a black top. (The casual version of her "uniform" swapped the blazer for a cardigan, in similarly TV-friendly jewel tones.) Dark blue banners with her "Liberty Green"–hued WARREN lettering cascaded down each leg of the Washington Square Arch, billowing as dusk fell on the city and the spotlights washed over the woman at the center of it all. From behind Frances Perkins's podium, Warren began "an important story about our past, and about our future . . ."

"We're not here today because of famous arches or famous men," she declared. "In fact, we're not here because of men at all." Cheers erupted. "We're here because of some hardworking women." More cheers. "Women who more than one hundred years ago worked long hours in a brown, ten-story building just a block that way. Women who worked at the Triangle Shirtwaist Factory." The crowd quieted, waiting for Warren to continue.

On a Saturday in March of 1911, a fire broke out in New York City's Triangle Shirtwaist Factory. "It took eighteen minutes for 146 people to die," Warren detailed. Some perished from the flames—they were trapped because factory bosses locked the doors to the stairwells and the workrooms. Others died from the jump out of the tenth-story ledges onto the ground below.

The dead were "mostly women," Warren went on. "Mostly immigrants, Jewish and Italian. Mostly people who made as little as five dollars a week to get their shot at the American dream." It was a tragedy, but it shouldn't have been a surprise.

"For years, across the city, women factory workers and their allies had been sounding the alarm about the dangerous and squalid conditions, fighting for shorter hours and higher pay. They protested, they went on strike, they got coverage in the press. Everyone knew about these problems. But the fat profits were making New York factory owners rich, and they had no plans to give that up. Instead of changing conditions at the factories, the owners worked their political connections . . . Nothing changed. Business owners got richer, politicians got more powerful, and working people paid the price. Does any of this sound familiar?"

A "yes" rang out from the crowd.

These were stories you didn't often hear from presidential candidates, or see much of in your history books. Researchers estimate that women's stories make up just 0.5 percent of recorded history. The stories of women that you *do* read are the tiniest tip of an insanely massive historical iceberg. But these were the kinds of stories you got when new people, who didn't look like or have the same lived experience as past contenders, entered the presidential arena.

It was something the Hillary Clinton team grappled with in real time: what stories, including the candidate's, we as a society tell and think are worth telling. Clinton campaign communications director Jennifer Palmieri wrote in her book *Dear Madam President* after the 2016 campaign: "Our history—the canon of American stories we treasured and told us who we were—were all based on men. Hillary didn't fit that narrative . . . I am embarrassed to say it now, but when I considered her life story at the time of the campaign, I didn't find it compelling. I didn't see anything remarkable in her upbringing," or in the struggles of her life. Those struggles have "to make sense to us, we have to recognize the struggle, it has to tell us a larger story we want told about America. It didn't work with her story. There wasn't anything in our history to compare to Hillary. I guess that's what happens to the people who are *making* history. We don't appreciate their value in real time."

Warren and her team were dredging up old *her*stories constantly. From launching her presidential campaign at a textile mill in Lawrence, Massachusetts, where in 1912 female workers went on strike to demand fair wages, to commemorating the legacy of Atlanta's Black washerwomen's 1881 strike that shook the city's white establishment in a speech at one of the nation's oldest historically Black colleges.

"A woman was visiting friends who lived in a townhouse behind me when the fire broke out," Warren continued, referring to where she was stationed, squarely behind the Perkins Podium. "She hurried into the street, joining the crowds as they ran across this park and headed to the Triangle Factory. When she got there, she watched. Watched as women on the ledge begged for help. Watched as they held each other. Watched as they jumped to their deaths. The woman watching was Frances Perkins. She was thirty years old and already a workers' rights activist, but that day set change in motion."

Warren described the marches that followed the tragedy at the factory, hundreds of thousands of people marching down Fifth Avenue to memorialize the women who were lost and commence the push for change for those who had survived as well as the many others still working in such terrible conditions.

"While the women of the trade unions kept pushing from the outside, Frances pushed from the inside," Warren said. "She understood that those women died because of the greed of their bosses and the corruption of their elected officials. So, she went up to Albany, ready to fight. She worked to create a commission investigating factory conditions, and then she served as its lead investigator. Remember, this was years before women could even vote, let alone play major roles in government. But Frances had a plan." Warren had made her connection.

"She and her fellow activists fought for fire safety, of course—and they got it. Next time you do a fire drill at school or work, or you see a plainly marked fire exit at work, think of Frances and the Triangle Women, because they're the reason the laws changed. But they didn't stop with fire safety . . ."

After the factory fire, Perkins rose through the ranks of state government in New York. Then, at the height of the Great Depression, President Franklin Delano Roosevelt nominated her to be secretary of labor—the first female member of the cabinet and the longest-serving person ever in this position. The Labor Department building headquarters in Washington, D.C., now bears her name.

"And what did she push for when she got there? Big, structural change." One of Warren's well-worn campaign slogans. "[Perkins] used the same model she and her friends had used after the Triangle Fire: she worked the political system relentlessly from the inside, while a sustained movement applied pressure from the outside. As Frances Perkins put it, the Triangle Fire was 'the day the New Deal was born.' So, what did one woman— one very persistent woman—backed up by millions of people across this country get done? Social Security. Unemployment insurance. Abolition of child labor. Minimum wage. The right to join a union. Even the very existence of the weekend. Big, structural change. One woman, and millions of people to back her up."

This was undoubtedly Frances Perkins's story, but it was also Elizabeth Warren's story. Her plan for governing and proof that women had blown through Washington to make change before. Sharing this narrative illuminated an often glossed-over part of our nation's history, one that was driven by women who were never given a seat at the table but made space for themselves anyway. They brought, as Chisholm advised, their own folding chairs.

While Warren was a woman telling stories of other women, showing she stood on the shoulders of their work and savvy strategizing, she was also using them to showcase her theory of how to effect political change. How *she* would force changes if she were allowed to be another female first in government.

All of the plans, all of the events through more than twenty states, all of the polling, all of the slowly climbing in the national consciousness through the summer of 2020, culminated in these remarks that laid out the North Star of the Warren campaign: rooting out corruption in the name of a fairer governing democracy and impacting big change in hard-to-move government structures. I'd watched nearly every speech and every town hall and interview for months, but this was both her clearest articulation of what it meant to be "in this fight" and an explanation for why she believed so deeply in grassroots organizing's ability to take on entrenched, insider systems of government. It was also the most overtly feminist I'd ever heard her.

At the peak of her popularity as a presidential candidate, Warren was arguing that women are the ones who pushed this country forward and toward progress and that she believed herself to be the next in this line of wily, uncowed, progress-minded women. "The tragic story of the Triangle Factory Fire is a story about power!"

And really that's what Warren's 2020 message was all about: power—who wields it and for whose benefit. Constantly trying to illustrate a system that Warren often described "worked for the wealthy and well-connected," usually at the expense of the non-white, non-male, non-monied Americans who made the country work. Disrupting these unequal power structures required leveraging grassroots movements—which was exactly what the Warren team invested in doing—and ensuring that a diverse slate of leaders were given a seat at the table, both within her organization and in the government she was campaigning to build.

Because it wasn't just Warren's ideas that made her disruptive. She was progressive, yes, and proposing massive government programs that would overhaul foundational pieces of America's social infrastructure. But her very existence as a woman meant that if she won, what had always been in American politics would be irrevocably changed. That would be true for Warren, for Amy Klobuchar, for Kamala Harris, Kirsten Gillibrand, Marianne Williamson, and Tulsi Gabbard. Even the women who weren't running on "big, structural change" represented a big, structural shift.

On top of that, Warren's message was gleeful when she addressed disrupting systems that worked for the monied interests and cozy capitalists. I mean, the campaign literally sold a mug labeled "billionaire tears."

That her naysayers were getting louder came with the territory of approaching front-runner status. It took people a while to call her that, despite it being true in many of the polls from the early primary states. The slow burn to achieve front-runner status meant attacks from rivals wouldn't truly come until fall—and when they did, the attacks would spur a polling slide Warren would never recover from.

But for now, she was allowed images like these: big crowds at rallies, followed by winding selfie lines. These were a campaign hallmark, dating back to her Senate reelection run in 2018. They were nonnegotiable, with Warren reminding staff that she'd consider an event a failure if she didn't get to say "hello" or take a picture with any person who wanted one. That was her argument after a sustained, if rare, disagreement with her campaign manager, Roger Lau. "It's going to take forever. And you're going to be tired. And it's going to be exhausting," he told her. She trusted him, but she trusted her instincts more. So, the lines came with her in the presidential race. Roger was proven wrong and has worn that badge with honor since.

The assembly-line-style mechanics that the team used to make these lines as efficient as possible were on full display in the park that night, too. One staffer greeted a supporter and took their things. Another staffer held on to the supporter's phone, passing it at the appropriate moment to Nora Kate Keefe—Warren's body woman and snapper of "selfies"—who always took more than one photo before passing the phone off to another staffer, who was waiting at the end of the line with the supporter's personal effects. The whole scene of whirring efficiency was so captivating that *The New York Times* once made a stop-motion graphic illustrating the anatomy of the Warren campaign selfie line.

Tonight, the team needed all the efficiency they could get. In their wildest estimations, they never thought the selfie line would get *this* long— or that they'd be arguing with the NYPD to let them make this event a success (by Warren's standard that no selfie go un-snapped, no "hello" unsaid) before the park's midnight curfew got them all kicked out. Staffers pled their case. They would break down the bike racks being used to section off the area, they said. Team members would start stuffing trash bags themselves to save on cleanup time, they offered. These moves bought them more of the time they needed, except that the line kept growing, not shrinking. Curious onlookers, or savvy supporters who had ditched the line and gone for a quick bite or home to do some laundry before coming back, were joining or rejoining the line. Ruthless efficiency extended to Warren's supporters, too, it appeared.

All the while, Andrea—the campaign's key event manager on site—

kept the calculator app up on her phone, punching the number of people left in line and dividing them by minutes left on the clock before midnight. "Go faster," was her only instruction, whispered to Nora, who was still dutifully snapping photos on strangers' cell phones. If they did seven seconds per person, Andrea estimated, maybe they'd make it. The line—when it was all said and selfie'd—lasted about four hours, made up of roughly four thousand pictures.

From an optics perspective, it was the perfect showing of enthusiasm around a candidate. Not to mention photos provided free advertising on social media. Selfies, after all, were the currency of the campaign trail. For many voters, especially those in the early states, collecting snapshots with the field of presidential hopefuls was part of the process. A sign that they were doing their due diligence around the massive field of candidates.

The lines served another purpose, though. It was a chance for Warren—and all the other candidates who took the time to do them—to take the pulse of the people. Sometimes, a supporter would press a letter into her hand; Warren would often read these letters during car rides between events. Other times, they'd tell her stories about the crush of student loan debt or healthcare bills piling up or the friend they'd just lost to an opioid overdose. In their own ways, they were asking for help; her help.

But requests weren't just made *of* Warren. Sometimes, she had her own asks to make. Asks of only the tiniest people waiting in line—usually, as they were holding the hand of a parent.

"My name's Elizabeth," she would say, kneeling and taking little girls' pinkies in hers. Her voice was soft but serious in these moments, never morphing into that high-pitched whine that some people make when they're talking to kids or babies. "And I'm running for president. Because that's what girls do."

On its face, it might have seemed silly. Selfies and pinky promises? But it was a solemn oath, one Warren had been making since her first run for the U.S. Senate in Massachusetts in 2012. "It matters a lot to me that little girls see themselves as future Presidents of the United States," she once explained. More brick-laying in the long road toward progress.

It felt like a continuation of the message Hillary Clinton had left women with when she conceded a race she'd won by the metric that didn't matter in November 2016: "To all the women, and especially the young women, who put their faith in this campaign and in me, I want you to know that nothing has made me prouder than to be your champion . . . And to all of the little girls who are watching this, never doubt that you are valuable and powerful and deserving of every chance and opportunity in the world to pursue and achieve your own dreams."

The selfie lines and pinky promises would continue until the very end of Warren's campaign, but her climb to the top of the field and front-runner status within it was fleeting. The rally in New York gave the campaign, and those of us following it, a taste of what *could* be—but that feeling never returned.

With the chill of fall comes a more serious phase of campaigning. Voters stop candidate speed-dating and start defining the relationship, sporting campaign buttons with candidate names proudly emblazoned and, in Iowa, filling out "commit-to-caucus" cards in earnest—the Iowa equivalent of a going-steady sweetheart pin. Candidates start funneling cash, if they have it, into ads that blanket TV, radio, and the internet. It's go time.

Warren began this period known for her plans yet lacking a critically important one: a clearly articulated healthcare policy; her own version of Medicare for All. Even though health care was *the* issue that Democrats rode to victory in the 2018 midterms, it wasn't a regular riff in Warren's daily stump speeches, nor did she prioritize rolling out a healthcare policy in the early months of the campaign. She laid out the mile marker early that she was "with Bernie" on Medicare for All, and that she believed health care to be a right, not a privilege. When voters asked, as they often did, about health care during town halls, that's what she would tell them. It was enough to get by at a town hall or even an early-in-the-game debate. Door-to-door with voters, it was a different story.

Warren's army of organizers, who canvassed front doors of voters across the early primary states daily, knew voters needed more—and fast. They were constantly asking for her actual plans on health care. They needed talking points, they told their bosses in HQ. During the polling surge over the summer, organizers planned what one described to me as "mutinies" on calls with Campaign HQ. Before one conference call between HQ and field staff, some staffers banded together to write Medicare for All into the pre-meeting document so that HQ couldn't ignore the trend on the ground. "All we're hearing is Medicare for All and we need answers," one organizer paraphrased the tone of the meeting to me. That's the thing about being on the ground: you can spot the surges in support before they happen . . . and you see the pitfalls, too.

By October, the problems organizers saw coming went mainstream. They began, as political problems often do, with a simple question that lacked a simple answer: Would Warren's Medicare for All plan raise middle-class taxes, as Vermont senator Bernie Sanders admitted his plan would? Being "with Bernie" was complicated, it turned out. And Warren's more moderate rivals planned to complicate it even further.

Candidates avoid direct answers to questions all the time. Rarely is a "yes or no" question ever answered with a "yes" or "no." But Warren had made direct engagement on policy issues her calling card, so the delicate dance of words made the omission of a simple answer even more glaring. The other Democrats in the field were quick to pounce on it. South Bend mayor Pete Buttigieg—who was raking in cash but nowhere truly noticeable yet in the polls—had been sowing seeds of doubt on the campaign trail, calling Warren "evasive" on Medicare for All.

During the next debate gathering—this one in Westerville, Ohio, on October 16, 2019—Warren's crowds, poll numbers, and plans made her a prime target for fellow members of the field who were looking to knock the for-now front-runner off her pedestal. And health care was the issue on which they sought to do it.

"Senator Sanders acknowledges he's going to raise taxes on the middle class to pay for Medicare for All," the debate moderator said, addressing Warren. "You've endorsed his plan. Should you acknowledge it, too?" She'd been asked some version of this question repeatedly since August 2019, including on every debate stage since the second Democratic debate in Detroit. Months later, she was still giving the same vague answer.

"The way I see this, it is about what kinds of costs middle-class families are going to face," she replied, her standard response. "So, let me be clear on this: costs will go up for the wealthy, they will go up for big corporations, and for middle-class families they will go down. I will not sign a bill into law that does not lower costs for middle-class families."

Asked his reaction, Buttigieg—correctly—called it "a yes-or-no question that didn't get a yes-or-no answer." An obvious, inartful dodge, meant to buy her campaign time to finalize their plan, allowing her rivals an easy slam dunk in the meantime. "Your signature, Senator, is to have a plan for everything," Buttigieg said. "Except this." Klobuchar, also championing a similar public option to Buttigieg's and Biden's, piled on: "At least Bernie's being honest here."

Sixteen days later—an eternity in politics—my phone rang. It was the night before the Iowa Democratic Party's famous Liberty and Justice Dinner and unfortunate personal timing, as I was the lucky recipient of a rising fever and rapidly oncoming flu. Having just touched down in Iowa and feeling terrible, all I wanted was to suffer through a shower, then roll into bed at the Renaissance Des Moines Savery Hotel. There's never a good time to be sick on the campaign trail, but this was a particularly inopportune moment. The "L-J" isn't your run-of-the-mill confab of the party faithful. It's a pyrotechnically tricked-out arena in downtown Des Moines packed full of hundreds of active Democrats from across the state, holding signs, cheering for their candidate, while also, sometimes, secretly open to being persuaded to the cause of another. The vibe is something akin to a combo of Harry Potter's Triwizard Tournament and the Met Gala. It is not something you want to cover while flu-ish.

My phone kept buzzing: Chris Hayden, Warren Campaign Deputy Comms Director. I almost didn't pick up, but then my competitive edge got the best of me. If it was a scoop and he gave it to another network instead . . .

"Hey," I said, faking my normal voice but still sounding stuffy and gravelly.

The Warren team was releasing their healthcare plan tomorrow and giving it out to select outlets on a strict embargo. Did I accept the terms?

"Yes," I croaked, gaining entry into the policy speakeasy.

Saloni Sharma—the keeper of all Warren plans released to the media in advance—would follow up with details for an off-the-record call with the policy team, as well as the plan itself, Hayden instructed. Giving out materials on embargo is common practice, not just on campaigns but throughout political circles, allowing reporters to pre-write pieces or do background research for coverage and letting campaigns or offices give context to better inform stories. I looped in my more policy-savvy colleague, Benjy Sarlin, for help. Healthcare policy vexed me on my best days—and this was decidedly not my best day.

Saloni sent the pages over around dinnertime. Sixty-three pages of documents. *Uggghhhh.* Nineteen pages of the plan's details. Twenty-eight pages from outside experts explaining how Warren calculated the cost of her version of Medicare for All. Another sixteen pages from outside experts backing up how her plan would not raise the cost on middle-class taxpayers. That was key: the answer to the sustained line of questioning she'd been dodging on debate stages and in campaign trail gaggles for months. My head swam with fever, multiple story drafts, and trillions in estimates.

While Benjy's focus was how this pushed the policy football forward, mine was how to explain dense healthcare policy on TV in a way that wouldn't force the audience's eyes to glaze over. Friends, as well as voters I'd met over the years on the road, told me they often felt ostracized from the political process because of how buzzword-y and complicated policy explanations often were. I wanted to do my part to address that, speaking clearly in Plain English and avoiding D.C. think-tank speak whenever possible.

Once our embargoed story was filed, I took the NyQuil that had been waiting for me on the bathroom counter and settled into sleep, naively under the assumption I would be doing no television the next day until after the Warren embargo lifted at noon.

I woke up from my NyQuil-induced dreams before my alarm went off, feeling even worse than I did when I went to bed but also like I was missing something. First order of business, as usual: check email, check Twitter, scroll alerts, send my mom a "good morning" text as proof of life for the day. Within a few scrolls the problem became evident: Warren's Medicare for All plan was public and Fox News had it—"exclusive."

I was pissed. *What about all the secret embargoed stuff—*

My next thought was more rational. There was no way a campaign whose candidate described Fox as a "hate-for-profit racket" had given the most important policy proposal of the entire primary to that network as an exclusive. I learned later that the campaign hadn't even briefed the Fox News embed assigned to cover them that the plan was coming. This was a rare leak—and a big one.

"Fox broke embargo," I texted Chris Hayden at 6:49 a.m. Iowa time.

Seconds later, Dafna Linzer, my boss and NBC News's managing editor of politics, was calling me. Her job was to keep us on top of big reporting and ahead of the competition. Right now, we had the reporting, but we'd agreed to the campaign's embargo.

"The embargo is broken," she told me matter-of-factly. She was right, of course. Our story was already written, and we could publish immediately. But this was a prime example of balancing relationships built over time with campaign sources with the churn of a 24/7 news cycle and the pressure to be first, or a very quick second.

Moments like this feel like you're on a speeding plane, knowing you're going to get pushed out the door when you haven't had time to check your parachute. They feel like the biggest things in the whole world, with only time giving you the distance to see how small it was in the grand scheme.

*   *   *

I was still in my pajamas while ping-ponging texts between my campaign contacts and my boss. While I texted, I dressed. There was only enough time for essentials: contact lenses, sweater, pants. Toothbrush (for about ten seconds), then a healthy layer of foundation and concealer because I was looking anything but healthy. I grabbed my backpack and jacket, then tore out of my room before taking two steps and doubling back for DayQuil. With the meds in hand, I sprinted toward the lobby.

We were moving to publish, I told Kristen Orthman, Warren's chief spokeswoman.

"We are moving up embargo," KO countered, trying to hold her roll-out plan somewhat together. "Do you think it can hold until then?"

I met my producer, Olivia Santini, and our crew, Mark and Frank Ringo, in the hotel lobby. They were referred to throughout the company as "the Ringo Bros," a title I always felt evoked the image of a three-ring circus, which was apt because life on the road with them tended to have a professionally chaotic cadence to it, akin to a bear riding a unicycle on a high wire.

"Today is about to get more complicated than we planned," I warned them. Olivia was already steering the ship, preparing for every possibility. She was always good in a crisis.

"We're going at 8:30," I texted KO, trying to maintain the relationship but knowing that frankly, this was their problem—not mine. "Fox made it so the embargo is broken," I said by way of explanation.

The weather was awful as we made our way outside for live shots for MSNBC. Rainy, icy Iowa on the first day of November. Everything was gray—and not just because I was feverish. That didn't deter the volunteers and campaign staff, lined up on Third Street outside the Iowa Events Center, holding signs and chanting for their candidate. Warren's team prided themselves on turning out for "viz"—visibility—the goal of which was basically a high school pep rally on big campaign days. Here, the hype was paired with grassroots organizing, collecting emails, phone numbers, and "commit-to-caucus" cards. There they were, dozens of twenty-something staffers, damp in person but not in spirit, decked in Liberty Green.

"We stan! We stan! We stan a woman with a plan!" they chanted.

Our coverage of Warren's Medicare for All plan finally dropped as we shuffled through the Skywalks, a labyrinth of indoor walkways that connect the buildings of downtown Des Moines and shield its residents from the brutal winter weather. We paused our gathering for another feature story we were working on and readied ourselves to be live on MSNBC hours earlier than we'd anticipated the night before.

"I never thought I would be describing a policy paper as 'hotly anticipated' but here we are in 2019," I began my hit. "The simplest way to go about explaining what's in this plan is to take it in three parts: you've got the cost, how she's gonna pay for it, and then the politics of it overall."

My execution of a detailed policy translated into Plain English for TV was as good as it could've been, save for my gravelly, congested tone. But the decision to not brush my hair that morning was a poor one, as was my choice of sweater—which I chose for warmth, but not for style. In boxes with my suit-clad colleague, Mike Memoli, and professionally made-up anchor, Hallie Jackson, both in studio, I looked out of place. As soon as I got off the air, I was (nicely) told to go find a less athleisure-looking outfit. That's showbiz for you.

For the next few hours, I stood shivering amidst the dancing, chanting, wet staffers, fronting live shots about complex healthcare policy while blocking out the noise. Warren herself showed up during my noon-hour hit, electrifying the dancing group of supporters and intensifying the frenzy around me. It made for great TV viewing, if not difficult TV making.

"This is the reception prepared by her campaign . . ." I half-yelled into my microphone.

"Outwork, out-organize, outlast!" chanted the crowd.

"This comes against the backdrop of releasing that policy plan . . ."

"Out-organize! Outlast!" the refrain growing louder.

". . . After the barrage of criticism from her fellow 2020 opponents . . ."

"Win with Warren! Win with Warren!" It was hard to fight against this din.

". . . talking about what her healthcare plan, Medicare for All, would mean in terms of its cost and in terms of how she'd pay for it."

At one point during my hit, a Warren supporter dressed in a cougar mascot costume danced in my periphery—a very niche reference to a theory briefly pushed by a right-wing conspiracy theorist that Warren once paid a twenty-four-year-old Marine for sex. Campaign staff were tickled by the absurdity of that. I briefly wondered if my fever wasn't getting the better of me.

After our live shot, my team and I followed the campaign horde across the street. Warren held forth with reporters in the shadow of a massive blow-up version of her golden retriever, Bailey. To this day, I wonder which lucky staffer will find that in their garage ten years from now.

While Warren was working the line outside the L-J celebration, former vice president Biden's campaign had responded to her plan, calling it, among other things, "mathematical gymnastics . . . geared towards hiding a simple truth from voters: it's impossible to pay for 'Medicare for All' without middle-class tax increases." Never mind that Warren, theoretically, had just shown exactly how she'd do it. And she'd certainly filled in more details than her progressive partner-in-policy, Bernie Sanders. I made my move in the gaggle.

"Senator Warren, you are building on Bernie Sanders's Medicare for All plan in this plan that you put out. Have you talked to him, or has he reached out to you?" I asked her, glancing up every so often at Blow-Up Bailey looming above us.

"I've called him, but he hasn't returned my call yet," she replied, though they would connect for a few minutes by phone later that day in a call that sources weren't too keen to read out at length, or even really talk about with reporters afterward. An attempt at preserving a détente on the verge of fraying.

Another reporter read Warren a part of the Biden team's response.

"Wow," she responded, pointing out that the people she used as validators to her plan were Obama-era officials, and that some of her mechanisms to pay for the plan were steeped in a little piece of Obama-era legislation called the Affordable Care Act.

"You know," her usual windup, "Democrats are not going to win by repeating Republican talking points and by dusting off the points of view of the giant insurance companies and the giant drug companies who don't want to see any change in the law that will bite into their profits." It was further than she'd ever gone in swatting back a rival attack, but she wasn't done. "But if anyone wants to defend keeping those high profits for insurance companies, and those high profits for drug companies, and not making the top one percent pay a fair share in taxes, and not making corporations pay a fair share in taxes, then I think they are running in the wrong presidential primary."

I kept going. "Do you feel like you, at this point in the race, had to put out a plan this detailed? Or do you feel like it was premature—too early in the campaign?"

"No, I'm delighted to do it. I've been working on it for a while. I think it's important."

What I was trying to ask, without asking, was if she felt this depth of detail was being asked of her because she was a woman. Or, put another way, if her male counterparts were being let off the hook on the details because they weren't.

Compared to the rest of the field, Warren *did* put out more for rivals to shoot at—something her campaign staff acknowledged was the ethos behind the campaign, but also something that made the race harder. "In a way, you're raising the expectations on yourself," Emily Parcell, a veteran Iowa operative and Warren senior advisor, said. "We put material out for people to shoot at, but that's the kind of campaign we ran."

In this case, the plan wasn't just lengthy for show; it parsed out, in detail, a Medicare for All policy that would expand coverage without raising taxes on the middle class. Her detractors gave Warren a specific problem; she gave them a specific solution. Moreover, she showed all sixty-plus pages of her work—including how much it would cost and how she'd pay for it. It was among the most detailed plans in the field—both its selling point and its flaw. Answers, even or especially nuanced, lengthy ones, often beget more questions in politics. And the field and the media both shifted the metric from "would it raise taxes on the middle class" to "okay, so how would you do it?" That plan came two weeks later, and Warren was back on the merry-go-round of press questions about the plan's actual feasibility, while progressives and moderates alike both feasted on what they hated about it.

That's what it is to be a presidential candidate: you put out your ideas and then you defend them, from other contenders' criticisms and from the media's built-in skepticism. And there was deep-rooted skepticism around Medicare for All as a policy overall even before Warren put her own spin on it. But some saw the burden of proof and bar for explanation as higher on Warren than on others to lay out and defend a complicated plan.

At the peak of this Medicare for All debate in the fall of 2019—and just before Warren released the point-by-point of her plan—Senator Sanders sat for an interview with my then-colleague at CNBC, John Harwood, who pressed the Vermont senator about how he'd pay for *his* Medicare for All plan, a bill he wrote.

"Do you think it's important to identify revenue sources for the other half? Or do you believe, as those who subscribe to modern monetary theory believe, that we've been a little bit too constrained by concerns about the deficit?" Harwood asked.

"We're trying to pay for the damn thing," Sanders responded with his usual gruff bravado. "At a time of massive income and wealth inequality, it is my view that the wealthiest people in this country, the top one-tenth of one percent, should be paying substantially more than they're paying right now. You have an insane situation. Let my Wall Street friends there tell me why it makes sense."

Harwood went on: "But you still have more revenue to go to make it fully paid for, yes?"

"The fight right now is to get the American people to understand that we're spending twice as much per capita, that of course, we can pay for it . . . I want to pay for it in a progressive way," Sanders said. "You're asking me to come up with an exact detailed plan of how every American—how much you're going to pay more in taxes, how much I'm going to pay. I don't think I have to do that right now."

"You think it's foolish Senator Warren is trying to?" Harwood pressed.

"I'm not saying it's foolish. All that I'm saying is that we have laid out a variety of options that are progressive. We'll have that debate. At the end of the day, we will pay for every nickel of Medicare for All, and it will save the overwhelming majority of the American people, who will no longer pay premiums."

But today wouldn't be the day for those details. And while Sanders earned some headlines about this dodge on his signature plan, eventually reporters seemed to accept that the man who "wrote the damn bill" wasn't going to speak to details and just sort of . . . stopped asking.

To some Warren staff, the questions—or lack thereof—posed to Sanders on issues where Warren over-explained were indicative of a double standard.

"How high a bar does a woman candidate have to jump?" Parcell asked me. "The assumption that a woman has to do the work and show her homework, where a man just has to give you an answer—is that implicit gender bias?"

I asked if it was, perhaps, less an issue of gender, and more Warren getting the short end of the stick on being toward the progressive end of the ideological spectrum. "It's not a fair comparison," she said. "Bernie didn't answer the questions. You can't compare apples to apples. If he'd answered, would he be equally attacked?"

Meanwhile, progressives and moderates alike attacked Warren's plan: it was shy of Sanders's progressive original and too radical for moderates, putting it in dangerous territory between the field's now well-established "lanes." That the plan fell between the lanes was also the whole point. It was an attempt at consensus building—a way to get to a Medicare for All system while acknowledging all the hurdles such a plan could face in gridlocked Washington. It built in pragmatic contingencies that would get more Americans covered, even if her administration fell short of full Medicare for All. It didn't work out the way the campaign hoped.

But the healthcare dilemma was illustrative of Warren's larger problem—one she would never successfully solve: she was playing the middle between Sanders's progressive lane and Biden's centrist one. And while voters don't vote by "lane"—plenty of voters' first and second choices made no clear ideological sense according to Lane Theory—knowing which category a candidate fell into was a foundational way to categorize the field.

Warren tried, in the campaign's last gasp, to make the strategy explicit, saying on a debate stage in February 2020 in South Carolina: "Bernie and I agree on a lot of things, but I think I would make a better president than Bernie. And the reason for that is that getting a progressive agenda enacted is going to be really hard and it's going to take someone who digs into the details to make it happen."

On the day she dropped out in March, she accepted that the dual-lane, high-detail strategy she'd employed didn't work. "I was told at the beginning of this whole undertaking that there are two lanes, a progressive lane that Bernie Sanders is the incumbent for and a moderate lane that Joe Biden is the incumbent for, and there's no room for anyone else in this. I thought that wasn't right. But evidently, I was wrong."

One Warren aide told me months after the race had ended that "the basic problem with trying to have it all" came down to potential. "There's potential where you thread it all together, and you're everything to everybody. But there's also the potential where you're nothing to nobody. And we were always being batted around through that."

All these narratives—plus others we'll get to later—were at play throughout the Warren campaign and lend to the explanation of why she was not the 2020 Democratic nominee. But there's also the reality that many of these strategic decisions were squarely within the campaign and candidate's control. The same campaign that picked its own branded color, chose to run on detailed plans, and built a Frances Perkins podium with such detail and specificity and meaning *also* fundamentally misread the policy priorities of the primary electorate and put the key issue of health care on the back burner. They saw the trees down to the leaves but missed the forest. And the candidate was burned for it. Was this the campaign's only *political* misstep, the thing that lost it all for them? No. But it was, in my estimation, a glaring miscalculation. One that evidenced a larger point: the Warren team ran the race they wanted to run, not necessarily the race they were actually running in.

Political watchers on both the Democratic and Republican sides told me repeatedly throughout the primary that they thought Warren's campaign was the most well-oiled, efficient, and clear in its strategy to win. But in running the race their way, they built an operation based on their ideals: against dark money in politics, with no outside Super PACs (until the very end, when it didn't really matter), little attacking of other candidates (until too late, when she was already trending downward), and lots of plans and explanations around the ideas they believed in, like anticorruption and focusing on who government works for (until the rest of the field bullied her into focusing on other issues, like health care, when the damage had already been done). It required the constant, careful balance between campaigning on the principles you aspire to, while campaigning in a reality that is far from that ideal.

In the end, in order to make change from the outside in; in order to show that big crowds do, in fact, mean big wins; and in order to live up to the forty-six-inch-tall podium made for the forty-sixth president of the United States . . . you first have to win.

6

Who We Take Seriously
The Qualification Question

NOVEMBER 2019

Sitting in a TV studio in Minneapolis in November 2019, Amy Klobuchar's team was torn.

A few days earlier, a story in *The New York Times* quoted Klobuchar as saying a woman with equal or less experience than South Bend mayor Pete Buttigieg would struggle to be taken seriously as a presidential contender. "Could we be running with less experience than we had? I don't think so," she told the *Times*. "I don't think people would take us seriously." She declined to say if Buttigieg was qualified but cast doubt on his limited statewide electoral track record.

That Klobuchar would go after Pete wasn't surprising. The story's headline—"WHY PETE BUTTIGIEG ANNOYS HIS DEMOCRATIC RIVALS"—was dead on because, well, the way Buttigieg grated on his rivals was all the press corps on the trail could talk about lately. And the Klobuchar-Buttigieg rivalry was well documented, too, from very public digs across multiple debates to the more low-key, like an email from Klobuchar staff to reporters making sure we knew the "interesting bit of context" that

Klobuchar's Fox News town hall garnered 500,000 more viewers than Buttigieg's. Not that they were counting.

The question now, as Klobuchar sat in a Minnesota greenroom readying for a Sunday show interview with CNN, was would she lean into the latest public twist in this rivalry—a potentially bumpy and heavily gendered rhetorical road—or pull a U-turn and head back for smoother pastures?

Some in Klobuchar's orbit were reticent about engaging further, worried that by continuing to speak honestly about this gendered dynamic would sound like she was complaining about a rival's rise rather than speaking to sexist undertones in presidential politics. Being a woman who was also in the race for president, complaining about the unfair dynamics faced by women running for president, could ring hollow or seem selfishly biased. One longtime Klobuchar campaign aide told me they worried it wouldn't be helpful to have the women who were experiencing sexism be the ones to call it out because the grievances were treated as "in the eye of the beholder" as opposed to an objective commentary. Never mind that this small crop of women were the exact people who could speak the most credibly regarding the sexism of the process.

Some were also concerned it would derail her campaign's message— which was decidedly and purposefully not woman- or gender-centric—into one that was. She'd fall into the same trap other marginalized candidates talked about falling prey to: being the woman talking about women's issues instead of the Minnesota senator talking about kitchen table issues and how she legislated around them.

But others on the campaign, including her national press secretary, Carlie Waibel, saw upside in her boss doubling down—not because it was the safe communications strategy (it probably wasn't), but because it was a chance to speak to the realities of the campaign in an authentic way. Because, really, a theoretical Mayor Paula would probably not have been allowed such a meteoric national, presidential rise as Mayor Pete. The bar *was* higher, the hills steeper, the pitfalls more plentiful, the shoes less comfortable for female candidates. These were just the facts. But ultimately, it was Klobuchar's call.

"Recent comments in *The New York Times* suggest that you don't believe that Mayor Buttigieg is *qualified* to be the president," the CNN anchor asked. "Am I reading that wrong?"

"Uh, yes," Klobuchar said, leaning forward in her seat. "I don't think I wanna dwell on various press articles, but I'll say this: I think any of the candidates that were on that debate stage were more qualified than the president of the United States right now . . . I like Mayor Pete but—"

"Do you think Pete Buttigieg is qualified—period?"

"Yes. But let me explain why I think I'm the better candidate. And by the way, we get asked this all the time. Welcome to politics. And that's what was in that article. Various candidates get asked about each other all the time and I made what I think was a cogent case. And that is that *I'm* the one from the Midwest who has actually won in a statewide race, over and over again . . . And that's not true of Mayor Pete. That's just a fact."

Carlie, the tip of the spear for the Klobuchar campaign's media operation, remembers what happened next as "everyone making it into this big moment: whether it's comparing herself to Pete or making this statement about women in the race. I was like 'she's just literally stating a fact,' and everyone blew it up." It then became something that required explanation.

"It wasn't something we were scared about or mad about or we didn't like," she said. "It just took up the next two days." Which meant two days off message. "And I remember having that moment of, 'fuck, is this exactly where we want to be?' No. But it's also a moment in time for women who are running in this race that Amy just said what she said . . . Amy felt it, Amy believed it, and someone's gotta say it."

Staff working for other female candidates were glad someone did, sharing a sentiment one person paraphrased to me as, "fuck yeah, someone had to say this."

It was risky, though. Comments like these, overtly made in self-defense, can come off as unlikable to voters—especially when female candidates make them. That poses a real risk to their electoral bottom lines, one that men don't face in the same way.

"We've repeatedly found women face a litmus test men do not," the Barbara Lee Family Foundation reported, finding continuity over years of their surveys, focus groups, and studies of female candidacies. "Voters will support a male candidate they do not like but who they think is qualified, but don't apply the same standard to women." It called to mind the dozens upon dozens of voters I met who backed Trump even though they didn't like his him, personally. "Women also have to do more to prove they are qualified," BLFF wrote. "For men, their qualification is assumed."

This was the whole Klobuchar-Buttigieg news cycle in a nutshell.

And regardless of what Klobuchar and her team decided to say that day about Buttigieg, the conversation around women, gender, and the "-bilities"—viability, electability, and likability—was happening anyway. Klobuchar herself had just been forced to participate in it earlier in the week in New Hampshire after a poll from *The New York Times* website *The Upshot* and Siena College exposed some curious, if not entirely unsurprising and frustratingly persistent, findings about voter sentiment toward female candidates.

The poll of key battleground states showed, as others did and would, that Trump was competitive against top Democrats. Sanders would tie Trump, the poll showed, while Biden would narrowly edge the president out, and Warren would lose to him by the same margins Hillary Clinton did in these states three years earlier. Democratic voters seemed to watch each new poll as if it were a horror movie, peeking through their fingers as they gorged on each new crosstab and cable news segment, trying to search for any sign—even just one!—that one candidate over another could definitely, certainly, beyond the shadow of a doubt, beat Trump. Certainty like that didn't exist in politics, but that didn't mean voters wanted it any less.

Any potential risk was too high. And paragraphs like this one in *The New York Times* screamed "risk!":

The results suggest that Ms. Warren, who has emerged as a front-runner for the Democratic nomination, might face a number of obstacles in her pursuit of the presidency. The poll supports concerns among some Democrats that her ideology and gender—including the fraught question of "likability"—could hobble her candidacy among a crucial sliver of the electorate. And not only does she underperform her rivals, but the poll also suggests that the race could be close enough for the difference to be decisive.

That point was underscored within the same poll. Forty-one percent of the voters that backed Biden, but not Warren—"disproportionately" working-class and male—agreed with the statement that women who run for president "just aren't that likable." These were the very kinds of voters Democrats were dedicated to winning back in their quest to rebuild the Blue Wall of the Industrial Midwest. Polls like this lent to the skepticism, however misguided, unfair, or antiquated, that Warren, the highest "tier" and best polling woman in the field, couldn't win because she wasn't liked by a substantial amount of the voters that she needed to win over.

Never mind, of course, that polls themselves are fickle metrics on which to premise electoral odds and coverage. Polls that show trends over time can be helpful, especially tracking public sentiment on issues. Horse race polls, though, are mere snapshots, yet they become daily installments of political gospel on cable news. We'd identified the risks and fallibility of polling in 2016, with many in the news media vowing to change both the way we poll and the way we cover polling, but both were promises easier to make than keep. In 2019 and 2020, polls were, once again, used by cable news and print outlets as an imperfect metric by which to impose some kind of rational order on a disorderly and irrationally large field of Democratic candidates numbering, at its peak, more than two dozen. Then the Democratic National Committee chose to use polls as a qualifying metric for primary debate stages. Most campaigns agreed this was a flawed system, though few proposed better ideas on how the party could winnow the field.

It was all connected. Polling well, or toward the top of the pack, meant more coverage—which likely meant a bigger dedicated press corps who would feed the hungry news beast and lend to a bigger footprint on the air and online. Top-tier campaigns or newsworthy candidates were assigned network "embeds"—like I was for Trump in 2016—dedicated to tracking their every event and statement, sending comprehensive notes to the network to inform and guide their coverage. On top of the embeds were assigned correspondents, like I was in 2020 for Warren and Klobuchar, who would bounce from state to state with the candidate to broadcast in hushed tones from the back of campaign events or bring viewers into a gaggle while live on the air. That kind of coverage—especially when sustained over time—signaled a seriousness from the networks about a campaign's prospects, one that those campaigns would then see manifest in dollars raised, endorsements given, and if all went right, a spike in the polls due to sustained time being seriously discussed on viewers' television screens.

Polling well, especially in the early months of 2019, relied on high national name identification and an ability to get coverage. The more name ID, the better the polls, the more coverage. The more coverage, the better the polls, the more name ID. And so the convoluted political chicken-and-egg game went.

Biden and Sanders were regularly considered in the field's highest echelons—both having run before and having extensive political networks and name recognition due to their long careers and previous bids. The field's oft-referred-to "lanes" were made with them in mind. Warren and Harris were also considered in the field's top tier, due to their ability to attract top staff, fundraise, and amplify their already-honed national profiles. Former representative Beto O'Rourke, after his hotly covered Texas Senate run, was also in the top layer of candidates at first. Klobuchar, New Jersey senator Cory Booker, and New York senator Kirsten Gillibrand were part of the second tier, with intrigue also paid to the governors of the field for their already-existing executive status—Montana's Steve Bullock, Washington's Jay Inslee, and Colorado's John Hickenlooper—along with interest in a little-known mayor from South Bend, Pete Buttigieg, and former Housing and Urban Development secretary Julián Castro. There were also the outsiders—Andrew Yang and Marianne Williamson—and the other electeds, mostly from the House and Senate, Congresswoman Tulsi Gabbard, yes, but also representatives Tim Ryan, Seth Moulton, and Eric Swalwell, Senator Michael Bennet, and New York City mayor Bill de Blasio, all of whom, at one point in the race, joked about how voters couldn't tell them apart because they were all white men of a certain age who looked, more or less, the same.

The New York Times's podcast picked up the likability thread found in their new poll, highlighting the steep climb still ahead for the women of the race. It's an important string to tug on and interesting data for listeners. I would've done the same, and at other points in the race, highlighted the steeper climb for these female candidates that was borne out in anecdotes and data from the road. Highlighting and calling them out could disrupt sexist narratives and level the playing field. But doing so also meant every listening voter considered, however briefly, whether the women running could really reverse the course of hundreds of years of history. Simply put, by bringing up the issue, *The Daily*—and anyone else who talked about it—made it more of an issue.

This narrative is both good and bad, if you're a female candidate or someone cheering for one. It reminds people that you're exciting, historic, fresh: the first potential female president of the United States. It also reminds people you carry the inherent risk of becoming something that has never existed before in American history: the first female president of the United States. As it turned out, voters had some questions about just that.

Two days after the poll and the podcast, a voter submitted a written question to Amy Klobuchar as she was campaigning through New Hampshire: " '[*The Daily*] said if the primary were today Biden would get the nomination because many people say they find the female candidates unlikable,' " she read, paraphrasing this particular voter's un-nuanced conclusion of the *Times*.

"Oooh." She looked away from the square in her hand, exaggerating a frown on her face. "That's not true, is it?"

From the stage, Klobuchar looked around the room, her shoulders slightly slumped and her arms outstretched in a small, exaggerated shrug. "So sad."

Then she straightened her shoulders. "I think we're really quite a likable lot," she chuckled, easing the comedy routine into more serious territory as the crowd chuckled along, too. She finished reading the voter's question on sexism in politics and what she could do about Americans thinking she was a member of a gender that was so gosh darn unlikable. Amy Klobuchar suddenly found herself responsible for proving why her entire gender could be liked enough to be president. Instead of that Herculean task, she opted for a more targeted defense of her fellow female senators with whom she still shared the presidential field.

"We have all had tough jobs, okay? Tough jobs. And really good, tough jobs that show that we know how to lead." Tough jobs, she said, require "tough decisions." They mean not everyone likes you. That *unlikability*—and the living with it—was a strength, as Klobuchar saw it. And one of several she sought to convince voters she possessed.

"We wouldn't be on that debate stage and where we are running for president if we hadn't been tough enough to have those jobs! So, I am just like, seriously? This is not a measure we use with men. And so, I find all of us quite likable, myself."

The voter's question in New Hampshire underscored that even though all the women were individual candidates, a knock on one of them could be a knock on all of them. All it took was one arrow through the electability armor of one fellow woman for them all to have to put their shields up and defend against it. Having a pack of six running was monumental progress, but it also presented the paradox of needing to run individually while still being seen as part of the collective pack. Klobuchar was so keenly aware of this that she would sometimes privately add up the polling scores of all the women running and marvel to her staff that even all together, their theoretical Frankencandidacy barely, if ever, led the field.

"We finally have these women out there and, yeah, we don't agree on everything—big surprise. Just like men don't," she said. But instead of focusing on the historically female field, Klobuchar wanted to focus on the experience that *she* alone—not the collective *them*—brought to the table.

"Experience should be valued, I will leave you with that," she said, turning back to a more comfortable pitch that steered toward concrete successes and not intangible gender metrics. "That matters in a man *or* woman. And I'm betting that that's where the American people are gonna end up. I'm just hoping and betting that they're going to connect that experience and ability not just with a man, but with a woman. Then: I win."

Klobuchar did well to hide any palpable frustration about the sexism in the race, but it's something Hillary Clinton told me she heard about from all the women directly at some point in their campaigns. They'd all run for the Senate, most in marquee toss-up contests, but the feeling—and the sexism—was different in the presidential arena.

"All of them, at one point or another, expressed their frustration that a lot of what they did *not* experience when they ran for the Senate—because running for the Senate, as you know, I've done twice, in a state where you can get to know people, where people can kind of size you up on a personal level—was so different than running for president. It was like one step removed," Clinton told me.

"All of the caricatures and the sexist comments and the press coverage and all of that played a much bigger role in how they felt they could present themselves and I thought that, you know, that was certainly my experience [when I ran for president]. And I was not surprised when each of them sort of expressed to me that that was what they were experiencing. Now, I think all four of them thought that they could avoid some of the worst of the sexist, misogynistic tropes and certainly some of the *ridiculous* press coverage that I endured. But I think that in each of her own ways they encountered some of that. And I was very sympathetic because I know what it's like."

But for Klobuchar specifically, the sexism her campaign encountered was in some ways more subtle than her opponents'. Harris endured moments like the Sparkly Jacket or being mocked for her laugh. Warren, at one point, had to defend against a story she often told on the trail that she was fired from a teaching job in her twenties for being pregnant. (The story was true, even as opponents tried to label her a liar because the school's official documentation for her departure didn't read "fired for being pregnant." Go figure.) But gender manifested differently in Klobuchar's bid. Advisors often talked about the ways sexism infested the Minnesota senator's foundational argument of electability—which we'll talk about next chapter. But the fracas that Klobuchar here found herself at the middle of also exemplified the way gender tended to tilt the intangibles of who we see as qualified to run in favor of the men running. Klobuchar versus Buttigieg was more than rival candidates getting on each other's nerves. Though it was that, for the record. Not just for Klobuchar but for most of the other campaigns watching the news cycles and headlines that gushed about his speaking five, nay six—or was it seven?—languages.

But it was also, for Klobuchar specifically, about who was given more leeway and credibility in being seen as qualified and able to successfully carry the mantle of Democrats' Moderate/Biden-Alternative from the Midwest. Because, like Klobuchar, Buttigieg also grounded his campaign in Midwest bona fides, steeping his run in a keen understanding of the heartland states from whence he, and Klobuchar, hailed. But where Klobuchar talked about being a thrice-proven statewide winner in purple Minnesota, in addition to being elected to races farther down the ballot before that, Buttigieg didn't extol his electoral experience . . . in large part because his resumé in elected politics was short. He had lost his only statewide race—a 2010 bid for Indiana state treasurer. He became mayor of South Bend two years after that.

The experience part of his stump speech instead focused on his service; Buttigieg was an intelligence officer in the U.S. Navy Reserve and did one six-month tour in Afghanistan in 2014, taking a leave from his mayorship. Asked by *The New York Times* in a November 2019 interview if he joined the military—his service being a focal point of his stump speech—knowing what it could mean for his future political career, Buttigieg said he'd asked himself the same thing. "There is a part of me that thinks, if the answer is yes, does that mean the service wasn't pure in some way?"

His time in the national political spotlight prior to 2020, though, landed with a thud. His briefly waged, insurgent bid to head up the Democratic National Committee failed, but it gave those who ran against him an early glimpse of his ability to make much media hay out of even a glimmer of exposure. Jaime Harrison, who would come to helm the DNC himself at Biden's request after 2020, ran against Buttigieg in that first DNC chair race.

"I had more hard votes and support, but he was able to turn limited opportunities into so much media coverage," Harrison told *Politico* in 2019. "And he impressed a lot of people that way." His then-rival's "ability to go viral," Harrison said in the article, was "a little frustrating for me."

The ability to go viral served the millennial mayor well in 2020, too. Perhaps most notably in his CNN town hall in March of 2019. Buttigieg catapulted himself into the national consciousness that night, calling fellow Hoosier, vice president, and Christian Mike Pence "a cheerleader of the porn star presidency." After an hour in prime time, the political world momentarily stopped on its axis and seemed to wonder collectively: who is this guy—and how the hell do I say that last name? The campaign quickly moved to establish some pronunciation devices (I was always partial to Boot-Edge-Edge over Buddha-Judge), as well as willingness to sit for multiple sweeping profiles born of access to the candidate granted by communications pro Lis Smith. The one-two punch of a solid, viral moment plus dozens of mainstream media profiles created the feeling that Buttigieg was everywhere, with everyone clamoring for more.

While Klobuchar reminded audiences that her message and brand had long resonated across purple Minnesota, Buttigieg campaigned on *the potential* that he could bring his soaring rhetoric and passion for creating "future former Republicans" out into the country in 2020. Where Klobuchar had earned Republican voters in a meaningful way in the past, Buttigieg was saying he thought he *someday* could. Where Klobuchar talked about the bills she'd passed and the bipartisan ties she'd forged with Republicans, including the late senator John McCain, Buttigieg shrugged off this brand of Washington experience, dismissing Klobuchar's hard-paid

Washington-honed dues as a way to buoy his outsider status—especially at a time when senators were readying for historic impeachment hearings against Donald Trump. That was an example of the very kind of tough situations Klobuchar wanted to sell in her pitch to be president: being at the center of critical battles, even if they don't always earn you friends or political expediency. Isn't that the job of a president, after all? To make the tough choices; to accept the hard calls?

"I also am someone who's passed multiple bills as the lead Democrat, important bills in Washington, D.C. He's had a different experience," Klobuchar said as part of her CNN answer that Sunday when asked about Buttigieg and the who-we-take-seriously debate. "We should be able to have those debates about candidates without being accused of being negative. All this is . . . Questions are asked. And the last point I made in that [*New York Times*] article? Was that of the women on the stage—I'm focusing here on my fellow women senators: Senator Harris, Senator Warren, and myself. Do I think that we would be standing on that stage if we had the experience that he had? No, I don't. Maybe we're held to a different standard. But my goal here is to get the best candidate to lead the ticket. I believe that's me."

There was yet another layer, though. One that I, as a woman, felt uniquely situated to see and understand. Because how many times have I, or my female friends, worked so hard to tick every box of necessary qualifications, shown our work, been exceptional . . . only to see a man earn the same or greater reputation or recognition having checked fewer boxes, shown half as much work, and done it less exceptionally?

Let's make something clear: Pete Buttigieg is an historically talented and unique candidate. Intellectually brilliant and politically adept. A man who served his country and continues to do so now in President Joe Biden's cabinet. That platform is one he's widely expected to parlay onto the presidential candidate stage again, if not as soon as 2024. And in 2020, this little-known mayor was the only person in the primary field who managed to break the rigidity of the tier structure, hopscotching out of the tier of little-known Also-Rans and into the top echelon of People Who Could

Actually Become President. He raised millions, built a massive national operation, and inspired thousands of voters, not just with his brand of politics but with his lived experience as a millennial who came of age in the era of mass shootings and economic tumult, and as an openly gay man. He was not the first openly gay man to campaign for a major party's nomination—that title went to 2012 long-shot Republican candidate Fred Karger, who fought in real time in 2020 to correct that narrative—but the first to come as close as he did. An important campaign in which many LGBTQ+ community members saw themselves reflected, and possibilities realized.

But it can also be true that Buttigieg benefited from white male privilege. And that a theoretical Mayor *Paula* would not have been able to do what the actual Mayor Pete did. It's both a feeling and a fact. Strategists, pollsters, and experts that I spoke with agree on that.

And Klobuchar, ever with her finger in the political wind, was aware of the landscape within which she was operating. She regularly reminded her staff—and later reminded me on one of the occasions that we spoke for this project months later—that "men get to run on potential and women run on experience." They must come armed with receipts: proof that they can do these jobs and, in the case of reelection campaigns, proof that they can continue doing them, too.

On its face: that's not unfair. As both a voter and a reporter, I love proof and proven records! But the metric is often not uniformly applied. Men are routinely given the benefit of the doubt on their qualifications and competency from the outset; women must actively clear that threshold to be taken seriously. Men can more easily run on the potential of what they *can do and achieve*; women must show and tout *what they've already won and done* to clear the threshold of seriousness required to be considered for leadership roles.

"You constantly hear: 'I'd vote for a woman if she were qualified' and nobody ever says, 'I'd vote for a man if he were qualified,' " veteran Democratic pollster Celinda Lake told me when I brought up this quandary of proven versus potential qualifications. She's been a respected polling mainstay for decades, working for Joe Biden in 2020 but with campaign stories that stretch as far back as Geraldine Ferraro's vice-presidential bid in 1984.

"What I was hoping for with so many women running, that the collective sense of them would reduce the burden on any individual proving that she was qualified," Lake told me. "Because there you had a head of economics, you had U.S. senators, you had AGs, you know, all kinds of women. And I was hoping that the collective would serve as an answer for all the individuals. But it didn't."

Yet having a larger collective—most of the female field were qualified and viable senators—could also serve as a sign of progress we've never had before. The conversation about who we take seriously in these spaces, and what barriers women must overcome in order to be, was central to the future, as much as it was to the present. Because even though the bar is higher for women, it's also true that to this point we've only really seen hyper-qualified women run for president in the first place.

"Only the really qualified ones run," Jennifer Lawless, author of multiple books and research on women running for office, said. "We don't know how a middling sort of female candidate would do." The four female senators who ran for president "were all top-tier or high-level second-tier candidates." And tiers aside, they all boasted impressive resumes. It begged the question of whether progress was really just . . . a numbers game, won when Average Janes ran in the same numbers as Average Joes.

"I don't think it'll be one or two high-profile women who are just sort of mediocre," Lawless concluded. "We're gonna just need it to be normal that lots of women run every election cycle."

The year 2020 could be seen as a start here, though. The model of Only Traditionally Exceptional/Qualified Women running expanded in 2020 to include two other women: author and activist Marianne Williamson and Hawaii congresswoman Tulsi Gabbard. Some have described them to me as the "problematic women" of the field who could never be taken seriously as presidential contenders in the way the female senators were.

In a word, yes.

Certainly, Gabbard proffered problematic views—most notably and well-known as it related to her willingness to advocate for murderous Syrian strongman Bashar al-Assad. She had a small, niche following of voters, some of whom liked Donald Trump or Bernie Sanders, but above all valued political outsiders and populist policy messages.

Williamson, for her part, had no government or elected experience whatsoever. She inspired more memes than minutes of devoted cable news coverage and her speaking style plus an ethereal, almost otherworldly vibe made her into an easy punchline. Some of it was warranted; much of it was not. But it struck me how quickly she was labeled a joke while we entertained Andrew Yang's pitch that "the opposite of Donald Trump is an Asian man who likes MATH." I'm not saying that pitch was going to get him elected president, but it did give him the polling and fundraising staying power to outlast even some sitting senators and governors in the field.

Gabbard and Williamson were unbolstered by traditional qualifications but ran anyway. They secured coveted spots on debate stages by meeting hard-to-meet donor and polling thresholds. They were ignored, to be frank, at the same rates as similarly unremarkably qualified men who ran. Considered sideshows, but still lending their voices to key issues in the race. Marianne Williamson, for instance, described herself as someone who has had a career "harnessing the inspiration and the motivation and the excitement of people." Those aren't traditional presidential qualifications, but it didn't lessen that she had an amazing ability to speak to sensitive issues of race relations, inequality, and reparations more eloquently than most of the other Democrats on the stage. And in the age of Donald Trump, some argued to me, what were "traditional presidential qualifications" anyway?

Williamson and Gabbard were never going to be president. But they are exactly the kind of women who could never have run in a system that wasn't becoming more comfortable with the idea of women—*all* types of women—in power. Their existence as part of the 2020 pack served to expand the leadership mold and allow new experiments in female leadership to take place.

In the same way that we've seen mediocre, or nontraditional, or underqualified men run for decades and in large numbers, we saw a glimpse of what it looks like when the women do the same—for better or worse.

And yet. What people like Celinda Lake saw in the field was a narrative, reinforced by the press, that still regularly questioned the qualifications and viability of the women in the race or framed their candidacies as having more significant barriers to overcome than the men. Questions like "are you likable enough to win?", which dogged Clinton during her 2008 and 2016 bids, morphed into more all-encompassing and less overtly sexist questions about overall winning ability. Are these candidates "electable"? Not an unfair question on its face, but one that, when posed to women, was imbued with the sense that their climb to the top was greater and more fraught than their counterparts'. Others had to answer for concerns over their age, or health, or even race or sexuality, too, but gender swirled most potently in the electability pot.

These two metrics—likability and electability—were both important political thresholds for candidates to be able to clear in the minds of voters and held a high potential for being co-opted and interpreted in gendered ways. Being likable and being electable, in many ways for women candidates, were linked. And it started with the very way these candidates told their political origin stories.

Amy Klobuchar began her political career by kismet, as she told it, inspired to make change after a "drive-thru delivery" forced her out of the hospital a mere twenty-four hours after giving birth to her daughter, who had to remain behind due to complications. This wasn't all that uncommon in the 1990s—a cost-trimming mechanism for insurance companies that shortened maternity stays—but it was the match to Klobuchar's political fire. She found other moms struggling with the same problem, Klobuchar recounted to crowds at her rallies, including one in Atlantic, Iowa: "And so, I went to the legislature and started advocating for one of the first laws in the country that guaranteed new moms and their babies a forty-eight-hour hospital stay." That work went on for "a long, long time," but taught many lessons.

Among them: "That when you're testifying in front of an all-male legislative committee with a few women, that if you say things that are really embarrassing about giving birth, they'll just go past it." But also, that powerful interests will leverage their power against you.

"In this case," Klobuchar explained, "the insurance companies were trying to delay the time the bill took effect. And so, what I did is I brought six pregnant friends to the conference committee, so they outnumbered the lobbyists two to one. And when the legislators said, 'Well, when should the bill take effect?' they all raised their hands, my pregnant friends, and said 'now.' " The bill took effect the day the governor signed it. "So, that's how I got involved."

It's really the perfect political origin story—and chances are, it was honed that way, over the years, on purpose. It showcases Klobuchar's biting wit and sometimes off-kilter sense of humor, easy ways to put an audience at ease, while building likability and showcasing authenticity. But part of what makes it so relatable and affable is that it introduces her as someone who entered the political arena to work on behalf of her community, not to serve her own interests. That's an important distinction—one that all the other female candidates in 2020 were also aware of and incorporated accordingly.

For Elizabeth Warren, it was being drafted into a fight for the Senate by Nevada senator Harry Reid and EMILY's List chief Stephanie Schriock, after being appointed to serve on the committee overseeing billions in government bailout spending. She regularly billed her plans to root out corruption and rebalance the economic playing field as a continuation of the work and research she'd been doing all her life, and framed her ideas as personal stories—not policy lessons—that could be applied to the shared struggles of fellow Americans. Child care, affordable higher education, housing and mortgage crises. She'd experienced these issues herself, researched them for decades, and now she was "in this fight" *on behalf of* others.

For Kamala Harris, her prosecutor's record that was the underpinning of her campaign—from the phrase "for the people" (a courtroom introduction used by some government attorneys) being amended into her slogan, to the executive experience honed by leading the nation's largest state justice department as California attorney general—was explained as a decision to change the system from within.

"I want to be in a place where I can be a voice for the most voiceless and humble," she often explained on the trail, campaigning first for president, then as Joe Biden's Number Two. Kamala Harris wasn't undertaking this bid for her; she was undertaking it for everyone.

So, too, was Kirsten Gillibrand, who ran on policies that impacted American families and framed herself as the maternal messenger. She regularly promised to "fight for your families the way I fight for my own."

Hillary Clinton had a harder task. She spent her pre-elected life in rooms full of powerful people, taking on volatile yet pressing issues like health care and women's rights. She rewrote the book on what to expect from first ladies by pursuing her own goals through an often-feminist lens that was not prevalent in the sociopolitical arena at that point. Those years spent in her husband's White House culminated in her own electoral career as a senator, presidential candidate, and secretary of state.

She branded herself, especially in 2016, as a representative of Democratic voters through policy and endorsements. A candidate defending others from Trump's barbs. A woman trying to break the glass ceiling in the name of all the women who came before, were watching now, and would come after. She was running on behalf of them, the messaging sought to show, not serving her own individual ambition. (Of course, as it is for male candidates, it was both.) Still, she couldn't shed the long-seeded suspicion in the minds of some voters and operatives that it was all part of the Clinton Dynasty's constant quest for power. Hillary's ambition was always treated differently than almost any other politician's, male or female. Maybe it's because she was one of the firsts, but it was almost always filtered through the lens that all the work she'd done before, all the moves she'd made, were in the name of winning power and obtaining more of it. And as experts have told us in these pages, that violates the norms of female gender stereo-types and results in an unshakably . . . unlikable feeling.

But for other women, the idea that they were moved to represent a larger community was a political and rhetorical strategy that sought to avoid triggering those gender biases in voters while also still showcasing authenticity. They led with their experience, but they also told stories that were of political *opportunity*, not outright political *ambition*.

"We often joke that women run for office to solve problems, not to seek fame and fortune," the Barbara Lee Family Foundation's executive direc-tor, Amanda Hunter, told me. "When some men look in the mirror and say that they would make a good-looking senator, a lot of times women kind of look around and all of a sudden they're running for office before they even realized what happened because something has affected them so deeply in their community."

Klobuchar's story of pregnancy policy origins fits this narrative—and eventually carried her from law in a private practice, to Milwaukee's Hen-nepin County attorney, to the Senate. She was in the mold of other women who saw personal reasons to get in the political fight, but was still without many role models for how to run and how to talk about policy once she decided to get into the arena.

During years as Hennepin County attorney, she looked to then–Kansas governor Kathleen Sebelius and then–Arizona governor Janet Napolitano as role models. "They were in redder states [but] they were some of the few women that were in a management job, which made sense to my county attorney job," Klobuchar recalled to me. "And they would set these goals . . ."

No accident. Goal-setting was a tool recommended by many experts to women running for office to help establish credibility, as is having external validators to bolster a female candidate's work. Through validators and "action-oriented," results-based leadership, leaders—men and women—could build qualifications and likability. But for women, these were neces-sary tools to overcome the overarching reality that it's just different to run as women. In some focus groups that BLFF and partners conducted, voters acknowledged that female candidates "are held to different and higher standards" than their male counterparts on qualifications and likability, "but many [voters] still actively participate in upholding those double standards." In other words: they know there's a double standard . . . but they still hold their candidates to them anyway.

Which means you must work around them.

Without even meeting Sebelius and Napolitano, Klobuchar leaned into their example of setting goals and proving how they met them. It was "accountability on steroids," as she called it. "I said, 'Okay, that's what I'm gonna do.' So, when I get into my first job [as Hennepin County attorney], I set these hundred-day and year-end goals and I show how we're going to do it. And I was the first woman in that job. The chief judge sends a letter to me that says, 'Amy, I appreciate and welcome [you] but I would like to point out with your hundred-day goals that this is a marathon, not a sprint in running the justice system.' I remember I wrote back: 'It is both a marathon *and* a sprint.'"

The list of goals followed Klobuchar to her presidential run, where, within four months of entering the race, she released an eighteen-page list of more than one hundred bullet points of what she hoped to accomplish in her first hundred days as president. Accountability on steroids. Climate change, voting rights, election security, lowering of prescription drug costs, antitrust actions, veterans' issues, $15 federal minimum wage, and immigration reform. Bluntly: it was every policy promise that every 2020 candidate would need to contend with over the next few months, a potpourri of buzzwords that would allow her to speak anywhere and promise to make [insert issue here] a priority.

But it wasn't the last time Klobuchar would take cues from her female colleagues as they grew their ranks in government.

"When I was running for Senate [in 2005], I totally remember looking at all of Hillary's ag speeches in New York," Klobuchar remembered of the race that made her the first female senator from Minnesota. "Not because she was Hillary, but because there weren't that many women to look at who had given rural speeches in a Senate race." She laughed at how crazy it sounded: the idea of scraping the stump speech barrel look-ing for someone—anyone!—who shared the same chromosomal makeup and desire to speak to rural issues as she did. It was a stunning reminder that even in just the last fifteen years, the women of the Senate have been remolding the image of what statewide congressional governance looks like, who gets to do it, and how they speak about it.

Nearly two decades later, we're still in a time of "firsts" and "never befores." Where some states—seventeen to be exact—have never had a female senator. Where nineteen states have never had a female governor. If we're still celebrating "firsts," of course the women breaking those glass ceilings are still putting together the road maps for how to do it success-fully; trying to find existing examples to mimic and learn from while put-ting their own stamp on it.

Klobuchar, even if she was reluctant to regularly filter her races through a gender lens publicly, was always keenly aware of the fields she was playing on. So, too, in 2020.

"This is a line that runs through so many of the women that were on that [2020] stage and running for president. That you just can't walk across the stage and declare 'mission accomplished' in a flight suit," she told me. "You have to actually show that you got all these things done—especially when you're running for president."

She saw it "in spades with Elizabeth, with her plans." In Harris (and herself) for their prosecutor's records. And in her own record of passing "all these bills." They ran on fights and their experience winning them. Biden, too, was running on experience—"but of course he was," she quipped to me. "He was the vice president!" The credibility of that experience speaks for itself. "Compared to a lot of the other men, they were really running on their ideas, and we did some of that, but it was a lot about how we had gotten things done to prove to the people we could do this."

Perhaps it was *all that* that put Buttigieg deep under Klobuchar's skin, griping about him to staff and reporters, and then eventually airing her grievance, shared by most of the 2020 field, in those November pages of *The New York Times*. And then, she said it even louder on the debate stage.

NBC's Andrea Mitchell presented Klobuchar again with her recent quotes: "Senator Klobuchar, you've said this of Mayor Buttigieg, quote, 'Of the women on the stage, do I think that we would be standing on that stage if we had the experience he had? No, I don't. Maybe we're held to a different standard.' Senator, what did you mean by that?"

Klobuchar thanked Buttigieg for the experience he brought to the race—yet another not-so-veiled jab meant to remind us that at a mere thirty-seven years old he didn't have nearly as much as the rest of them— and then she doubled down, again.

"I am honored to be standing next to him. But what I said was true. Women are held to a higher standard," she said plainly. "Otherwise, we could play a game called 'name your favorite woman president.' Which we can't do."

Buttigieg nodded and smiled, waiting to see where she'd take this next and if he would have the chance to jump in. She left no such opening.

"Because it has all been men and"—the applause grew louder inside the debate hall—"including all vice presidents, have been men. And I think any working woman out there, any woman that's at home, knows exactly what I mean. And that's a fact. But I wanna dispel one thing. Because for so long why has this been happening?"

No one was even thinking about Pete now. It was all eyes on Amy. From my seat in the spin room full of reporters—all eyes glued to screens and fingers fused to keyboards—I was rapt.

"I don't think you have to be the tallest person on the stage to be president. I don't think you have to be the skinniest person. I don't think you have to have the loudest voice on the stage—I don't think that means that you will be the one that should be president."

That image we called to mind of a suit-clad, tall, male president? Klobuchar was forcing us to challenge it, calling it out.

"I think what matters is if you're smart, if you're competent, and if you get things done."

She'd passed over a hundred bills as the lead Democrat on the leg- islation during her time in Washington, she reminded us. She had won elections in red counties and purple counties, she declared. This was Klobuchar's pitch to an electorate skittish and scared of four more years of Trump: proven electability and an overflowing bag full of legislative receipts. Take them or leave them.

"I govern both with my head and my heart," Klobuchar finished. "And if you think a woman can't beat Donald Trump? Nancy Pelosi does it every single day."

A debate, and I'd argue candidacy, defining moment—in less than ninety seconds.

Afterward, I staked out an area in the crowded room of over-caffeinated reporters, all trying to push their way to the front to get their faces and questions in front of the candidates. I texted Klobuchar's aides, as did every other reporter present, making sure they knew where I was and that I wanted time with her. And then we waited, using the time it took for candidates to make their way off the stage, to their waiting aides and family members, and then over to us one production stage away to game-plan questions with my producer, Molly Roecker. We'd spend every waking second together from this point forward until the inauguration—she was the first person I'd see when I got in the car in the morning and the last person I saw before we'd close our hotel room doors and set a meet-up time for the following morning to do it all over again—but at this point in Atlanta, we were strangers.

Standing with our crew at the ready and Amy Klobuchar finally in front of me, I went for it: "You had a pretty feminist moment out there tonight, though, when you talked about the double standard that female candidates face. What do you think the larger impact of that is, calling it out on this stage?"

I asked, expecting Klobuchar to jump feet first into the feminism pool. You don't make a point like that on the stage without knowing the questions you're going to get afterward, right? But that's not Klobuchar—and she was about to remind me.

"Well, what was interesting, and somewhat surprising for me, is that I am someone that has not run in that way. And I am not doing it now—

and I will explain that in a minute," she told me. My cameraman orbited around us, but we ignored his moving lens and the bobbling boom microphone above. "I have never run as 'hey, elect me because I am a woman.' Yet, I was the first woman in both my jobs as a DA and then also as the U.S. senator from Minnesota. I always ran on my merit."

Ever the storyteller, Klobuchar launched into a shorter-than-usual memory of campaigns past: "I remember standing in a room of steelworkers and saying to them, you know what, I am not running just to be elected as a woman; I am running on my merits. And last time I checked, half the voters are men, so if I was just running as a woman, I wouldn't win. It really made no sense, but they finally put their arms down and were open to me."

I wondered afterward why she didn't think about the other half of the voters who were women, and if she meant that running on gender was at odds with running on merits, as some conservative candidates might argue. "So, that is not how I am going to run," she concluded. But not running "as a woman" doesn't mean you aren't still treated as one. And that's why Klobuchar decided she had to say something.

"I had this moment after months of watching all this happen, and seeing how people perceive you differently, and seeing my media clips where people actually said, 'I don't know if she looks presidential.' " Klobuchar wasn't the only woman of 2020 hearing that, either. She continued: "I remember [former Maryland senator] Barbara Mikulski saying, 'You want to know what a senator looks like? You're looking at it.' So, what I wanted to basically say on that debate stage, 'You want to know what a president looks like? You are looking at it.' "

Months later, with the primary long in the rearview mirror and Biden just weeks away from ultimately winning the 2020 race, I reminded Klobuchar of this moment in Atlanta.

"I was arguing, 'I'm the one that can win, and guess what, a woman can do this!' " she recalled. "It was almost responding to the entire United States history of women not serving [as president]. But I had, in fact, always run, and I think in this race *did* run, based on my experience. Based on the fact that I could win and bring people with me, as opposed to 'put the first woman in.' And I wasn't really making that argument in Atlanta. It was more of—while it was a feminist moment, and important moment for the country, and I hope it's helped Kamala [Harris] on the ticket and all kinds of things that came out of it—I did it because I realized 'boy, we're not gonna have a chance of doing that if we don't make this argument.' Because it's still in people's heads."

Just as she delighted in the memory, so did I. The moment in Atlanta was, and remains, one of my favorites. It injected theories of feminism into real-time politics. Theories that were playing out regardless, but that the women being impacted by them reframed and co-opted as they occurred. Perhaps this kind of real-time game theory made change harder in the immediate term—reminding voters of the theoretical pitfalls hardened them into realities—but it also may have made the ground firmer for the women who would come next.

7

Can a Woman Win?

The Electability Question

JANUARY 2020

W hat a night!" Elizabeth Warren said.

It was past 3 a.m. on Iowa Caucus Night and we were barreling through the air from Des Moines to Manchester. At the back of the plane, the press corps was exhausted, contorted into resting positions in our seats but too scared to fall asleep for fear that the candidate would come to the back of the plane. And then there she was. Warren coming right toward me, clad in a dark blue campaign-branded hoodie and brandishing party-size bags of Smartfood popcorn and Doritos. I was both too tired to eat and not given a choice, the candidate holding the bags in front of my face until I dunked my hand into a bag of cheesy powders. The rest of the press corps, most of us women, followed suit, and then draped ourselves over the seats, craning to be in view of the candidate and straining to hear her above the thrum of the jet engines.

She seemed to be in a good mood, even though this was not the Caucus Night she, or any of us, had imagined. Mostly because it was the Caucus Night that wasn't. We left Iowa, along with the rest of the field, not knowing who had won, but surmising it likely wasn't Warren. The already-complicated caucus process went completely haywire on Caucus Night, with the Iowa Democratic Party's app not reporting the results from multiple precincts. The breakdown led to each individual campaign culling its own counts from organizers across the counties.

Amid the confusion, some—namely Pete Buttigieg and Bernie Sanders—announced themselves as the winners, gleaning from their own internal data that they had likely won. Klobuchar, too, made the most of the moment, jumping on stage at her own victory party to declare "we know there's delays, but we know one thing: we are punching above our weight." Ultimately it was Buttigieg who won Iowa if you were going by who won the most delegates, and Sanders if you were judging by percentage of overall votes earned. But really? Nobody was a winner given the way it all shook out. Neither candidate got to bask in the famed post-caucus springboard of media attention, with potential now affirmed by actual votes, and polling boosts typically earned from an Iowa win. Instead, all the candidates left Iowa in a state of chaos. And Warren was left to recalibrate what her own victory could look like, having her campaign's Iowa-centric strategy upended and with the biggest question of the primary freshly laid bare for all to see just a few weeks prior.

Warren hosted more than one hundred campaign events in the Hawkeye State once it was all said and done, but her final gatherings and media appearances hinged around a simple and centralized message: women win.

"Guys, we just have to face this," she said. "Women candidates have been outperforming men candidates in competitive elections" in the post-2016 era. "We took back the House, we took back statehouses around this country because women ran for office and women showed up to make those elections winnable. So, I say all that just to level the playing field a little bit, right?"

After the event, I asked her, "Is that your closing pitch? Women win, period?"

"It's a big part of it," she told me. "People ask in different ways. They ask about it, I'm glad to talk about it right up front, 'cause you know what? Women win."

She may have been glad to talk about it. But Bernie Sanders—and the News Gods—hadn't given her any other choice.

Ten days earlier, the words hit the air like wet mud hitting a wall: "Can a woman beat Donald Trump?"

It was a rhetorical question—in the context Warren was using it in, anyway—but that it even had to be uttered on a debate stage, especially one this consequential in January 2020, was a depressing marker of gender's inextricable link with the presidential political landscape.

Of course, it's always been there. When voters or pundits or operatives wondered about "likability" or "viability," what they were really asking about was "electability": can this person *win*? And gender informed those answers in an incalculable, but substantive, way. Especially in 2020, when the question wasn't just about winning; it was about beating Donald Trump.

In a way, I was sort of surprised it took until January 2020 for the question to be publicly grappled with, given this had been The Question since the day Hillary Clinton conceded to the New York real estate mogul and former reality TV show star in 2016. And it wasn't just voters or reporters trying to dissect it. Candidates were consumed by it, too.

Warren and Sanders talked about it over a now-infamous dinner in Warren's Washington, D.C., apartment several weeks before the 2020 primary kicked off in earnest. Gathered in Warren's downtown D.C. home, the two progressives discussed the path to the presidency ahead and the higher-than-ever stakes of the election. They discussed their nascent candidacies and planned to keep the discourse civil, so as not to harm the broader progressive ideals they espoused and movements they fostered. Then the topic of 2020, Trump, and who could beat him was laid on the table—and the since-reported accounts of what happened at the dinner began to differ from there. Sanders and his allies contend he mentioned the ways Trump would try to defeat another female opponent, given how

he took on Hillary Clinton. Warren and her allies say the Vermont senator was saying a woman couldn't win, even as the Massachusetts senator
made her case for running. Publicly, the story wasn't heard from again . . .
until the nearly year-long Sanders-Warren détente started to fray in full
view of the political world at a critically important moment.

Sanders's campaign seemed to light the spark, going "negative on the
doors," which meant they were speaking badly about Warren when their
volunteers went door-knocking to recruit voters in at least two early-voting
states. Not unusual, especially for this point in a campaign. Once *Politico*
broke the story about a script the Sanders campaign was using that highlighted her pitfalls, I asked Warren about it after she finished a stop in
Marshalltown, Iowa. It was two days before the scheduled debate and just
over two weeks until the Iowa Caucus.

"Senator Warren," I began when she swiveled her head in my direction, as she usually did, to signal she was ready for questions. "There's
reporting from my colleague in *Politico* this morning"—I gestured behind
me to the reporter—"about the Bernie Sanders campaign and the way
they are talking about you at the doors here in Iowa. Basically, saying
that your voters are people who will vote Democrat anyway and you don't
bring new bases into the Democratic tent. Why is he wrong?"

I'd asked questions about Bernie dozens of times before and Warren
usually swatted them away. So, I tried to frame this as something she
couldn't wriggle away from. Turns out, this time, she wasn't trying to
wriggle away from anything.

"I was disappointed to hear that Bernie is sending his volunteers out to
trash me," Warren responded, clearly angry. "Bernie knows me and has
known me for a long time. He knows who I am, where I come from, what
I have worked on and fought for, and the coalition and grassroots movement we are trying to build. Democrats want to win in 2020. We all saw
the impact of the factionalism in 2016 and we can't have a repeat of that."
This was a not-so-veiled reference to Sanders's splintering of the party in
2016 when he ran against Hillary Clinton, and then, some say, even after
dropping out, he never truly embraced her as the nominee.

The so-called "Bernie Bros" only lent credence to this criticism from mainstream Democrats for their continued targeting of Clinton well past the Democratic National Convention. Their moniker—a sign of praise or contempt, depending—referenced Bernie's largely white male supporter base, but it also spoke to an age divide among the kinds of people who backed Bernie over Hillary in 2016. The young and the fratty, vehemently defending their candidate in the vast, online expanse of Twitter. That's not just a male candidate thing, by the way. Every journalist learned the sting of the pro-Kamala "K-Hive" online if they were to write a less-than-glowing story or offer anything even mildly critical about Harris. And even now, well after the initial emergence of the Bernie Bros, there is a view that this moniker applies to any ultra-progressive male who is out-spoken in his views and vehemently, even aggressively, defensive of mainly male progressive candidates or their ideals.

But in 2016, and now, the Bernie Bros' attacks were seen by some as more than political; they felt especially gendered.

In a viral post that was actually more of a primal scream (most of it was literally written in ALL CAPS), writer Courtney Enlow captured it:

THE DAY MY HUSBAND TOLD ME HE LIKED BERNIE, HE SAID, "I mean, how great is it to have a president who just doesn't even care how his hair looks" AND I EXPLODED "DO YOU THINK THERE EXISTS A WORLD WHERE A WOMAN COULD EVEN CONSIDER THAT?" . . . I'M NOT SAYING THERE AREN'T REASONS SOMEONE SHOULD DISLIKE HILLARY OR PREFER BERNIE. THAT IS FINE. THAT IS YOUR JOURNEY. BUT LET'S NOT PRETEND FOR A SECOND THAT THERE WOULD BE *THIS MANY* ISSUES WITH HILLARY IF SHE WAS A GODDAMN MAN . . . IT IS ABSOLUTELY GUT WRENCHING THAT THIS BADASS, IMPORTANT WOMAN HAS BEEN DIMINISHED AND WRITTEN OFF AND HATED HER WHOLE CAREER, HER WHOLE EXISTENCE AS A PUBLIC FIG-URE. YOU LIKE BERNIE BECAUSE HE DOESN'T PLAY THE GAME, BUT FOR HILLARY RODHAM CLINTON, FOR A WOMAN, SHE HAS HAD NO OTHER CHOICE.

So, when Warren talked about the "factionalism" of 2016 . . . that's the mindset some people harkened back to.

Looking to lower the temperature on the Warren situation the next day, Sanders said he had "hundreds of employees" on his campaign and that "people sometimes say things that they shouldn't." As for him? "I have never said a negative word about Elizabeth Warren, who is a friend of mine," he said. The publicly friendly sentiment between the two progressive campaigns was restored—until just before noon the next day.

I was sitting in Java Joe's Coffee Shop in downtown Des Moines, covering Senator Cory Booker's departure from the race that morning. He was ending his campaign, one that centered around a message of love in a campaign that was mostly about fear. Many Democrats, donors included, liked him personally but shrugged their shoulders at his love-first approach to this national campaign, wary that it could work and not eager to give the cash Booker so badly needed to stay in the race.

The New Jersey senator was far from the winner in 2020, but he was a joy to be on the campaign trail with. Following candidates who enjoy campaigning—and don't openly despise their traveling press corps—makes the job a lot easier, the frigid temperatures of Iowa worth braving, and the countless nights spent away from home a lot less depressing. From what I could tell, Cory Booker really loved campaigning. Also, selfies. One night I got off a plane from South Carolina to see him crouching and craning to fit himself and a voter in the frame of the iPhone lens. It was nearly eleven o'clock at night and we'd just capped off an insanely long day of campaigning. Yet there he was.

"Always taking selfies," I said to him as I hustled by, eager to get in an Uber and get home for a rare night in my own bed. Never moving his arm from its prime elevated selfie position, he shifted his head to smile and wink, then readied for yet another close-up.

But between live shots about Booker—and midway through a sip of oat milk latte at Java Joe's—the cable news banners started popping up. CNN was now reporting the long whispered-about, but previously private, 2018 dinner between Warren and Sanders. There went Cory Booker's day of campaign *in memoriam* coverage.

Sanders, in a statement, called it "ludicrous to believe that at the same meeting where Elizabeth Warren told me she was going to run for president, I would tell her that a woman couldn't win." He said people talking about this conversation now were "lying" and that while Trump was a "sexist, a racist and a liar who would weaponize whatever he could," he "of course" believed a woman could win in 2020. "After all, Hillary Clinton beat Donald Trump by three million votes in 2016."

The Warren team, meanwhile, was sending my calls to voicemail. *If they leaked this story,* I thought, *wouldn't they confirm it more readily?* While I texted and dialed and got "off the record, but . . ." from sources, Sanders's campaign manager, Faiz Shakir, upped the stakes.

"I believe strongly what we are talking about here is a lie," he told my colleagues at NBC who covered the Sanders beat in a phone call. "I believe that [Warren] should come out and say 'yeah, that is not my recollection of events. Of course, Bernie Sanders does not believe that. Bernie Sanders has been a friend and supports—and has always supported me when I needed him.' "

That same day, Shakir also went on CNN and said he wanted to hear from the Massachusetts senator. "I knew what she would say," he posited. "That [the story] is not true. That it is a lie."

Behind the scenes, the talk was along these same lines. The campaign space is full of friends competing against friends; former coworkers now working for separate bosses. That was certainly true for the folks that made up Sanders and Warren Worlds. Texts were flying between the two camps, with members of the Sanders team urging friends on the Warren team to say this was a lie . . . even when she and her camp believed it wasn't.

Around 7:30 p.m. in Iowa, Kristen Orthman, Warren's comms director, sent me Senator Warren's response. It did not read at all like the one Faiz suggested for her. "Among the topics that came up was what would happen if Democrats nominated a female candidate. I thought a woman could win; he disagreed," Warren said, on the record.

Soon after, the Sanders camp sought to soften their claim that the story was a "total fabrication" to an explanation that "wires crossed apparently about this story." Both sides agreed the dinner tale was taking on a life of its own. The word of the evening soon became "de-escalation." At least, publicly.

Behind the scenes, candidates and staffs alike were fuming, with fingers pointing and accusations flying about who leaked this news and what ends it served them in doing so. Among some there was the view that it was Warren's team who put it out there, looking to reignite her stalling campaign while knocking off the man who carried the progressive mantle. Sanders's allies calling the story's timing—mere weeks before the Iowa Caucus—suspect, maligning the Warren campaign in anonymous quotes to reporters that called the meeting leak "disgusting." The Warren team, meanwhile, closed ranks but saw the Sanders denial and the aggressive posture of their response as a betrayal. More than that, they were angry about how the media seemed far more willing to give Sanders the benefit of belief than Warren, who had also put herself on the record with her account of the story.

The morning of the debate, my colleague and longtime friend Shaquille Brewster and I wrote a story that spoke to the vibe across the campaigns before Debate Night: "This isn't how the home stretch before the Iowa Caucus was supposed to go."

As much as Warren's team was not relishing the prospect of a public, progressive blowup on the stage, the other campaigns were also none too thrilled to publicly wring their hands about electability through the lens of gender, inevitably summoning the sexist specter of Hillary Clinton's 2016 loss less than three weeks before Caucus Day.

The male candidates had to bolster the electability of their female rivals or risk looking sexist and out of touch, while the women now had to answer the hidden question that lacked a satisfactory answer and had dogged them from the start. And it was all happening in full view of an electorate, mere days before they voted, on one of the most consequential debate stages yet.

Texting with one Democratic operative about their reaction to this being "The Fight" leading up to Debate Night, they replied: "heavy sigh."

Amy Klobuchar, the only other woman set to appear on the debate stage that night, weighed in on Twitter before the candidates took their podiums: "There is a lot of talk today about if a woman can beat Donald Trump. As I said on the debate stage, Nancy Pelosi does it every day."

It took roughly forty-three minutes of debate for the topic to come up that night. The moment we'd all been waiting for. Every reporter in the spin room perked to attention and readied for fireworks.

"CNN reported yesterday, and Senator Sanders, Senator Warren confirmed in a statement, that in 2018, you told her that you did not believe that a woman could win the election. Why did you say that?"

"Well, as a matter of fact, I didn't say it," Sanders parried. "And I don't want to waste a whole lot of time on this, because this is what Donald Trump and maybe some of the media want. Anybody who knows me knows that it's incomprehensible that I would think that a woman couldn't be president of the United States. Go to YouTube today. There's a video of me thirty years ago talking about how a woman could become president of the United States. In 2015, I deferred, in fact, to Senator Warren. There was a movement to draft Senator Warren to run for president. And you know what? I stayed back. Senator Warren decided not to run, and I, then, I did run afterwards. Hillary Clinton won the popular vote by just shy of three million votes. How could anybody in a million years not believe that a woman could become president of the United States?

"And let me be very clear: if any of the women on this stage, or any of the men on this stage, win the nomination—I hope that's not the case, I hope it's me—but if they do, I will do everything in my power to make sure that they are elected in order to defeat the most dangerous president in the history of our country."

"I do want to be clear here," moderator Abby Phillip followed up. "You're saying that you never told Senator Warren that a woman could not win the election?"

"That is correct."

Abby turned her attention. "Senator Warren, what did you think when Senator Sanders told you a woman could not win the election?"

The room erupted with laughter. In the spin room, I saw some jaws drop, incredulous. Sanders shook his head. I thought about the nerve it took for Abby to ask the question that way, and how another moderator might not have.

"I disagreed," Warren replied. "Bernie is my friend, and I am not here to try to fight with Bernie. But look: this question about whether or not a woman can be president has been raised and it's time for us to attack it head-on. And I think the best way to talk about who can win is by looking at people's winning record. *So, can a woman beat Donald Trump?* Look at the men on this stage. Collectively, they have lost ten elections." She paused briefly to let the stat sink in before moving on. "The only people on this stage who have won every single election that they've been in are the women. Amy and me." Applause rang out.

"So true," Klobuchar said with a chuckle. "So true."

"And the only person on this stage who has beaten an incumbent Republican anytime in the past thirty years is me. And here's what I know: the real danger that we face as Democrats is picking a candidate who can't pull our party together or someone who takes for granted big parts of the Democratic constituency. We need a candidate who will excite all parts of the Democratic Party, bring everyone in, and give everyone a Democrat to believe in. That's my plan and that is why I'm going to win."

Abby asked Klobuchar her reaction to those "who say that a woman can't win this election?"

"I hear that," Klobuchar said. "People have said it. That's why I've addressed it from this stage. I point out that you don't have to be the tallest person in the room. James Madison was five foot four. You don't have to be the skinniest person in the room. You don't have to be the loudest person. You have to be competent . . . I have won in the reddest of districts. I have won in the suburban areas, in the rural areas. I have brought people with me . . . And finally, every single person that I have beaten, my Republican opponents, have gotten out of politics for good."

"Just to set the record straight," Bernie interjected, "I defeated an incumbent Republican running for Congress."

Warren asked: "When?"

"1990."

Warren paused to do the math again. In the spin room, some reporters closed their eyes (I presume, to count) while others *tap-tapped* to their
calculator app. For my part, I felt betrayed. I was told there would be no
math in journalism.

Dispensing with the calculations, Warren made another pass at the
electability question. "I do think it's the right question: How do we beat
Trump? And here's the thing: Since Donald Trump was elected, women
candidates have outperformed men candidates in competitive races. And
in 2018, we took back the House, we took back statehouses, because of
women candidates and women voters. Look, I don't deny that the question
is there. Back in the 1960s, people asked, could a Catholic win? Back in
2008 people asked if an African American could win. In both times the
Democratic Party stepped up and said 'yes,' got behind their candidate,
and we changed America. That is who we are."

Warren had been thrown into the center of the electability gauntlet
and was trying to disrupt the cycle before it chewed her up and spat her
out. A 2021 Stanford University study of the gender dynamics of the 2020
Democratic Primary field would show just how intense the sexist undercurrents were that she, and the rest of the field, was fighting.

Seventy-six percent of likely Democratic primary voters, they found,
believed it would be harder for a woman to win the 2020 election against
Trump compared to a man. Nearly four in ten said they thought most
Americans weren't at all, or were only slightly, ready for a female president. And half thought Warren and Kamala Harris—two of the women
specifically polled by Stanford—were less electable than Bernie Sanders
and Joe Biden. The data underscored electability as a problem for both
the General Woman Candidate and specific, real-life women candidates.

But the study found that these perceptions translated into how voters actually voted. The researchers called it "gender-shifting" and they
found "evidence that participants who most wanted the woman candidate shifted to the man candidate because they were concerned with the

woman candidate's electability." Making electability the foremost thought for voters "decreases voters' intentions to vote for candidates who are perceived as less electable, such as women candidates." This study built upon a 2019, real-time version from Avalanche, where pollsters asked voters who they'd choose as their nominee if they had a "magic wand" versus who they'd vote for if Election Day were today. Warren led the field with "magic wand" voters. Biden ran away with it among "horse race" voters. When asked what the "magic wand" candidate (Warren) could change to make themselves more likely to win, the most cited attribute by respondents: gender. And of the people citing gender, a whopping 69 percent identified as female themselves.

Electability concerns, Stanford found out, came from multiple places. More than nine in ten poll respondents said many Americans are not yet ready to vote for a female president. They also said that "electability of women candidates is undermined by gender biases in the culture at large, including higher requirements for proving themselves (94%), biased media coverage (77%), and harsher (87%) and more effective (79%) criticisms by polling opponents." Finally, they also found "a sizable minority of voters thought that women lacking the experience required for the presidency (26%) and not being tough enough (25%) were reasons why it would be harder for women to win."

Yes, the undercurrents were strong, and long-lasting. They were more prevalent in primary cycles than generals, and in races for executive positions (mayoralties, governorships, the presidency) than legislative spots "since the former are more clearly at odds with traditional gender stereotypes, and representation in these positions has historically been lower for women." They were on display on the pre-Iowa debate stage. But the Stanford data also tested ways to break out of the riptide.

"Presenting evidence that women earn as much electoral support as men in U.S. general elections increases the likelihood of intending to vote for a woman president," they wrote, and while the effect size was small—3 percent higher intentions to vote for a woman candidate—"it's worth considering in light of the small margins observed in many U.S. primary and general elections." Electability intervention could, on a small scale, disrupt the cycle and level the electability playing field.

A reminder—as Warren was delivering here on the debate stage and as Klobuchar, Harris, and Gillibrand had done as well—of female electoral successes was essential. Women do win . . . but if, and only when, you vote for them.

The electability argument wasn't over just because the debate was.

Candidates departed their podiums and outstretched their hands. As Pete Buttigieg shook hands with Tom Steyer and chatted with Biden, Warren and Sanders met center stage.

"I think you called me a liar on national TV," Warren said, a hint of anger in her voice as she ignored Sanders's outstretched right hand.

"What?" he replied, caught off guard. All the while, the audience applauded.

Hands grasped in front of her, Warren repeated: "I think you called me a liar on national TV."

Sanders put his hands up in protest as billionaire Tom Steyer—the man with the best, or worst, timing in the world—put his hand on Bernie's shoulder. Steyer would later explain to me that he "just wanted to say 'hi' to Bernie."

"Let's not do it right now," Sanders said to Warren, ignoring the billionaire's touch. "You wanna have that discussion, we'll have that discussion."

Warren opened her mouth and gestured as if to say *bring it on.*

Sanders continued. "You called me a liar. You told me—"

Tom Steyer had now dropped his hand and was blankly staring at the scene—held captive by social niceties that made him an awkward, accidental third wheel to this very uncomfortable interaction.

"All right, let's not do it," Sanders cut himself off and walked away.

Warren, too, exited the stage—furious, and evidently unaware that her microphone was on the whole time. We'd all find out later that the exchange was clearly audible and would be televised.

Concern existed within the Warren camp's ranks over splintering the progressive movement or alienating Sanders supporters who could still choose to back her, but there was also the competing feeling of satisfaction of watching a woman speak her truth, be called a liar, and stand up for herself forcefully. That America got to see an authentic reaction not meant for TV made it all the more compelling to some in the Warren campaign.

"She walked up, hands folded, 'Hey, I think you just called me a liar on national TV.' He's like, 'What?' She's almost like, 'Did I stutter?' " one top staffer excitedly recalled, well after the primary dust had settled.

Female staff saw this as an unguarded moment that showed how *real* their candidate was. This is why they went to work for her, many told me. They felt validated and excited. Some thought of moments where they hadn't stood up for themselves and filed this away as a touchstone to come back to. A powerful person doing what they wished they could have done. But that didn't mean the campaign could capitalize on this display of confidence the way they had in similar viral moments. There was no rush to print "I think you called me a liar on national TV" T-shirts and no mugs emblazoned with "So, can a woman win?" as they'd done before with mugs labeled "billionaire tears" after a billionaire became emotional on TV while talking about how upsetting it was to see Warren vilify the billionaire class. Some staffers joked about how well these new shirts would've sold.

"But you can't do that," a senior aide acknowledged. For the obvious reason that Sanders and Warren were both progressive darlings, trying to lay very similar policy bricks down as they built their path to the White House, and to throw that level of shade would have alienated Bernie's base too much. Plus, the move would have looked ugly on a female candidate. And while some in the media chalked up the entire issue to personal emotions spilling into public view between candidates, others grumbled that Warren's anger wouldn't play well, even if she had every right to feel angry.

Hillary Clinton was watching this debate moment, too. "I believed her because I know Sanders and I know the kind of things that he says about women and to women," she told me, her distaste for her 2016 opponent still palpable. "So, I thought that she was telling an accurate version of the conversation they'd had."

I asked what she thought about the hot mic moment.

"I wish she had done it on mic," Clinton said. "I wish that she had pushed back in front of everybody. I think it weakened her response that it was after the cameras were supposedly off and, you know, they were just standing there. I think it's important that you call it out when it happens and that was my only regret for her. That I wish she had just turned on him and said, 'You know, it's one thing to mislead people about your healthcare plan. It's another thing to tell someone to her face that a conversation which you know happened didn't happen.' I mean, that would have been, I think, a really important moment for her."

In one (rare) study called "Putting Sexism in Its Place on the Campaign Trail" on how candidates can respond to sexism, pushing back on mic the way Clinton wished may have helped Warren to disrupt sexism cycles or recruit voters, even as the conventional wisdom goes that voters, and some in the media, recoil at women showing aggression in moments such as this. It's an imprecise science, one that still requires candidates to be seen as acting *on behalf of* other women and girls as opposed to doing what's best for her campaign's political considerations, but the 2021 study by the Barbara Lee Family Foundation found broad support for women calling out sexism when faced with it, calling it "an opportunity for a candidate to demonstrate her strength and leadership."

In fact, the research suggests that turning a blind eye to sexist moments could result in potential blowback, with 25 percent of respondents suggesting they would lose confidence in a candidate if she ignored a sexist incident, "citing her complacency and weakness in failing as a leader to address a serious problem." But there are rules to responding. Respondents responded best to responses that were calm and confident. "For voters," BLFF wrote, "the only thing worse than ignoring overt sexism is reacting by lashing out in anger or retaliation." No matter if that sexist moment really does piss you off.

Ultimately, it didn't matter whether Warren purposefully capitalized on the moment on mic, off mic, or not at all. Sanders's supporters mobilized online at the first whiff of disloyalty, lashing out at Warren with snake emojis and using #NeverWarren to organize their response. It was 2016 redux. Back then, it was #NeverHillary or #NeverClinton, a hashtag that persisted throughout the primary, past the convention, and into the general election. Now, it was #NeverWarren. The hashtag revived and revamped to fit another female candidate who dared challenge Bernie and the Bros.

To some in Warren's orbit, the trend felt like a perfect collision of gender and politics. Sanders's acolytes, a senior Warren staffer said, were fine with Warren "making her own sandcastle, as long as it's not encroaching on his."

But above all else was the crux of the exchange itself, somewhat muddled and morphed when it was broached on the debate stage but still dredging up an important and central question about female electability. Even as field staff were knocking on doors and introducing early-state voters to Warren in the first days of the primary race, the electability question always came around.

One Warren organizer remembers door knocking around Des Moines with a young female colleague. Upon arriving at a door with a peace sign in the yard, and greeting a sixty-year-old white woman, the resident "looks both of us in the eye and goes, 'Oh sweetie, this country will never have a woman president.' I lost it . . . But that was the vibe, women and men alike, both as explicitly as that but also implicitly would just say, 'Look, I think it's great what you're doing . . . but America—it's just not gonna happen.' "

When Sanders said during the January debate, "Does anybody in their right mind think that a woman cannot be elected president? Nobody believes that!" this organizer was incredulous.

"Knock one door, please, in the state of Iowa or anywhere in the U.S., because every single person believes that!" they said. "I think what he meant was that no one believes that a woman cannot serve and be president and serve in that role. As in, obviously women have the brains. Of course, people believe *that*. But I don't think that people believed that a woman could become the president by winning an election . . . I think that was the worst moment," this staffer concluded. "Because it was just like, what planet is this person living on? This is what we deal with every single day."

The organizer was right, Sanders never said publicly that a woman couldn't win the presidency, though the issue here was if he made that judgment privately and in regard to facing off against Trump.

And it was understandable, too, that the question of women's electability and then their electability against Trump would come up, given the forty-fifth president's proven and consistent propensity toward gendered and racist language. Trump felt no shame in weaponizing negative tropes against any of his opponents, including female candidates, who he would mock and attack only to proclaim five seconds later that he "cherish[es] women." It was fair to expect that he'd try to use a potential female opponent's gender or race against her. In the 2016 GOP primary, it was attacking conservative businesswoman Carly Fiorina for "that face." In the 2016 general it was, among other things, saying Hillary Clinton didn't have a "presidential look" and calling her "Crooked Hillary."

None of the women who ran in 2020 lived 2016 under a rock. Most of them even campaigned for, and with, Hillary Clinton, seeing firsthand the double-edged sword of seeking to break gender barriers while competing against a male candidate who was a caricature of hypermasculinity and lacked traditional qualification metrics for the presidency. These women knew what to expect, having played supporting roles in the case study of the first female nominee for president from a major political party. And that Stanford study referenced above talks about the ways Trump complicated an already-fraught electability metric for women candidates even further.

Not only had they watched Clinton versus Trump, but these women had been first themselves their entire career. And, once in office, they knew they were required to be more prepared than their male counterparts because they were typically given less benefit of the doubt or room for mistakes. Staffers who can compare working for male and female bosses told me, by and large, their female lawmakers asked more specific and probing questions during policy sessions or pre-interview preps than male ones. To pretend these women of 2020 hadn't thought about how to leverage their gender as an advantage, or to neutralize Trump's easily anticipated lines of attack, is unfathomable. And given this, the more-informed question we all should have been asking was: Were these women *ready* to have gender used against them and did they have a plan to beat Trump at *that* game?

That would have, at least, been a question they could more tangibly answer. Instead, most reporter and voter questions about gender were framed from the negative perspective, as an albatross to be overcome, with no satisfying solution in sight.

"What blows my mind a little bit about the electability conversation and how it relates to this cycle is that all these women were elected officials," Kirsten Allen, a former campaign aide to Kamala Harris, told my colleague Deepa Shivaram at one point late in the primary. "They're clearly electable." Scholars pointed that out to me, too. Not just about the four female senators, but about Representative Tulsi Gabbard as well. "All of them who are in Congress have already cleared several bars," author and academic Jennifer Lawless told me.

"The qualities of leadership don't discriminate between men and women," Allen said. "You are discerning, intelligent, thoughtful, and all those things can be described in a man or a woman. And we, as an electorate, have to open our minds up to where that is the case."

A hope for the future, but not the case in 2020. Whatever Bernie meant when he told (or didn't tell) Elizabeth Warren that a woman couldn't beat Trump—that *she* couldn't beat Trump—the timing for this airing of grievances could not have come at a worse moment for the female candidates in the race, all of whom had been contorting themselves to answer the electability question in a way that would placate a nervous electorate. And all of whom would now have to spend the twenty days between now and Caucus Day making their final pitches to a group of voters grappling with a nagging, truly unknowable question: Could a woman win, in an election where winning was the only thing that mattered, with an opponent so unpredictable?

For Harris, Warren, Klobuchar, and Gillibrand, their runs were all rooted in being female candidates. Even as they all ran in different ideological and strategic ways, they all shared the same collective onus of having to answer an unanswerable question. Spending time on the campaign trail that male candidates didn't have to spend proving this metric that couldn't be proven until voters actually cast their ballots—and by then, it would be too late.

Harris would call it "the elephant, or maybe even the donkey in the room" during her events, saying this gender-race-electability ghost has come up "in every race I have ever, and here's the operative word, won."

"I heard it when I ran for district attorney and people said, 'They are not going to be ready for you. No one like you has done it before. Not based on your race. Not based on your gender,' " Harris said to voters for the first time at a Coralville, Iowa, rally in September 2019, right as her poll numbers started to plummet.

"Let's just look at the numbers," Warren said in January 2020 in Des Moines. "When people ask the question—can a woman win?—what does this mean? . . . Look at the numbers. Since Donald Trump has been elected, women candidates have outperformed men candidates in competitive races." Warren would echo Harris now with this truth bomb.

Up against sliding poll numbers and a shortage of funds, both candidates—despite different political ideologies and after running campaigns that danced around gender as both an ancillary and a central theme—ended their races leaning into electability in the same way; an unofficial "playbook" of sorts for how female candidates could tackle the issue.

"I think it is harder as a woman," Klobuchar told me after the race, of proving this metric. "It shouldn't be, but it is. Why? Because [voters] want to win. So they have to go to their muscle memory and the actual facts about, well, who *has* won?" She, like the rest of them, tried to counter that on debate stages and at her events. "That was just something I had to confront. And whether I could've done it differently, I don't know. But that was in people so much. [They] wanted to win. And I think that did make the task harder."

Ultimately, after these candidates gave multiple options and explanations, voters answered the electability question for them.

"These four women," Clinton said of the four female senators who she watched run in 2020, "they've been elected by their states—and big states! Lots of people have voted for them and they are distinguishing themselves in the Senate. Then they decide to run for president and all of a sudden, I'm going to rewrite their history? I'm going to look at them differently? Why is that happening?"

The inability of the women in 2020 to translate favorability ratings or voter intrigue into tangible electability at the ballot box was a letdown for many who'd been in the political space for so long.

"In the past, who you liked and who could win, they merged," Celinda Lake told me. "In 2016, if you were [for] Bernie, you thought Bernie could win. For Hillary, you thought she could win. That was not true this time around. It was a separate dimension. There were a lot of Boomer, women voters in particular, who said, 'I want a woman, I was a supporter of Hillary, but we gotta beat Trump and I'm not sure a woman can win.'"

Emily Parcell, the senior Warren aide, saw the same thing. "It's just so counterintuitive to see high favorability ratings not also be translated into being someone voters think can win. It was so stark and bizarre."

After 2016, Lake's (and others') explanation for the outcome was "it wasn't women; it was Hillary. But after 2020, I think that it's a really profound question." Blaming Clinton's polarizing figure was a salve for some in 2016. Now, though, it was clear that our failure to elect a woman was more than just a Hillary Problem.

"What was sobering about 2020 was you had so many different kinds of women run," Lake told me, sounding a little deflated. "So, if you didn't like a tall woman, a short woman, a blond woman, a brunette . . . And I think it was really sobering for those of us who have been working for this for a long time . . . 2020 was just a very sobering reminder of how tough it still is."

Clinton felt that, too.

"I was very happy there was more than one woman running because I thought that would expand the understanding," she said. "We come in all sizes and shapes, different heights, we have different hairstyles, and yes, guess what? We have different experiences and maybe even different policy ideas. But none of the women won anything. And it was a real disappointment."

In the end, that Sunday night in Cedar Rapids, Iowa where Warren first argued "women win" said it all. No sooner did she finish her pitch to voters like Torina Hill of Muscatine, who was "tired of old white guys making all of the rules," than a white man with graying hair walked up to the microphone to ask a question.

"How do you convince white men—who aren't as smart as me—how do you convince those white men over fifty that Elizabeth Warren's the candidate?"

In the end, she couldn't.

And back on the plane, hurtling into New Hampshire, down but not yet out, she knew at least one explanation for why. Deepa, our Warren embed, brought up the "women win" messaging and the fact that, at least in this Iowa Democratic Caucus . . . they didn't. She didn't. Where did that message come from, Deepa asked, and why was it important to speak to gender now?

"I'm responding to what people wanna hear," Warren told us plainly, with a characteristically biting edge in her voice. She spoke sometimes as if all the annoyance and frustration she had about the political system simmered right on the edge of her words, teeming on the top of her teeth, threatening to spill over.

We'd talked about the dynamics of Iowa, her competitors, and the pressure she put on herself not "to screw this up." But here and now she offered her plainest view of the landscape yet: "Everyone comes up to me and says, 'I would vote for you, if you had a penis.' "

8

New Hampshire
Reckoning with the Inevitable

FEBRUARY 2020

Before I covered politicians, I entertained becoming one.

The dalliance was brief. I tried once, failed, and quickly tucked the experience away. Until, at a packed campaign event in Nashua, New Hampshire, a few days before the February 11th primary, Amy Klobuchar declared—as she often did—that she'd "won every race, every place, every time," including in fourth grade.

"Guys, they boast about stuff all the time on the debate stage. So, this is my thing," she said, grabbing my attention as if I hadn't heard this line dozens of times before. "Back then my slogan, which I have since abandoned, was 'All the way with Amy K.'" The crowd roared. "I don't think that's where we wanna go right now, but that was it."

Klobuchar had been nailing this joke on the campaign trail for months, a comic routine steeped in the truth that this *was* her "thing." Winning in races that weren't necessarily easy electoral layups for Democrats and breaking the Minnesota glass ceiling back in 2006 as the first woman to represent the state in the U.S. Senate. She won then as she ran now: as a candidate who "bridged the river of our divides" and brought voters along through pragmatic policy, with a workhorse, not show horse, mentality, and a folksy-with-a-biting-edge persona. Winning was winning. And wasn't winning—as opposed to the gender you are when you win—the part that really mattered?

I was not a winner. "Amy K" was reminding me of that. In 2007, Amy Wagner and I embarked on an ill-fated presidential bid to be co-presidents of our entire high school. The most executive of executive roles Briarcliff High School in Westchester County, New York, had to offer. As seniors, our brands were well-known. We were established in the minds of the electorate as hardworking "smart girls"—which, as other smart girls reading this may know, is a moniker that's not always a compliment. We both brought past leadership experience to the table, Amy as thrice-elected secretary of our class, while I was editor of our school yearbook. We also held positions of leadership on the well-respected, more-successful-than-the-boys' Varsity Girls Soccer Team. Where Amy was sometimes shy, I was outgoing. The press—had we had any—would have deemed her a "political insider," while I brought "outsider" calculus.

I can't remember many people urging us to run, but research tells us that's not uncommon for young women first getting into elected politics. Both avid organizers and planners, Amy and I painstakingly decorated posters and made flyers, plastering them around the brick walls of our school, leaving piles of glitter in our wake.

Our opponents were a male duo, fellow athletes who also took many of the same Advanced Placement classes that we did. They were shy and self-effacing, but ambitious and roundly liked. What they lacked in hand-painted and hand-glittered posters, they made up for in charisma, especially during formal, in-person speeches to the student body in the auditorium. The room loved the "aww shucks" style they brought, tempered with humor. Our speeches, by contrast, were neither unassuming nor funny. But wasn't this a serious job?! Why should that be disqualifying? We were campaigning seriously—glittered posters and all.

On Election Day, I whipped votes between classes, moving shark-like between rows of lockers, seeking to drive up turnout among key parts of our electorate and earning assurances of support from across cliques—I mean, voting blocs.

It almost goes without saying that we lost. A win was never really in the cards given the way we ran—unabashed, touting our credentials, "leaning in" to our ambition years before Sheryl Sandberg even coined the phrase and well before mainstream media "stanned" or YAAAAS'ed female candidates. It was before the age of the "girl boss" and before female leadership was cool. Hell, I didn't even know I was a feminist yet!

While the details of our race are fuzzy, I'll never forget the armchair punditry when it was over. One classmate said we had *too many* posters. Someone complained that Amy's handwriting—the kind of looping lettering that you can now monetize on Etsy—was *too perfect*. Our advocates and validators, mostly female friends and soccer teammates, had been *too loud*. The knock on the Wagner/Vitali ticket was, in essence, that we did, and were, *too much*. Our opponents, by comparison, won with a laid-back attitude that made it clear they didn't care *too much* about governing at all.

I never ran for office again. No one ever told me I should, either. That doesn't make me special. As researchers Jennifer L. Lawless and Richard L. Fox found in 2013, political ambition among young people is low, but "Young women are less likely than young men ever to have considered running for office, to express interest in a candidacy at some point in the future, or to consider elective office a desirable profession." Their data further suggests "that the gender gap in ambition is already well in place by the time women and men enter their first careers."

Lawless and Fox see that gap in political ambition taking hold over time. In their 2015 book *Running from Office*, they found the gap for high-school-aged people, ages thirteen to seventeen, to be relatively insignificant. Less than 10 percent of kids across genders have political ambition during that age range. But at age eighteen, there's a spike in young male ambition, while young women remain well below 10 percent. Once college-aged, men were twice as likely as women to report that they'd be interested in running for office.

It manifests across specific offices, too—the higher the office, the greater the gap. Men were more than twice as likely as women to express openness toward running for Congress. They were three times more open than women to running for president.

And Fox and Lawless find this imbalance is even evident in social spheres. Young women (eighteen to twenty-five years old) report less political discussion and exposure than men, in media, in school, or among friends. They are less likely than men to have anyone suggest they run for office and are less likely than men to think they're qualified to run for office, even later in life with careers established.

My meandering mind steered its way back to the stuffy room in Nashua just as Amy Klobuchar was wrapping up her stump speech. Standing at the back, I shared this whimsical, long-forgotten high school memory on Twitter. Responses flooded in.

A woman named Susan called my story a "repeat of 2016," projecting her own view of our race and the boys we ran against (who were actually very nice guys), saying: "Instead of voting for the smart girl in front of the class that did her homework and did all the extra credit, they voted for the loser in the back of the class that blew spitballs, looked up all the girls' skirts, and cheated on every test."

"I was voted 'most likely to be president . . .' even though I lost every election for class president each year of high school—to a boy," a woman named Courtney tweeted back at me.

Another user advised that "voters sense when you're trying too hard . . . a campaign needs to have that effortless quality but be backed up by a genuine lack of effort as well." *Perfect.*

Thirteen years after our election loss, I randomly texted Amy Wagner. It was a shot in the dark: Did she remember our failed bid for BHS class president in 2007? Her response was instant.

"We ran against two guys that were relatively charismatic and showed up with an okay speech and won and that was that vs. our tremendous amount of effort and ideas. Either of us probably would've won had we run for secretary . . . but the jump to president led to defeat," she concluded.

The biggest indignity, though, came a few months after our loss, when my high school classmates voted on senior superlatives. Our yearbook-commemorated awards were things like Class Clown or Most Likely to Marry for Money. I was voted . . . you guessed it . . . Most Likely to Become President. My classmates had an ironic sense of humor. I was electable—in the annals of high school yearbook history, anyway—just not when I wanted the job of president in real life. I had campaigned *too* openly; shown I wanted it *too* obviously; spoken in favor of my own ambition *too* brazenly.

The lessons of Briarcliff High School's 2007 class president election were playing out on a much more consequential stage, more than a decade later. Instead of complaints about too many posters and too perfect handwriting, now it was complaints about too shrill a voice, too much emotion, too much anger, too little anger. The Warrens, the Harrises, the Klobuchars, the Gillibrands, the Clintons, the Doles—just like the Vitalis and the Wagners—were, all in their own ways, just *too*. And winning required being Goldilocks. You had to be just right.

In December 2019, *The New Yorker* finally found the perfect prototype of "The Electable Female Candidate." Citing a recent Gallup poll that found a whopping 94 percent of Americans would vote for a woman for president, they posed the question at the core of this book: "Why haven't we had a female in the White House? Simple! We haven't had the right candidate."

The right candidate? Goldilocks was staring us right in the face all along, really. Claire Friedman, the piece's author, finally fleshed her out for all to see: "She knows how to fire a gun, but also has never held a gun, and doesn't know what a gun is." And "she's able to radically reshape society, but moderately." And "she wears sensible shoes that are hot . . . Her breasts are large but not obscene. Her rear is juicy. The only symptom of her period is that it makes her skinny. She glows in the dark, but in an extremely healthy, nonradioactive way."

Referencing the many stories of Klobuchar's demands (or outright abuse) of her staff and the reporting that she'd once eaten a salad with a comb because a staffer forgot to bring her a fork, Friedman went on: "She would never eat a salad with a comb, because she knows that the only acceptable non-hair related uses of a comb are scratching your back and playing it like a kazoo."

Of Warren's early misstep of taking a DNA test to prove her Native American ancestry after months of Trump calling her "Pocahontas": "She has never taken a DNA test, because she already knows that she's a hundred per cent that bitch."

"She is everything to everyone," Friedman writes. But perhaps most important on this laundry list of hilarious-if-only-they-weren't-true paradoxes for this perfect would-be woman president: "She would be pleased to be President, but she is not ambitious enough to run."

Every time I read it, this story hits me like a punch in the gut. The balancing act that women are taught from the time they first understand what running for office is continues until the time they become too old to run for office anymore. To do it, you gotta want it; but to get it, you can't show anyone how hard you'll work for it.

My classmates' ironic sense of humor persists, too, in the electorate writ large. A slew of polling and studies showed fertile ground for female candidates after the 2018 midterms—at least, theoretically. One study conducted at the end of 2018 set the stage for a diverse Democratic primary field, wherein researchers Gabriele Magni and Andrew Reynolds found: "At least in the 2020 Democratic presidential campaign, candidates are likely to be viewed more favorably for being nonwhite and nonmale."

This electorate, their findings said, had a "strong preference for women over men (plus-6.8 percent) and for minority candidates. Compared with whites, Black candidates received an advantage of 4.2 percentage points, Latinos 2.2 percentage points, Asians 0.4 percentage points and Native Americans 4.5 percentage points." Gay candidates, they found, "face a slight penalty compared with straight ones."

Female voters liked female candidates 8 percentage points more than male candidates. Male voters also preferred female candidates, by 5.3 percentage points, over male candidates. And while we already know that women win at the same rates as men when they run, Magni and Reynolds rightly point out "that's only because the women who enter races tend to be better candidates independent of gender." And certainly, most of the women in the 2020 field had proven qualifications to run on, just as the women who'd run before them had in spades.

So, this study spelled good news for the theoretical female and non-white candidate in 2020. But real-world politics isn't theoretical and doesn't happen in a vacuum. It doesn't let voters judge solely based on gender, or race, or gaffes, or singular debate performances. It's a holistic view of a person that's oftentimes informed more by "vibes" and psychology than by polling or policy, especially during primaries. When faced with real people, with real backgrounds, and with real personalities, voters . . . didn't vote for them. Which is a possibility Magni and Reynolds left open.

"It's possible," they wrote, that "Democrats stick with white men because of subconscious biases that affect their judgements of the character, history or 'likability' of women or minority candidates." These researchers allow that maybe "Democratic primary voters who prefer a non-white, non-male candidate believe it's safer to choose a white man for the general election" despite fears that this business-as-usual candidate wouldn't sufficiently electrify the Democratic electorate. All this despite their prediction that "when the field narrows, our survey suggests that a nonwhite or nonmale candidate is likely to emerge as a real contender—and when that happens, their identity will be a selling point rather than a hindrance."

Once names and bios and physical, tangible, specific people were applied . . . the enthusiasm in that polling proved to be *too* hypothetical. The reality, and the irony, was that the only thing the women of 2020 never seemed to have *too much* of was ultimately the thing they needed most: the belief—or even the benefit of the doubt—from voters that they could win.

In 2020, much of that stemmed from what, and who, came before.

While the January debate had laid bare the question of *can a woman win*, the truth is that conversation had been happening from the moment Hillary Clinton conceded to Donald Trump four years earlier *because* Hillary Clinton had to concede to Donald Trump. The Iowa debate stage in January made it splashy between Bernie and Warren, but *IT* was always there. The Hillary hangover. The most recent data point that affirmed any doubts about women being able to win the presidency, and win the presidency against Donald Trump, specifically.

Of course, the entire premise was somewhat mystifying on its face. Yes, Trump had beaten Hillary Clinton (by the metric that mattered, anyway), but he'd also beaten *fifteen* Republican men (as well as the GOP field's one woman, Carly Fiorina) on his path to winning the GOP nomination. Either we seemed to collectively forget that, or it didn't give us nearly as much pause as one woman, losing to one man, in one general election, once.

Over more than four hundred days of following every twist of the 2019–2020 primary cycle, I don't think any Democratic male candidate was asked about concerns he had that *a man* couldn't win. Male candidates were asked if *they* could win, sure. Did they have the name ID, the fund-raising prowess, the policy prescriptions, the personality, the ability to go toe-to-toe with Trump? But they were not asked if their entire gender needed to convince the country that they could prevail in the fight ahead, after having failed before.

Female candidates, meanwhile, were asked regularly. Could *they*—as individuals and women, *collectively*—win? It was framed as a negative almost every time; a problem in need of a solution, as opposed to a selling point.

Men had been losing elections for hundreds of years. And more than that, falling short—losing—was actually a good way to ensure you were next in line, especially among Republicans. For Ronald Reagan, for George H. W. Bush, for John McCain, for Mitt Romney . . . they all ran, and lost, only to be the party's next heir apparent and next best chance at victory. Their past runs made their "electability" battle-tested, not permanently or irrevocably marred. That was also true for Joe Biden, who'd run for president twice before 2020 to little success.

But women were only a few decades into mounting presidential bids—

and thusly new to losing. The hand-wringing over their electability in 2020 was the penalization cost from one woman, Hillary Clinton, who was first, who fell short, and who wasn't even on the ballot again now. But the women of the 2020 Democratic primary were tagged with her electability baggage anyway. The female candidates, the Democratic primary electorate seemed to decide, were *too* risky in large part because they were *too* like Hillary—which is to say, *too* female. Of course, the comparisons weren't necessarily that explicit. Even before her bid was official, one *Politico* headline declared: "Warren Battles the Ghosts of Hillary." Chalk that one up, Clinton told me, to "a limited imagination about what a woman running for president can be."

One thing was a direct comparison, though: these candidates were heading for a rematch with Trump—for whom the nickname "Teflon Don" fit perfectly and who was known for scorched-earth campaign tactics against all opponents and detractors—which made that skepticism even greater.

"He was looming over everything," Amy Klobuchar told me. "That caused me, especially, and a few of us, Biden, to be making this argument: that what matters is that we 'win big,' in my words. That we bring people with us. That we cross—in my words—'the river of our divides to get to a higher plane' and to make that a central theme, because people wanted to win so badly."

That was her primary pitch. "That of course leads me to the corollary to that, which is that I *then* have to make an argument that a woman can beat Donald Trump. And that's why I would say things like 'if you think a woman can't beat Donald Trump, Nancy Pelosi does it every single day' . . . To show that I was the one who had won in these swing districts, Republican areas, red districts, that became so central."

But Hillary Clinton made those arguments, too. Over three debate stages that showcased her breadth of knowledge and experience; in consistent (and, it turned out, very wrong) polling that led the country to believe the 2016 election was a foregone conclusion; and in terms of her outright qualifications and preparation for the job of president. It wasn't a question of competency. It was a question of skepticism about the person, more than the candidate. About "but her emails" and James Comey's investigation and the history of scandal that has followed the Clinton name since the 1990s. It was mistrust (some of it understandable), and unlikability, and concern about a woman on a long-term quest for power. It all led to a lack of enthusiasm among key portions of the electorate in critical swing states—places like Wisconsin and Pennsylvania. People stayed home, thought her win was all but assured, and were shown just how wrong they could be.

After the shock of 2016, the lack of a true understanding about "What Happened" left Democratic voters in 2020 with broken candidate compasses, unsure of what polls to take seriously (if any), what gaffes or missteps from Trump to read into (if at all), and what metric by which to measure the field of Democratic hopefuls (if that even existed). Policy was important, but it could come later. There would be no time for policy if they didn't first unseat Donald Trump. They needed to win. This desire, paired with more than twenty candidates who sounded mostly the same on policy, made the left ravenous for consensus and petrified of risk of any kind. The female candidates—despite clearing viability and credibility and qualification thresholds in spades—still carried an air of risk. Because it wasn't just that two hundred years of history never showed a woman atop the U.S. government structure, it was that the woman who was supposed to finally make it there . . . didn't.

An advisor to one of the women who ran in 2020 told me that before the primary truly began in 2019, they'd already found themselves in an angry headspace akin to "the most deranged and full-of-rage Hillary supporter at the end of the 2016 primary." Already facing questions about electability and gender, already bracing for the ways it could manifest and leave the women of the field playing from the start at a disadvantage.

Democrats were also coming into this election having just experienced a 2016 election cycle rife with sexism, which meant it was top of mind. Sexism in politics existed well before that, of course, but the collective rage over it—mostly from Democratic women—had been unleashed anew with Trump and during his presidency. There were women's marches and the #MeToo movement, lending to the feeling that women were not willing to let their righteous and rightful rage take a backseat anymore. But when the time came for Democrats to leverage that anger into a nominee in 2020, they found Joe Biden's all-in-moderation persona as their pick.

"You know me," Biden would tell voters, the well-known gleam in his eye crowded now by more wrinkles. During the campaign—primary and general—Biden's elder statesman persona reminded voters what it was like to have a president who they didn't have to think about every day; who just did the job; who was a little boring. Moderate and moderating, in all senses of the words.

But he was hardly the only one who could offer that. Klobuchar consistently sought to remind voters that there *was* more than one moderate with a tangible record that they could get behind. After all, she shared similar beliefs to Biden's on health care and took regular shots at Medicare for All. She prioritized infrastructure—one of the few, consistently bipartisan policy themes left in Washington—to the tune of a trillion dollars in the first policy plan her team rolled out. She pushed election reform to build more confidence in the security around our voting systems. Her entire pitch hinged on wins: legislative and electoral. But even as she tried to keep them separate, gender was always tied up in it; neither metric could ever be considered on its own.

"She'd make her case for electability, proactively bring it up . . . and then the reporters' response would be 'but a lot of people have concerns about whether a woman can win,' " one Klobuchar aide recalled. It was a feedback loop that constantly forced them to question whether to engage or ignore, where ignoring was to leave it to others to fill in the blank and to engage was to enter another news cycle of female candidates talking about running as women. Klobuchar preferred to *prove* women's electability, not talk about it.

"Look what we did in 2018," she'd riff in her regular stump speeches, restating some version of the same message multiple times a day for voters. "We won with congressional candidates by uniting all over the country, the left, the middle and more conservatives in our party and we were joined—and this is my key argument—by independents and moderate Republicans to win in those races, take back the House. That's how we won the governorship of Michigan with Gretchen Whitmer and Laura Kelly in Kansas. That's how we win those races, so I think the proof is in what just happened."

And with the electability question so inextricably tied to Trump, Klobuchar was more than willing to talk about him—how she'd take him on, and how he'd gone after her. Referring to her presidential announcement, which I covered in below-freezing temperatures while getting covered in fluffy snowflakes, Klobuchar regularly reminded crowds that Trump called her "snow woman." "I wrote back: I'd like to see how your hair would fare in a blizzard."

It was another piece of evidence, however childish the barb-trading, that she was using to build her case as the nominee. She could win, she could get attention, and she could fight back.

"You have to be able to think in the moment and be able to respond to what he does and to be able to show grace under pressure, which I hope you saw me do in the Kavanaugh hearings," she'd tell crowds across the early states. "Where the nominee [Kavanaugh] actually had to take a break and apologize to me. And so, I think these are important tasks of who we want as our candidate, and we want heading up our ticket."

The Trump question was so ingrained that even during "veepstakes," vice-presidential contenders were reportedly asked during their VP vetting interviews what they thought Trump's nickname for them might be. (For some, Trump had already answered that question. For Kamala Harris, he opted for Obama-style birtherism claims in lieu of a traditional nickname—though he did often mock or mispronounce her name.)

"Everyone remembers how Donald Trump vanquished the primary candidates in '16 and then how he took on Hillary and the negatives he reinforced," veteran Democratic strategist Hilary Rosen told me. "If Amy Klobuchar had run and if [John] McCain had been the candidate in the

GOP, or Romney, I think we might've actually had a better chance of a woman candidate. But somebody as bold, brash, and insulting as Donald Trump? I think people believed the worst of the [2020] campaign."

Still, with every chance Amy Klobuchar got—from the very snowy beginning of her campaign to her final rallies in rooms like the one I stood in in Nashua, New Hampshire—she was reminding people of what she and her advisors saw as her biggest asset: she could win. And that could come to include Trump . . . if voters believed enough to give her the chance.

With days to the New Hampshire primary, and with a field thrown totally into flux after Iowa's Mess, Klobuchar was finally getting a real look from voters. Her campaign joked about "Klobmentum" or, as I called it, "Klobomentum." Whatever you said, there was no denying the momentum was there. She'd put in the work on the ground in New Hampshire for a year. But Klobuchar's big boon came because she closed out a stellar debate performance in Manchester, days before voters went to the polls, with a story.

"There's an old story of Franklin Delano Roosevelt. And when he died, his body was put on a train and went up across America. And there was a guy standing on those tracks, along with so many Americans, and he had his hat on his chest and he was sobbing. And a reporter said, 'Sir, did you know the president?' And the guy says, 'No, I didn't know the president, but he knew me. He. Knew Me.' I will tell you this: there is a complete lack of empathy in this guy in the White House right now. I will bring that to you. If you have trouble stretching your paycheck to pay for that rent, I know you and I will fight for you. If you have trouble deciding whether you're gonna pay for your child care or your long-term care, I know you and I will fight for you."

She said each word with the full weight of her body behind it. "I do not have the biggest name on this stage. I don't have the biggest bank account. I'm not a political newcomer with no record, but I have a record of fighting for people." She was emotional, but strong. "I'm asking you to believe that someone who totally believes in America can win this. 'Cause if you are tired of the extremes in our politics, and the noise and the nonsense, you have a home with me. Please, New Hampshire, I would love your vote."

It was an emotional plea of politics and persona at a critical point in the race. After successfully framing her Iowa fifth as a better-than-anticipated success, she parlayed this moment on the next debate stage into more of the same. The following day, starting in that room in Nashua, I was forced to think about the electoral barriers I'd experienced and seen, but I also watched Klobuchar challenging and co-opting them.

"She knows me," one man, there with his wife and kids, told me. He was likely going to vote for her.

The debate gave Klobuchar a badly needed jolt—on the trail, and in the bank. Her once-perpetually dry campaign coffers were now filling up with badly needed, record-breaking cash. Enough of it that she could stay in the race through the end of the early contests, but never enough to allow her to build a campaign with as many boots on the ground across the country to rival organizations like Sanders's, Warren's, Buttigieg's, or especially billionaire Michael Bloomberg's.

Still, the debate performance, followed by ramped-up cable coverage showcasing bigger-than-ever crowds, skyrocketed Klobuchar to a third-place finish on Election Day in New Hampshire, proving that voters *are* sometimes willing to reward female candidates for stand-out, aggressive debate performances. No small feat, given how Klobuchar's female rivals had previously fared. Where Kamala Harris had been perceived as *too* mean-spirited going after Biden on busing, or Warren, in Iowa, as *too* angry or emotional for taking on Sanders and losing some progressives over it, Klobuchar showed she could be . . . Goldilocks: toeing the invisible line of electability and likability *just right* as she attacked and contrasted against her opponents.

As Klobuchar rode her post-debate surge, Biden abandoned any hope of redemption here in New Hampshire and absconded to the warmer pastures (and warmer receptions) of South Carolina hours before the polls closed in Manchester.

Elizabeth Warren, the other powerhouse struggling with underwhelming results, stayed put, hoping against hope to stave off another electoral night of failure. Her campaign was floundering after a middling finish in Iowa and now this, a dismal fourth place in her neighboring state of New Hampshire. But she was also suffering from what several would tell me was "Warren erasure," a lack of coverage that came immediately after her disappointing Iowa finish.

After Iowa, the focus was all about the B's: Buttigieg and Bernie for their first-place tie, and Biden for just how poorly the field's man-to-beat had been, well, beaten. The resulting coverage in the days after included cable news chyrons like: SANDERS & BUTTIGIEG LEAD IOWA RESULTS, BIDEN IN 4TH. Even someone as mathematically challenged as I knew there was a number missing—and Warren's allies and supporters were vocal about it, seeing the field's top vote-earning woman as sidelined from the conversation without explanation. Sources called me to gripe and I could only shrug. Campaigns often complain about (a lack of) coverage, but in this instance, I couldn't say they didn't have a point.

The trend continued when Warren performed even worse in New Hampshire than she had in Iowa: a top-tier candidate, with top staff, top fundraising, and top ground game who was very much at the bottom of the pack. She had company there. Joe Biden also came in with all the expectation of a top-tier candidate and rolled out of the first two voting contests with none of the electoral goods to show for it. Both campaigns were failing, disappointing even the most modest of expectations. But some failures, it appeared, were more interesting than others.

It was hard not to read it as the field's top-tiered woman fulfilling the prophecy that women couldn't win; and many in the media counting her campaign as "out" before they were even close to making that call for themselves. One (messy) caucus is hardly a holistic view of the field, yet when Warren underperformed in Iowa—which is to say, she didn't win— it may have confirmed some bias about her *unviability*. She fell short, so she's less viable, so she warrants less coverage, the subconscious decision-making process may have gone. Meanwhile, Biden fell short, too, which meant he should also be perceived as less viable. But both because of who he was (a former VP) and the expectations of him (that he was the most electable, in a general), coverage of him persisted, and he benefited from a deeper well of benefit of the doubt.

New Hampshire has a tendency of laying cold truths bare. In 2020, it gave and took from two women showcasing two entirely different platforms and strategies toward the nomination. It was the second stake through Elizabeth Warren's presidential aspirations but also a brief, much-needed validator for Amy Klobuchar.

And for me personally, it was a series of days packed with new revelations. About the implicit biases of my industry, but also about the pressure I felt in ensuring a level playing field and uniform metric of assessment for the female candidates I was covering. It dredged up my oldest memories about politics, however low the stakes then, and forced parallels between those old days at Briarcliff High School and the gyms, debate halls, and polling places I was frequenting now.

I was still one of "the smart girls," only now, I would joke, there were more of us. I grew up to be "a smart girl covering the smart girls" who were running for president. It was still double-edged—disqualifying and inspiring at the same time. And there were still layers of irony.

That these women could earn small wins, but not the ultimate victory. That when they fell short of their goal, the electorate who had spurned them as possible presidents then embraced them as potential VPs. That even as they showed what women could achieve when taken seriously, we still couldn't see them as anything other than obscured by the cloud of the woman who'd most recently come before them.

9

Nevada

Going Down Swinging

FEBRUARY 2020

"This is the kick in the ass they needed," a Warren ally told me as her New Hampshire Not-So-Victory Party cleared out and the reality of just how poorly she was doing sunk in.

It was without joy that this person shared this assessment—and very unlike my days covering the Trump campaign, when staffers relished backstabbing each other in the press and trying to play armchair psychoanalyst to the candidate himself in the pages of *The New York Times*. No, in Warren World they believed deeply that their candidate *should* become president—but that she desperately needed to change things up if she had any hope of actually doing so.

New Hampshire's fourth place was an embarrassment, given Warren's status as the Senator Next Door in Massachusetts. But it was also an additional sign of how her campaign's early-state strategy had fallen flat. The truth was, they needed more than a kick in the ass. They needed to pull a rabbit out of a hat and then have *that* rabbit pull a rabbit out of its hat.

But with rabbits and hats scarce, the team and the candidate settled for a change of strategy—one that was soon evident to all of us who'd spent the last year following her.

Warren rose to national prominence as Warren the Fighter but did relatively little combat with her rivals during her 2020 campaign for president. She gaggled with us, her traveling press corps, almost daily, but when we would try to bait her into contrasting herself with her rivals in the field, she typically balked, dodged, and shook her head in the name of not going there. She wouldn't alienate any potential voters, a strategy initially built with Iowa's ranked-choice caucus system in mind.

That's not to say there weren't moments of contrast, even ones that got a little feisty in their delivery. But they tended to be steeped in some larger policy principles, like an irritation at candidates who pressed for what she saw as too-slow, incremental policy change or rivals who were using the traditional fundraising apparatuses that leaned heavily on big-dollar donors, bundlers, and PACs.

Usually, these moments of contrast came on the debate stage. Sometimes—like in Detroit in July 2019 when she took down Congressman John Delaney for attacking her "fairytale economics" and progressive ideas—Warren's precision on the debate stage was applauded.

"You know," she said then, "I don't understand why anybody goes to all the trouble of running for president of the United States just to talk about what we really can't do and shouldn't fight for."

In December 2019—two months after Buttigieg helped lay bare her lack of a healthcare plan and her unwillingness, or inability, to answer whether her plan would raise taxes on the middle class—she turned up the heat on Mayor Pete over a fundraiser he held in a Swarovski crystal–adorned, Napa Valley wine cave.

"We made the decision many years ago that rich people in smoke-filled rooms would not pick the next president of the United States," Warren said on that debate stage. "Billionaires in wine caves should not pick the next president of the United States."

Buttigieg fired back that Warren used to fundraise for her Senate campaigns this way and that she transferred millions from that effort to her presidential campaign coffers. "Did it corrupt you, Senator?" Buttigieg said. "Of course not."

In the early days, when I'd ask advisors why she wasn't willing to contrast more consistently—especially when it was clear she needed to differentiate herself from Bernie Sanders—they brushed me off, reminding me that the strategy was to push her ideas and plans, not cast down the plans and personalities of others. Especially not Sanders, who was Warren's policy ally and friend (by Washington standards), but who, more importantly, had a lot of sway and overlap with voters that Warren needed to win. By not attacking, or even actively contrasting, the team thought they were keeping the focus on her message. But they were also missing an opportunity to elevate their candidate above the field—which, in the end, *was* the goal.

Eventually, I asked Warren herself about this when she joined her traveling press corps on the press bus in between campaign events days before the New Hampshire primary—a typical move for politicians, but a new one for Warren, who usually preferred to engage the press on neutral turf, like at a campaign event venue, as opposed to on our mode of transportation and traveling workspace.

"Isn't there a point that you have to say, 'Well, my policy on health care is better than, say, Amy Klobuchar's or Joe Biden's'? Or 'my policy on X is better.' Don't you have to be explicit?" I asked.

"I have laid out what my policies are and they're not the same as everyone else's," she replied, facing backwards and standing in the aisle as we sat forward-facing, like kids on their way to school. She pivoted to talk about her wealth tax, but I jumped back in.

"Do you think you'll be able to run through *the whole primary* without drawing that explicit line of attack?"

"It's not an attack," she replied.

Warren used to joke that she only officially practiced law "for forty-five minutes," but it was in moments like this I was reminded that she never actually stopped arguing for a living. She just did it with lawmakers and colleagues and the press as opposed to judges and, apparently, on school buses instead of in courtrooms.

"Differentiation, contrast, okay," I replied. *Sustained, counselor.*

But even the change in word didn't bring about a real explanation in response to my question. Some spun it as simply choosing her battles. "She picks smart fights, she doesn't just pick every fight," Adam Green, the head of a Warren-aligned progressive group, Progressive Change Campaign Committee, explained to me once.

The other side of this coin is that Warren *likes* drawing contrasts. It's how she ascended into the national consciousness: as the woman who beat incumbent Republican senator Scott Brown in 2012 with a message focused on how "the middle class is getting hammered!" and, once in Washington, didn't shy away from taking on, well, anyone regardless of party if she felt they fell short of her ideals on policy and governance. The lawmaker who carved up bank CEOs with no-holds-barred lines of questioning on behalf of the American consumer. The regulation-minded progressive who colorfully vowed that she wanted "a strong consumer agency" in the Consumer Financial Protection Bureau (CFPB) that was her brainchild or "no agency at all and plenty of blood and teeth left on the floor." Most of her 2020 campaign stump speeches ended with her explaining why she was "in this fight." But that fight, apparently, was only about ideas and taking on Republicans, not the Democrats she'd have to beat to get to the center ring.

Once the campaign was over, some would point fingers over the "fluffy-ifying" of Elizabeth Warren. "Blood and teeth" traded for plans and politics played (mostly) nice. The blame was laid by some at the feet of her chief strategist, Joe Rospars, which amused him as he once describe himself as "lighter fluid, not a fire extinguisher" on her instincts. At one point there was even a conspiracy theory circulating on the far left that Rospars made Warren get a dog for the presidential campaign—literally making her "fluffy Warren." Of course, Warren and her husband, Bruce Mann, had had golden retrievers for years prior.

Warren's selective holding of fire was meant to preserve the primary approach of being the candidate between progressive and moderate lanes, but it also protected her from the double-edged nature of going on offense as a female candidate. Aggression in the name of individual female ambition is not often met with cheers, studies and recent events have shown us. Attacking in advancement of your own political ambition—as opposed to in defense of a constituency or an issue—can often be met with resentment from voters or foment a negative narrative in the still mostly male-dominated press. Even basic policy contrasts, if stated with too sharp or snarky a tone, can be read as bitchy or sassy and unlikable to voters on the fence. And we all remember that being liked is essential for female candidates to be able to win.

"We are uncomfortable with women vying for power," Kirsten Gillibrand's campaign communications director, Meredith Kelly, told me plainly. Meaning it required more consideration on the part of these female candidates and their campaigns when attacking, contrasting, and differentiating. And considering—more than white male candidates had to—if it was worth the heightened risk.

It wasn't just aggression that earned women demerits for style or likability, though. It was that attacks from opponents were also harder for them to shake; controversial decisions from the past harder to explain away then move past.

Gillibrand, for example, was dogged by a decision that predated her presidential campaign. Voters across Iowa and New Hampshire—where Gillibrand spent most of her five and a half months campaigning—told me they were mad at her for saying that former Minnesota Democratic senator Al Franken should resign his seat in 2017 after more than half a dozen women alleged that he inappropriately touched or kissed them. Ultimately, thirty-six of his fellow Democrats in the Senate called for him to resign before an ethics investigation could take place. Some said it was Democrats eating their own, subjecting themselves to rules Republicans would never govern themselves with. To others, it was the party living their values even when it meant going against a colleague.

Gillibrand, to much media fanfare, was simply the first to speak her mind. The way voters told it, it's as if one junior senator's decision tipped the rest of the party's dominos on the issue. And while she represented a crack in the dam at the time, it's hardly true that in an institution of one hundred senators who pride themselves on making their own decisions that Gillibrand herself was the reason dozens of senators threw in against Franken. She did—in part because she was a "she"—create a permission structure, though, for others to follow suit.

But as I traveled the early states in early 2019, voters weren't over it. They saw Gillibrand's actions as betraying a friend, as ganging up on a fellow Democrat, losing the party a critical voice (and vote) on the Judiciary Committee during an administration that would consider multiple Supreme Court justices. And who's to say there wasn't some of that at play. But the way the backlash manifested and lingered felt . . . uniquely gendered.

On the fundraising circuit, Gillibrand aides recall the issue "came up constantly," with some donors declining support "because Franken." Some Democratic operatives whispered about it as a political move, meant to neutralize a potential 2020 rival and a sign of just how opportunistic Gillibrand could be.

"The opportunism would've been to step away from it!" one top Gillibrand advisor argued. "There is no one, including [Gillibrand] or anyone who worked for her, who thought taking on Al Franken was some political panacea." If anything, this person told me, it was the opposite. "She's seen women take on powerful men and get the short end of that stick. There's no way she thought it was a winning position [politically] for her."

Gillibrand herself said "it was hard to overcome it," when we spoke over Zoom several months into the pandemic. She explained her inability to shake the Franken moment as opponents kept it in the bloodstream to harm her, chalking it up to opposition research. But I could tell it vexed her on a deeper level.

"I think someone smarter than me would have to figure out why" this stuck to her so specifically, Gillibrand said, an edge in her voice. "Because I don't really know."

"You can agree or disagree with her decision, but Bernie Sanders quickly followed Kirsten [in calling for Franken to resign] that same day. So did literally every senator on the stage," Meredith told me. She was right. All the other senators (not just the women) who ran in 2020 also said Franken should resign his post or that he made the right decision after he did so. And those candidates were all asked about Franken at various points in the campaign. But Gillibrand, Meredith recalls, "was asked in the beginning and the end. Why did so many reporters feel the need to ask? I think it's because they all felt entitled to making a woman defend why she stood up to a man."

By contrast, top male contenders who had evolved in their positions over the years were allowed to play defense for past statements during the race . . . and then move on. Bernie Sanders was frequently criticized by colleagues on the left for past votes against bills that would've established national background checks for Americans trying to buy a gun and for backing protections for gun companies from lawsuits. These questions persisted in 2016, with Clinton using them to attack her opponent in that primary. In 2020, these criticisms were briefly revived, but never with any real staying power.

The same went for Sanders's heart attack in the fall of 2019. While some speculated the health scare would end his campaign, Sanders instead rallied a coveted endorsement from Representative Alexandria Ocasio-Cortez and pressed on with renewed energy. The health questions waned over time—including qualms over the transparency and disclosure of the scare to the press—and public discussion dedicated to them did, too, even as concerns persisted when he began notching wins in early-state primaries.

Joe Biden, too, was allowed the space to shift and play defense in the primary. On a litany of issues—from the Anita Hill hearings to his authorship of the controversial 1994 Crime Bill, to allegations of unwanted touching and, later, one sexual assault allegation—Biden was able to hold fast against critics and opponents, weathering these storms and eventually moving into clearer skies. The controversies were not forgotten, but pushed to the background; questions were asked, answered, and then filed away, baked into his candidacy as he forged forward. So, too, for policy changes, like an abrupt U-turn on his long-held support for the Hyde Amendment, which put him out of step with his party and banned federal funding for abortion, most negatively impeding access to abortion care for poor women and people of color. He was asked to explain the change, a welcome one for most Democrats and their voters, and allowed to evolve without too many more questions.

For Warren, an aggressive campaigning style was a double-edged sword. It's what she was known for, and yet her team saw their attempts to parry attacks from rivals or strike chords of contrast met with negative coverage and speculations about her motives. They complained that when she responded to barbs from other candidates or drew her own lines of contrast, they were met with articles describing her as a "murder-suicide" candidate—i.e., landing the punch on a rival even as she hurt herself in the process. Anything to keep someone else from winning, as opposed to the view that she was attacking to put herself ahead. Like that debate stage moment with Buttigieg over wine caves. It was chewed over in the press and among operatives as Warren attacking Buttigieg to take him down, as opposed to elevating herself and her principles.

Warren was surrounded by a loyal group of longtime staffers, so you could chalk this sensitivity up to staffers bruised by a tough-fought primary that didn't go their way. It's partly that. But consider their point of view.

Take, for instance, Biden, during the fall 2019 days of heated debates over Medicare for All, describing Warren as having "an elitist attitude" and calling the way she argued in favor of her own healthcare plan (and against his) evidence of "an angry, unyielding viewpoint that has crept into our politics." For her part, Warren responded by suggesting the former VP might be "running in the wrong presidential primary" because of his "repeating Republican talking points." A zinger, for sure, but calling Biden—whose moderate policy portfolio was his main selling point—a Republican hardly carried the same weight and possible impact as words like "angry, elitist, and unyielding" do for a female candidate.

The moment harkened back to Barack Obama dismissively calling Hillary Clinton "likable enough" during a 2008 debate, after a moderator literally asked Clinton what she'd say to those concerned about "the likability issue" (despite voters agreeing that Clinton was the field's most experienced and "electable" candidate). Or Donald Trump attacking Clinton for lacking "the strength and stamina" to be president. Or bringing women who accused Clinton's husband of sexual misconduct to one of their 2020 debates. Repeatedly, I met women on the road in 2016 who stated some version of "if she couldn't control her husband, how can she control the country?"

These words play upon sexism that may already exist in voters' minds. Hillary tried to laugh it off with Obama, and to act unfazed with Trump. Warren showcased her qualifications by campaigning on highly detailed plans and opted to call out the sexism of the anger and elitism claims. Her team blasted out a fundraising email:

> *Over and over, we are told that women are not allowed to be angry. It makes us unattractive to powerful men who want us to be quiet . . . Well, I am angry, and I own it. I'm angry on behalf of everyone who is hurt by Trump's government, our rigged economy, and business as usual.*

I flagged the email to NBC's Political Distribution List, with context. "Most women will 'get' this stereotype of women being described as angry as a way to invalidate or attack them," I wrote. "That Warren would call this moment out, bringing it further into the mainstream, is fascinating. For the academics amongst us on this thread, this kind of mainstream discussion of female rage may as well go on your Gender & Politics 101 syllabus."

"You are channeling so much 'good and mad' vibes in this email, and I am HERE FOR IT," Deepa Shivaram, our NBC embed following Warren, wrote back to me, referencing Rebecca Traister's book *Good and Mad*, which focused on the social and political power of female rage.

I was kind of mad, for what it's worth. Not on behalf of Warren—I cover her, I don't defend her—but because I, like most women, know too well the harmful impact of being called words with deeper, double meaning. So did Deepa. So did Molly, my producer. So did several of the other female colleagues at NBC who replied to my email with texts or direct messages. Seeing it play out at work makes your blood boil. Watching it happen on the biggest political stage in the world can make it bubble over. But calling it out publicly channels that rage in the hopes that once everyone sees it as illegitimate, there will be less misogyny to deal with in the future.

While female candidates had to temper or explain or spin their emotions on the trail, Biden led with them. And in that there is progress. Traditional embodiments of masculinity have only recently come to include a man's ability to cry or show empathy. Those were the best parts of Biden—both the man and the candidate. His empathy and ability to connect, especially on the deeply intimate feeling of loss, was a clear comfort and selling point for voters, showcased in repeated rope-line interactions and now, as president.

But the other emotion Biden showed was anger. Anger about the course of the country in the Trump-led era, anger about the racism and sexism and anti-Semitism that have been all too frequent but emboldened themselves over the last four years, but also anger when challenged in ways he thought were unfair. At one point during the lead-up to the Iowa Caucus, Biden reacted to an Iowa voter's questions about his age, and his son's foreign entanglements, by calling him a "damn liar" and challenging him to "push-ups together, an IQ test, or run." He defended himself against a perceived slight, angrily and using hypermasculine feats of strength as the metric. In response, there was head-shaking and finger-wagging—it's not advisable, after all, to berate the voters—but the outburst did not invalidate Biden as too emotional to lead or too quick to fly off the handle to be president.

A few months later, during a March tour of a Fiat Chrysler plant in Detroit, a worker challenged Biden's stance on the Second Amendment, wrongly claiming that Biden was "actively trying to take away" those rights. Biden promptly told him . . . he was "full of shit." When a staffer tried to end the exchange with an "all right, thank you," Biden put his hand up and shushed her, proceeding to defend his record. "I did not say that," Biden said. "I did not say that!"—his frustration greater by the second.

The exchange was stereotypically macho. The resulting coverage was neutral, with some even reasoning that this kind of heated exchange might *help* Biden with voters. Former Obama speechwriter–turned *Pod Save America* host Jon Favreau said on MSNBC afterward that in focus groups he'd conducted, "Biden talking to them like a normal person would talk to them at worst [is] a wash, and at best it might help him."

These unscripted moments on the trail showed strength and passion and that classic Biden, off-the-cuff fire. It's part of his appeal as an emotional and authentic politician. It's also the very kind of unscripted moment female candidates rarely have, and must be wary of, for fear that they could be seen as unable to control their emotions or likened to the shrill controlling woman, usually a nagging wife or mean teacher. And Black female candidates have the added concern of being painted as an "angry Black woman." For women, anger and passion are emotions not so easily spontaneously deployed.

And in fact, they're exactly the kind of thing that the women *apologized for* on the debate stage in December 2019. All seven candidates were given the choice between asking for forgiveness from one of their rivals or offering them a gift. It was a curveball of a question. First, entrepreneur Andrew Yang offered a copy of his book, noting that Warren was already giving him the honor of reading it. Buttigieg liked the idea of the book, saying, "I should probably send my book around more, too," but instead offered the gift of a future with any Democrat on the stage becoming president and beating Trump. Then Elizabeth Warren answered, and the entire mood shifted.

"I know that sometimes, um, I get really worked up," Warren said, speaking softly. "And sometimes I get a little hot. I don't really mean to. What happens is when you do 100,000 selfies with people, you hear enough stories about people who are really down to their last moments," like the Nevada voter she met who was sharing an insulin prescription with three other people who needed it. Warren, by the way, has authored more than a dozen books.

Biden followed, offering the gift of help and empathy for Americans who are hurting. Then Sanders gave "any one of *four* books that I wrote," paired with a different vision for America going forward after Trump.

"Senator Klobuchar?" the moderator intoned.

"Well, I would ask for forgiveness any time any of you get mad at me. I can be blunt. But I am doing this because I think it is so important to pick the right candidate here," she said. "We have to remember as Democrats, and if I get worked up about this it's because I believe it so much in my heart that we have to bring people with us and not shut them out. That is the gift we can give America in this election."

Billionaire environmentalist Tom Steyer capped it all off with "the gift of teamwork."

"Only the women apologized," I said, incredulous in the spin room to colleagues after the debate. This often unspoken, murky dynamic for women in general, and especially female politicians, had just played out in the national spotlight.

After the debate, Klobuchar advised inquiring reporters not to "read that much into" the fact that only the women opted for forgiveness while the men proffered gifts. "Maybe we're humble," she posited, not such a bad thing given "the guy in the White House right now."

But operatives for Klobuchar's and Warren's campaigns all remember this moment the way I do: stunning. "Only women leaders have to do this," Alencia Johnson, Warren's national director of public engagement and later a consultant for the Biden team, told me. "It counters the point that women are emotional leaders and therefore aren't good. You *want* people to have emotion because they can empathize." But emotion remains one of the most gendered and risky metrics in politics.

All the women, whether their campaigns overtly said so or not, were challenged by this invisible, unpredictable dynamic. To emote, but not too much; to attack, but not too harshly; to differentiate yourself from the rest of the pack, but not offend anyone while doing so. That's not to say they weren't still aggressive or authentically angry or passionate, but that was more the outlier than the trend. Because overt emotion—anger, sadness, seriousness, fighting spirit—is unpredictable in how it plays.

It's a dynamic that many of these staffers never saw until they came to work for a female candidate, which is a trend I've heard from nearly everyone I spoke to for this book. People who worked for male, then female candidates felt smacked in the face by how obvious the double standards were, from media coverage to the way female candidates asked more questions in prep briefings to be ready for anything and everything.

For some on the team, coming to work for Warren gave them a new appreciation for Hillary Clinton's team during the 2008 primary.

"I didn't see it until I read [former Clinton advisor Jennifer] Palmieri's book and thought, 'That's what they were so apoplectic about in 2007,' " one Warren advisor told me. "They could never attack. And Obama attacked all the time. And when Obama attacked, it got through the filter as 'strategic Obama drawing contrast' and when she attacked it would be 'unlikable, risk-taking Hillary looking nasty.' "

With the benefit of that very recent hindsight, they remained vigilantly on the lookout for traps.

"It's not like we had a meeting about gender . . . but it's factored into all the strategic stuff. The way that people respond. If every time she draws contrast, she gets a lot of negative coverage for it, it influences your next decision about whether you're going to draw contrast," the advisor told me.

But in their attempts to avoid the traps, Warren's team also sacrificed one of their candidate's best assets to stand her apart from the field: that she *was* an adept rhetorical fighter. And after a lackluster performance on the debate stage in New Hampshire, followed by an abysmal finish there, and a sinking feeling threatening to tank the whole enterprise, they knew they'd held punches for too long. It was time to start *really* getting in the fight.

Roughly a dozen of Warren's top aides gathered in a suite at the Bella-gio for prep, their room looking down on the bright neon lights of the Rio Hotel and the mountains that brushed up against the wispy clouds above The Strip. Their task, as always, was fine-tuning Warren's responses into a memorable performance that would keep their electoral hopes alive. It being Vegas and all, they believed Lady Luck was on their side for no other reason than former New York City mayor and billionaire Michael Bloomberg was joining the stage for the first time. "If you were to design a candidate to run against EW," one advisor said, using the nickname for Warren that her entire team employed, "he would be it." The perfect foil.

Most of Team Warren's debate prep sessions on the road took place in empty hotel rooms: chairs and podiums (or the occasional music stand) arranged in half-circles with aides looking head-on at the session, quarter-backing each exchange and honing the candidate's delivery, as well as the message. For the most part, the prep team drilled her by topic—campaign finance or health care or immigration—and tried to keep her within the allotted sixty- or ninety-second time frames. In the rarer, full mock de-bates, advisors played the field. Policy guru Jon Donenberg took some turns as Bernie Sanders; at times, Deputy Policy Director Bharat Rama-murti played Pete Buttigieg. Advisor Ganesh Sitaraman was usually the team's Joe Biden stand-in, but in these sessions, he was among those who took turns playing Bloomberg. Standing a few podiums down, Political Director Rebecca Pearcey performed her best Tom Steyer—which effec-tively meant just standing there smiling and taking in the show. After watching Warren launch torpedoes at "Bloomberg," Pearcey remembered thinking, "Is this our let EW be EW moment? This is great!"

EW being EW meant quick-witted, sharp remarks. It meant academic, even nerdy, policy explanations. It meant expecting the most from staffers and a sometimes-tense environment that required constant preparation. It also, sometimes, and mostly in the privacy of her closest advisors, meant straight-up sass that juxtaposed her publicly professorial persona.

Like in the latter months of 2019 when Facebook's Mark Zuckerberg targeted Warren for her plans to break up Big Tech—including his own company. "Fuck this guy and his fucking hoodie," sources close to Warren recalled her saying during one conversation about Zuckerberg's taking her to task, before then pivoting to how they would publicly respond to the tech CEO's grievances. Now, she couldn't exactly say *that* to her naysayers on the debate stage . . . but her team knew she had the range.

As Warren bounced between Vegas debate prep sessions and campaign events, I took the pulse of voters between live shots on MSNBC. "Do you want to see her get a little more aggressive on stage?" I asked Sandy LaBoy, a female voter waiting in Warren's selfie line after a well-attended town hall event in Henderson, Nevada, the day before the debate.

"That's a tough one," she said. "I think women get a really bad rap when they get to be a little too aggressive. I loved Kamala Harris and as soon as she got aggressive, people thought, 'No, that's just a little too much.' So, I think she can be assertive, but be careful with being aggressive. It's that fine line."

"It's a double standard," I offered. She agreed.

I walked farther up in the line and found Castille Ritter waiting for a Warren selfie with her boyfriend, Jack Hawkins. She loved Warren; he was still deciding between Warren and Sanders. I asked if they thought Warren needed to be more aggressive this time around.

"Are people asking the male candidates the question, if guys need to be more aggressive?" Castille asked me. *No.* "I think a woman can stand her ground without having to be told she needs to be more aggressive, or she needs to be more passive."

I wanted Castille to be right. But I'd seen even in my own experiences— not running for president, just simply running around as a reporter on the campaign trail—that even basic interactions of self-advocacy could be met with hostility from male managers who, for some reason, didn't like the way their female workers asked questions, or made suggestions, or offered different opinions from theirs.

After the Henderson town hall where I met Sandy and Castille, I met up with the Warren campaign for her last event of that day. It was at Cardenas Market, a Latin American–style grocery store in East Las Vegas, and poorly attended by roughly half a dozen, mostly Hispanic, voters. The room was flat, no buzz and no excitement. The last stop on the campaign train after a very long day, with a candidate who was sagging in the polls and lagging in her campaign's coffers.

Molly's and my energy level matched the mood of the event. We'd been up since 5 a.m. local time, reporting live on MSNBC throughout the day and attending Warren events, thinking we'd be in bed by now because our call time was just as early the next day. But I'd been offered exclusive time with the candidate. So, we set up for our interview in the "Central American Food" aisle, a *La Cocina* sign as our background and, over my head, a Tecate beer sign floating in and out of our cameraman's viewfinder.

"There's a debate coming up, I'm sure you've heard," I joked to Warren as she came over for the interview. She nodded. "I was talking to some women at your event earlier today and we were talking about how you could be potentially more aggressive on the next debate stage. And they pointed out that there's sort of a double standard between women being seen as potentially too aggressive or maybe not aggressive enough. Do you feel that when you're on the debate stage? Is that something you're thinking about?"

"You know, I'm thinking about how can I best get out there and fight for the people that I got in this race to fight for," Warren said.

This was her usual answer. And it's what made interviewing her hard: she was always so damn disciplined and on script.

"But do you feel like you could be seen as *too aggressive* in doing that?" I interrupted.

"You know, this is what women face all the time. It's always too much of this, too much of that." Her hands emphasized the point, pointing in opposite directions. "But you put your head down, you do your job, and you keep on going. Or you might say, we persist."

We'd had conversations about gender's role in the race off the record on the plane, and she'd alluded to it in her Iowa riff about "women win," but this felt like a new level of candor on the topic. Like she'd had enough and just wanted to lay her reality out there. It was refreshing, as it had been with Klobuchar and her candor over who we take seriously, to hear a powerful woman speak succinctly to the double-edged sword women struggle with everywhere. We were all grappling with biases that were unfair, that were out of our control, but that we had to push past to keep going. She was just doing it under the biggest spotlight there is.

On the debate stage two nights later, the spotlight would only get bigger.

At this point, Bloomberg was benefiting from being a somewhat known unknown. While the rest of the field traipsed through the early voting states for over a year, Bloomberg remained off to the side—first declining to run, citing a "really narrow" path "with Joe in the race," one source told me in March 2019, and then reversing course and running in November 2019. His campaign team knew they got in the race too late to make any headway in Iowa or New Hampshire, even Nevada and South Carolina, so they decided to skip the early states and set their own personal start date: Super Tuesday, March 3rd.

They earned lots of media coverage for their risky, nontraditional strategy while also avoiding the bruising battles, on the trail and on debate stages, that made up the race so far. Bloomberg had the money to go the distance, which lent to his feasibility, and he had the reputation of a smart businessman who always made informed, data-driven decisions. He wasn't just jumping in willy-nilly, the thinking went, he must *know something* that proves he'll get a return on this very costly investment. Plus, having avoided debate stages, he had yet to be dinged by his rivals. And by not competing in early-state contests, while the rest of the field over- or underperformed expectations, Bloomberg remained above the fray, expectations untested but growing.

While Warren and Biden were underwhelming in their Iowa and New Hampshire results, Bloomberg was coasting on a parallel track, campaigning in states like Texas and Florida and plastering millions in ads all over the airwaves there. Voters in the early states told me they didn't like what Bloomberg was doing, but what they thought didn't actually matter since Bloomberg wasn't competing for their votes anyway. He'd circumvented the early-primary-state gauntlet.

The strategy was separate from the fact that Bloomberg entered the Democratic primary having not always been an actual Democrat. His first mayoral win came as a Republican, and then he switched his party registration to Independent, and then he re-registered as a Democrat right before announcing his presidential run. By that point, though, he'd thrown hundreds of his millions behind Democratic causes to combat climate change, enact commonsense gun laws, and flip state legislatures blue. In the Trump era, he was among the most vocal of critics, his barbs elevated because he, too, was a brash New Yorker of the monied class—though with more money than Trump, it must be pointed out.

When he entered the race eight months after counting himself out, it was with great concern about Biden faltering as progressive candidates, like Warren and Sanders, rose. It was Bloomberg—not Biden—Bloomberg's inner orbit concluded, who would be best positioned to take on Trump. His team cited polls showing Democrats still without a consensus pick, and were licking their chops at the two-thirds of voters in the fourteen Super Tuesday states who had yet to make up their minds and liking the way voters in states that had already voted were making their minds up as late as they could. Immediately upon announcing, speculation about his *potential* fueled him. He immediately apologized for his controversial stop-and-frisk policing policy when he was mayor of New York, and the questions about it quickly faded from the press corps—not that we were offered much opportunity to ask him regular questions, anyway.

Bloomberg was covered as the long shot because he was. But he was a long shot who was willing to do—and spend—whatever it took to beat Trump. Bloomberg was quickly added high up on the unofficial list of Candidates Who Could Be an Alternative for Moderate Voters If Biden Choked. He had bona fides in areas that breed immediate respect—money and business—and he could stake a claim to boosting myriad progressive causes, like climate change and sensible gun reforms, in addition to having helmed one of the largest liberal cities in America.

Bloomberg, in those first few months, was all potential. And Elizabeth Warren was not having it.

While she hesitated to attack other Democrats, she never hesitated with Bloomberg. "This election should not be for sale," she warned in a gaggle soon after Bloomberg threw millions into TV ads in November 2019. "Not to billionaires, not to corporate executives. We need to build a grassroots movement. That's how democracy is supposed to work." Those remarks would look tame compared to the premeditated political murder she had planned for him on Debate Night.

Roughly 120 seconds into Debate Night and Warren brushed aside the moderator's original question, quietly brandishing a razor-sharp rhetorical knife. "I'd like to talk about who we're running against," she began. "A billionaire who refers to women as fat broads and horse-faced lesbians. And no, I'm not talking about Donald Trump."

A collective *huh?* hit the room where I was sitting.

"I'm talking about Mayor Bloomberg."

The audience let out a shocked "ooouuuooh."

"Oh shit," I said, definitely in my head but possibly out loud to my fellow NBC colleagues who were sharing a circular table with me backstage at the debate. Warren's team, meanwhile, was giddy. Knowing what was coming didn't make her top staffers laugh any less as they watched this takedown happen. Warren didn't pause for the audience's reaction, nor did she look to her right where Bloomberg was standing, stone-faced, before pressing on.

"Democrats are not going to win if we have a nominee who has a history of hiding his tax returns, of harassing women, and of supporting racist policies like redlining and stop-and-frisk," Warren said. "Look, I'll support whoever the Democratic nominee is but understand this: Democrats take a huge risk if we just substitute one arrogant billionaire for another."

Some applause started again, cautiously. In the same way Warren had been tagged as a risk—and harmed by it in the eyes of the electorate—she was trying to do the same to Bloomberg.

"This is not just a question of the mayor's character," Warren said later in the debate, returning to Bloomberg. "This is also a question about electability. We are not going to beat Donald Trump with a man who has who-knows-how-many nondisclosure agreements and the drip, drip, drip of stories of women saying they have been harassed and discriminated against. That's not what we do as Democrats." Here Warren was, flipping the electability script perfectly, introducing tangible risks to a Bloomberg nomination.

Warren wasn't the only Democrat attacking Bloomberg that night— he was a convenient foil for almost all of them to score political bank shots off—but she was the one who left the most indelible mark.

In the spin room that night, Bloomberg's aides were peppered with questions about his seeming lack of preparation and the political rustiness he exhibited on stage. His unmarked armor of potential was chinked, and while his next debate stage performance was less deer-in-the-headlights, his air of inevitability was erased. Which was exactly what Warren was hoping for. Not just because she hoped to save herself—though some part of her still hoped she could win—but because she also felt it was her responsibility to stop Michael Bloomberg.

"It was about Bloomberg," Warren told me when I asked her if taking on Bloomberg was about making sure he was not the nominee or if it was meant to revive her own struggling campaign. "If Michael Bloomberg wants to run for president or Tom Steyer, that's fine. Yeah! Get out there, throw out what your credentials are. But you'll go raise money like everybody else. You'll go do democracy like everybody else. You'll go shake hands and do town halls and take questions and ask people for ten-dollar contributions and build a grassroots movement." But that's not what Bloomberg did.

Bloomberg was not just a billionaire coming in with his own billions;

he was eschewing grassroots donations. Of course, it made sense why. It's a hard sell to ask Americans for $5 or $10 when you've got a net worth of more than $50 billion. Nevertheless, everyone else who ran had to tie themselves in knots to earn the requisite number of donors that allowed them to qualify for debate stages. That requirement was waived by the DNC before the Nevada debate and Bloomberg was allowed onto the stage by qualifying with just poll standing.

"He skipped the first four contests," Warren reminded. "All that democracy stuff, like shaking hands and town halls and press avails. He wanted to skip all that. And because he was a billionaire, he could buy enough TV advertisements that it made him, he believed, a plausible candidate. So, for me, I think that is a threat to our democracy. Because . . . if all we're going to do is like people who can gather up enough money, or already have enough money that they can run a billion-dollar ad campaign on TV and not do any of the rest of it—not build the grassroots machine—then the government will become completely divorced from the people. Democracy will be nothing more than voting for people on a reality show."

"So [taking him on] was your idea," I asked.

"That was how I felt about it," she said, hearing my question but blowing past it. Bloomberg was only Part One. "Number two, this question about electability. Think about who Michael Bloomberg was." She was back on the stump, but from her Washington, D.C., living room on Zoom with just me. "Here's a man who had said genuinely terrible things about women . . . Here's a man who would not release his taxes. Does any of this sound familiar? Who blamed the 2008 financial crash on people of color, right? Here's a man who pretended to be shocked to hear that stop-and-frisk fell disproportionately hard on Black and brown men, when he had been told it over and over and over and over and over." Even all those months later, she was still pissed. Mostly because, despite all the wrong she saw with it, she watched Bloomberg's play work—at least for a few months.

"If he had been at zero in the polls and there was just no threat that this was happening, if the Democratic Party said, 'Sorry, [if] you don't show up and shake hands and answer questions from the press and meet people? You're not getting up on the stage. You don't get to do this.' He was a serious alternative at that point. And so, my view on this is no, he does not belong in this race. He does not belong on this stage. If you remember," she concluded, "that is basically what I said."

Basically. Sure.

Most Democratic strategists I spoke to relish the Bloomberg/Warren moment. Staffers who worked across other presidential campaigns were similarly grated by the way Bloomberg entered the race, the media coverage he immediately got, and the way the Democratic National Committee bent the debate stage rules for him to join the pack on stage. One operative told me Warren never got enough credit for this moment of "public service" to the field, in the name of democracy (and Democracy). Feminists and progressives cheered her, with some thanking her for halting Bloomberg's thus-far unscathed ascent to viability in the minds of voters. Others lauded her successful execution of a much-needed memorable performance because of the dire political straits she herself was in. And for some, it simply felt good to watch a very ambitious billionaire get brought back down to reality with a good old-fashioned debate stage smackdown.

The money wasn't a bad upside, either. The Warren campaign raked in millions—$17 million total, when it was all said and counted—making the hours and days after that debate their most lucrative ever. This is a fundraising haul any campaign would shout about from the rooftops. But an FEC filing that dropped the day after showed it was also a haul that the Warren campaign desperately needed. The campaign finished January with $2.29 million cash on hand . . . after burning through $22 million that same month.

But even as the money and praise were flowing, some still saw Warren as a kamikaze pilot. CNN's Chris Cillizza wrote of only two possible reasons why Warren would go after Bloomberg instead of targeting front-runner Bernie Sanders during this debate: either she "knows she can't win the nomination and is on a mission to destroy Bloomberg" or she wants to be Bernie Sanders's VP.

Let's unpack these arguments.

Cillizza reasoned that destroying Bloomberg was "sort of a culmination of her life's work" given his billions and her commitment to righting wealth inequality. On this, Cillizza is right. That's exactly what it was—and Warren told me as much herself. That's also not a sinister or shocking answer for anyone who spent even a little time watching Elizabeth Warren, whose entire campaign focused on a set of principles that Bloomberg's candidacy flew in the face of.

But on the latter explanation—that Warren just wanted to be a veep—he describes it as "slightly more Machiavellian . . . Warren may already see the writing on the wall that Sanders is the very likely nominee," he wrote. Deflecting attacks away from Sanders and focusing her ire on Bloomberg could be a way to curry favor when Sanders's team began considering VP picks. On its face, there's nothing wrong with suggesting that Warren's motives are self-serving in some way. This is politics. But would Buttigieg be described as "Machiavellian"—believing that it's better to be feared than loved as a leader—for saying things on a debate stage that served Joe Biden, in hopes of being *his* VP? Would any of the other male, Biden-alternatives be described in a way that made them out to be politically calculating with an implied negative tilt?

The frames Cillizza used to put forward these uninformed guesses are packed with sexism. That she's power-hungry in a "Machiavellian" way. That she's self-serving and acting purely in furtherance of her own power quest. That she's really in this for the Number 2 slot—something I heard about every single woman who ran in 2020 and, prior to that, in 2016. That she's just angry at Bloomberg's success, so much so that she'd torpedo her own efforts just to stop him.

These frames cast Warren's actions on the debate stage, which were both politically strategic and based in her own personal beliefs, in negative terms. And the analysis didn't include the fact that the debates were—just as they were with Harris and Biden or Buttigieg and Klobuchar—about, well, debating. And about debating aggressively. Narratives like these made it so that even when she was winning—and Warren did win this debate—she was also somehow losing, too.

10

And Then There Were None

Opportunity, Lost. Again.

MARCH 2020

What if you don't win here?"

I could sense instantly that Senator Warren was less than thrilled with my question. These are the kinds of things you notice when you talk to a candidate almost every day for a year.

New polling showed Warren neck-and-neck with Bernie Sanders here in her home state of Massachusetts, and the Sanders campaign had just made a big show of campaigning—with a big crowd—on Warren's turf days earlier. They did the same in Amy Klobuchar's home state of Minnesota, a power move in those crucial days before the biggest delegate haul of the Democratic primary: Super Tuesday.

"Why would you ask me a question like this at the beginning of the morning when we're going down to vote?" Warren said, her voice high and tight, betraying an uncharacteristic tone of irritation. I felt like I was a kid in trouble. There had been some tense news cycles this campaign, but this was the first time she'd shown outright annoyance at one of my questions.

Warren had only one option: she had to win here—or anywhere!—on

Super Tuesday, because she had yet to do so and because everyone knew her campaign was in trouble. This was it. The final test for her pitch of Big Structural Change. The last chance for a candidate trying to find a lane somewhere between moderate Joe Biden and progressive Bernie Sanders.

"This is the best part," she finally answered. Her sternness dissipated with each word, regaining the usual brightness that rounded out her tone. "This is the best part of democracy."

She turned back to her supporters now, hundreds of whom had gathered outside her Cambridge home to cheer her on as she walked to her polling location and cast a ballot for herself, moving handshake by handshake toward the elementary school down the block, which also happened to be where she would vote. Warren was both a dedicated handshaker and a dedicated media ignorer when she was working a line of supporters. She wanted to give them—not me, or my crew—her attention, but her staff had told her to stop for a question from me. I wondered if she regretted listening to them.

"Thank you, Senator," I said, shimmying off the uneven brick sidewalk and trying not to wrap myself, or anyone else, in the cord that connected my microphone to my camera crew.

I didn't know it then, but this was one of the last crowds I would ever "sorry" and "excuse me" my way through before COVID-19 hit. Looking back, it's not a bad way to go out—if you must stop going out, that is. I was stressed, I hadn't slept in weeks, and the campaign was taking on that out-of-control-train-car-careening-off-the-tracks feeling that often accompanies the end. Questions of "what will I do next?" had seeped into my dreams and I was still nursing a deep cough that had appeared back during the Nevada Caucus. But every single Liberty Green wearing person out there that day had so much hope emanating off them that I couldn't help but soak in it. This *was* the best part. The part when everyone believes that everything is still possible.

The producers for MSNBC's 9 a.m. show were working feverishly to get my Q&A with Warren ready in time for me to share it with viewers. While they worked, I set the scene on the air: "This," I said, walking the line of supporters and straining to talk over the cheers, "is exactly the kind of send-off you want on Election Day."

"Sound is in," a voice from the New York control room told me while I was on the air. I pressed my earpiece into my ear to hear more clearly and thought, *great!*, rewriting my report in real time in my head in order to toss to the "SOT"—sound on tape—of me and Warren. Quick wrap-up. Then a brisk walk up the street to Graham & Parks public elementary school. Warren was already there, walking in amid more than one hundred supporters and falling flower petals that cascaded from the windows, tossed by her constituents—those of voting age, and far younger. Then walking out and mounting the bed of a parked pickup truck, surrounded by supporters and media. Looking up from the street outside, we could see little faces popping up in the windows, taking in the chaos, and waving with tiny hands.

"I am so happy to be in the place where Bruce and I have been voting for twenty-five years," Warren said. "We've been here to vote every time with that spark of hope in our hearts that the vote will matter, that we will build a better country. That's what this election for me is all about. 2020 is a moment we've been called to in history. And it is a moment not just to get rid of Donald Trump, it is a moment to build the America of our best values."

Election Day was no exception to the near-daily gaggles I'd become accustomed to. Her head swiveled in my direction. I'd also gotten used to her always looking to me first when we assumed our usual positions in the gaggle. It was both a basic way of signaling that she expected to hear from me—I always had a question to ask, after all—but it was also a way of shifting a stereotypically male process in favor of the women in her press corps. Scrums and gaggles favored the loudest and most aggressive reporters in them. The ones who could physically push to the front of the pack (which, at five foot two, I was great at) and the ones who commanded attention when they shouted for the candidates' attention. "Senator! Governor! Mr. President!" It was a chaotic process that often lent to, and rewarded, stereotypically male traits. Warren was hyperaware of those dynamics, and I was often struck by the way she leveraged her power as the candidate to empower the women who covered her to get their questions answered. She didn't favor us, but she did make sure the field was level. More than once, she stopped louder male reporters with their deeper and louder voices from talking over me.

On one occasion when she'd already called on me and I was halfway through asking my question, a male reporter from a local station physically put his microphone (and arm) over me and just started in on his query. "I'm talking to Ali now," she told him, retraining her eyes on me and ignoring his stunned silence. I'd never had a candidate do that before.

On another occasion, she asked me why—instead of everyone crowding closer to her and squeezed uncomfortably together—we didn't just all take a step back to make more room, alleviating the issue of physically jockeying for position. "That would require trust," I told her, half-joking, something that competing networks didn't often have for each other. At the next event, there was a taped-down semicircle for our gaggle to better space us out.

There was little space here, though, and as Warren dismounted the truck, we all crunched in around her.

"How was voting?" I asked.

"It was great. I really liked voting today," she said, standing at the center of a giant scrum. She faced squatting correspondents (me) brandishing microphones, still photographers clicking from ladders above and on their knees below, video journalists and embeds just trying to find stillness for their shots amid the scrum. Behind her, Kristen Orthman stood—steely in black sunglasses, phone outstretched recording the exchange in case they'd need it later. Molly snapped a picture of the scene that *Glamour* magazine soon made a meme: "Me," they labeled Warren, looking out into a sea of dozens of faces and lenses expectantly turned toward her; "All My Unread Work Emails," they designated us.

"Talk about what a metric for success tonight looks like," I asked. "I know it's about delegates, but broadly what does that mean? What does success look like?"

"It's to compete everywhere," Warren said, then launching into an explanation of her no-donors-just-campaign-stops strategy that I'd heard dozens of times before. The rest of the group hesitated, so I took advantage: "What should we read into the fact that you're gonna be in Michigan tonight, which is a March tenth state, not a March third state?"

"Well, because it was just next on the schedule to get out there and talk to people. I don't think you should read anything special into it. But I'm delighted to be there."

Sure, it was next in the schedule . . . because her campaign dictated the schedule. But the message it sent was clear: there was no Super Tuesday state they seemed confident enough in to make it the location of their Tuesday night rally. So instead they pushed the Massachusetts senator . . . out of Massachusetts, sparing her a home-state speech that would've underscored her inability to win a state as a presidential candidate—even in a state that had elected her to represent it twice in the Senate.

A chorus of "Thank you, Senator" followed the gaggle as Warren departed and KO joked that it was "the Ali gaggle." I hustled into a waiting Uber to Boston's Logan International Airport, where Molly and I scarfed down some limp salad leaves and boarded the plane to Detroit to begin the process all over again. Rental car, Google Maps, speed to the campaign event site to make it for another live shot. The 20-degree wind whipped through us as I updated NBC's political director and *Meet the Press* anchor, Chuck Todd, on my latest reporting before shuffling inside for what we all knew, deep down, was the last Elizabeth Warren town hall we would ever cover.

Inside, the mood was uneasy. I approached Jon Donenberg and Ganesh Sitaraman as they surveyed the half-full event space. We didn't talk about the stakes of the night, or the politics of the moment—not directly, anyway. Instead, we talked about what would come next after Super Tuesday. Not because they were looking for an exit—Warren's core team was deeply loyal and wouldn't jump to join another campaign when hers ended—but their hunched shoulders and gallows humor betrayed the heaviness of the night that extended from advance staffers, to embeds, to senior staff who were rarely on the road but were present tonight. All were soaking it in and mentally preparing for it to be over.

Everyone was.

Campaigns are unpredictable, but staffers and journalists seek consistency wherever they can find it. Don't underestimate the intimate pull that sameness can bring when you're disconnected from friends and loved ones for months on end, shuttling to a new state and city and hotel room every night in the name of coverage or a cause. Most days you contemplate what city you're waking up in because you don't immediately remember. That can be exciting as much as it can be jarring, disorienting, even sometimes depressing.

For me, and for the rest of us in that room that night, normalcy came in seeing the same candidate every day, predicting the ebb and flow of a campaign event, knowing all the people who stood around you in the gaggle or piled into the minivans that Warren and her traveling mostly girl gang typically cruised around in on the road. It came from the group texts and knowing each other's coffee orders and the shared mental and physical exhaustion with the people whose lives were also controlled by the movements, words, and plans of Elizabeth Warren. A campaign ending meant a total disruption of all of that. It meant having to find a new consistency in an unpredictable churn.

For the press corps, speculation was starting about who of us was moving to which campaign next. 'Twas the season of jockeying behind the scenes for the best next assignment even as you followed your current one to its conclusion. One of Warren's senior aides admitted to me after the campaign ended that they'd felt since the fall, even before the Medicare for All debacle, that they were just staving off a loss. But they still projected a public posture that if Warren could net just enough delegates on Super Tuesday to be competitive at a theoretical contested convention, and no other candidate got the requisite number of delegates needed to clinch the nomination outright, then they still had a chance. But it was nearly impossible to imagine any candidate walking into the convention and making a real case for the nomination when they hadn't won any states outright.

From my perch on the press riser in Detroit—one ear on Warren's rally and the other on MSNBC's live air—Biden's sweep of the electoral map was stunning. Democratic voters who had resisted any kind of cohesive coalescing for a year had, in the seventy-two hours after Biden won South Carolina, decisively lined up behind him. As did all the other candidates who were one-time Biden alternatives—Klobuchar, Buttigieg, Beto—who lined up to endorse him, furthering his air of inevitability. Apparently one win after losses in Iowa, New Hampshire, and Nevada was all it took to affirm Biden's long-talked-about electability.

Warren, in the end, netted dozens, not hundreds, of delegates on Super Tuesday. She lost her home state, not to Bernie Sanders but to Biden—who had no campaign infrastructure in the Bay State and hadn't even set foot there to campaign, yet earned 33.6 percent of the vote to Warren's 21.4 percent. Put plainly: Biden was cleaning up. On MSNBC and CNN, it was over. The cable narrative had moved on to the victorious Biden news cycle it had been storing up for months.

Inside Warren's rally, though, you could've been forgiven for forgetting the biggest night of the primary was happening. The candidate didn't even say the words "Super Tuesday." Instead, Warren gave her standard stump speech and got on a plane back to Cambridge as soon as she wrapped. The decision to cancel the selfie line that night told you everything you needed to know. The tension was only more obvious when two network embeds, NBC's Deepa Shivaram and CNN's Daniella Diaz, waited outside the event venue near Warren's idling rental minivan—a standard, if not slightly stalkerish, campaign coverage practice—only to be shooed away by campaign staffers and angrily chastised for being "practically in the car with her." (Deepa denies trying to get in the car with the candidate, for what it's worth.) For a campaign that regularly made the candidate accessible and rarely got publicly worked up about anything, this was a departure from the norm, a sign that emotions were running high.

When the campaign plane arrived that night in Boston, Warren and Bruce Mann stood at the door, doling out hugs and thanks while staff deplaned. Warren was known to love a good, deep hug, but a line of such hugs wasn't the usual practice to cap off a campaign trip. Some staff traveling on the small charter took it as another sign.

My night was only beginning, though. Sitting in the passenger seat of our rental car in an unlit parking lot outside the event venue, I worked my sources, killing time until my 2 a.m. live shot and fighting gravity's pull on my eyelids. More of my sources were up late and answering texts than usual. Some responded with unprompted and uncharacteristic phone calls. There was a lot of "off the record . . ." followed by frank assessments from top campaign brass of where the campaign had left to go from here (nowhere but out, was the consensus). Some wondered aloud if maybe they could continue another week, wait for the upcoming debate. Maybe Biden or Bernie would make a mistake. Maybe the nation would see the need for the third path that Warren had been pitching. It was empty-calorie chatter. They weren't trying to convince me as much as they were trying to convince themselves.

I flew back to Boston on a 7 a.m. flight from Detroit. Warren's weary press corps made up the bulk of American Airlines' travelers that morning. We all knew what was coming, and most of us hadn't slept more than three hours, so the air was thick with exhaustion and anxiety.

With no time to wait for a rental car, Molly and I took an Uber to Warren's home in Cambridge as soon as we landed, pulling up just before 10 a.m. and trying not to think about how weird it was that every major TV network was . . . waiting outside the candidate's *house*. Eventually the campaign stationed Gabrielle Farrell, the traveling press secretary, in the driveway, a watchful sentry for her holed-up boss. She was missing a much-needed hair appointment to be camped out in her Jeep, she told us, but she was there "in case we needed anything"—and to keep an eye on us, too.

I put my makeup on in the passenger seat of our soundman's car, trying unsuccessfully to draw straight lines of eyeliner. Nothing will humble you on the daily like this exercise. My hair was unwashed, and my contact lenses were peeling off my dry eyes as they often did when I was low on sleep. My phone pinged. Warren was "reassessing" what came next for her campaign, a source told me.

I called Dafna Linzer, my boss and NBC's managing editor for politics, to clear my sourcing. This was the normal operating procedure for reporting on major news moments: telling our editorial managers the news that we had, and describing the anonymous sources who told us about it, ensuring that it met our standards for reporting. The public doesn't know who "sources familiar" or "people with knowledge" are, but journalists always do.

While I handled our approval process on one phone, I tapped out an email on my second device to send to our political distribution list—the constantly moving bloodstream of the network's campaign coverage. "REPORTABLE," I labeled it in the subject line. "Warren is talking to her team to assess the path forward, a Warren aide tells me." When Dafna "approved" on one phone, I hit send from the other.

"They want you now," Molly called to me seconds later, the cause and effect of my email now clear. She was standing next to the camera setup, juggling her own phones and talking to the control room. Our luggage was scattered around her, making it look like she was setting up a campsite near Warren's lawn.

"Coming." I pulled my earpiece out of my pocket and clipped it on the back of my coat before dousing the front parts of my hair with spray to keep it from flying in the whipping wind.

"Ali, this is Audio. Can you hear me?" a deep voice intoned from 30 Rock through my earpiece.

"I hear you, Audio."

A producer got in my ear. "Ali, it's Essa." She thanked me for being so quick to the camera. The show would come to me very soon. "Stand by."

Minutes later, an all-staff memo from campaign manager Roger Lau was forwarded to me by a Warren staffer. "Didn't get this from me," they warned. *Of course not.*

"Elizabeth believes in her ideas and in the big, structural change that is badly needed to root out corruption in Washington and will decide what she thinks is the best way to advance them," Lau wrote to his campaign teammates in the forwarded memo. When I got off the air, a few more forwards of the memo were in my in-box.

I stood outside on the corner the rest of the day, reporting various nuggets of news and contextualizing them, knowing that we were just killing time before the inevitable became official. At one point, Daniella Diaz from CNN thought she saw Warren through a side window, creating the biggest buzz of the otherwise uneventful day.

From the corner across from Warren's house, I watched notifications roll in that former New York City mayor Michael Bloomberg was dropping out. His spend-everything-but-campaign-little approach had failed. Several strategists texted to point out (and gloat) that Warren had outlasted him, basking in whatever glory they could get given the glum mood over Warren World.

When I finally got back to the hotel that night, I showered and collapsed into bed. But the anxiety over the news still to come kept me lying awake. This was all ending tomorrow. It had to. I didn't Know that yet, but I *knew* it. And knowing the end was coming didn't make it any easier.

Because here's the truth about my job: covering a candidate is exactly like being in a really overbearing, one-sided relationship. You think about them all the time, you talk about them constantly, you wonder what they're doing when you're not around. When you're not with them, you're wondering when you'll see them again. And I get paid for this. It's bizarre.

Paid to get to know these people. Their policies, positions, and statements—absolutely. But also, what kind of *person* they are. How do they treat their staff? How do they treat their press corps, especially when they're being pressed on hard moments or questions in the campaign? How do they talk about their opponents off the record? Do they really know their policy? Who the heck do they think they are to be president of the United States? *Who are they, really?*

The even more honest truth is sometimes you're assigned to cover a candidate who you get to know and find you can't respect. I've covered those candidates. But sometimes you also get assigned to cover candidates who you get to know, and you learn that they're basically good humans. For my fellow *Bachelor* Nation members, they're "here for the right reasons." They're still politicians, and your job is still to vet them, but by and large you enjoy covering them because the person you're following is challenging, intelligent, and committed to bettering the country you're both citizens of. That doesn't mean they're always nice; this isn't about mean and nice. These are still politicians questing for power and you're still there to hold them to account. But while you're doing that, you can also respect the good ones for what they bring to the table.

Around midnight, Molly and I set our alarms for 6 a.m. on Thursday. We were exhausted and didn't have to be live until 9 a.m., but we were too afraid we would sleep through any news or incremental updates. "Living in fear of the guillotine" was what I texted Deepa and Molly in our group chat. When the next day dawned, we grabbed my oat milk latte and Molly's black coffee and stationed ourselves outside Warren's house. Just after 10 a.m. Thursday, my phone rang. Warren was going to drop out, one of her top aides told me, embargoed until she told her staff on a call at 11 a.m.

The news broke in *The New York Times* twenty minutes before Warren could make that phone call. Once the embargo was broken, I hit send on an email I'd pre-drafted for this moment: "Elizabeth Warren is suspending her campaign, a source familiar tells me," I wrote. "She will be announcing the decision on a call with her campaign staff at 11. Warren will do a media avail here in Cambridge, MA. We expect it around noon, but timing remains fluid so bear with us."

"Bear with us" is the mood of every reporter during any breaking news. It says: *I'm trying, I'm working as hard as I can and I promise, I'm not keeping any secrets about what I know, I want to get the latest and best reporting. Did I mention I'm trying? I'm really tryyyinnngggg!*

In this instance, though, I had everything I needed.

Interrupting a segment about concerns mounting over the still-seemingly-far-away coronavirus, the anchor, MSNBC's Hallie Jackson, pivoted back to politics and teed me up. "Ali, she's gonna be announcing the decision pretty soon apparently?"

"Yeah, Hallie, I just heard from a source familiar with the senator's thinking who says that she's going to suspend her campaign, informing her full staff in a phone call in just a little while . . ." I stayed on the screen in a matrix of ever-multiplying boxes as more reporters and analysts joined the panel, repeatedly glancing down at my phone as I continued to text sources and repeatedly snapping back to attention when the control room nudged me that I was "on cam."

Elizabeth Warren was dreading that all-staff phone call, thinking about the people who had given up jobs, apartments, time with family, basically their lives to help elect her president. But she was dreading coming out to talk with the press even more. That would make it official. That would mean that she'd have to publicly admit that the plan hadn't worked, that there would be no big structural change—at least not as they'd imagined it, anyway.

"I want all of you to hear it first," she told hundreds of staffers on the call, "and I want you to hear it straight from me: Today, I'm suspending our campaign for president. I know how hard all of you have worked. I know how you disrupted your lives to be part of this. I know you have families and loved ones you could have spent more time with. You missed them and they missed you. And I know you have sacrificed to be here."

As Warren spoke to her staffers, I spoke to MSNBC's Craig Melvin at the start of his show, the last hour of coverage now bleeding into a reset at the top of this new one.

"Craig, she's probably on a call with staffers right now. We know that was set to start at eleven . . ."

I don't think I've ever felt more stressed. No, it wasn't stress. It was pressure. I'd never felt the weight of another moment more. I told my mom frequently in the primary season's waning weeks that as one of the network's few female "Road Warriors" on the road daily, and the one tasked with covering the field's two remaining female candidates, it was up to me to give these women their due. Not to be complimentary, not to be overly harsh, just to show them for who they were as candidates: competent and qualified women. It meant a lot to me to highlight the policy—which I had learned inside and out—and the politics, but to also showcase the humanity. Tell people how it felt to be on the road with Klobuchar and Warren; what it was really like to watch them interact with voters as they tried to convince them that they should be the first female commander in chief. Being the girl covering the Smart Girls Who Wanted to Be President meant reporting on the politics as usual, but also bringing a gender lens to these moments and explaining them that way, too. As a reporter, I had watched the sexist dynamics in play—the subtle and the overt—and I was determined not to fall into those traps. As a feminist, I was committed to contextualizing this female moment in history. As a woman, I simply did not want to get this moment wrong.

Separate and apart from that pressure was my predisposition to cry *at everything*. Stress, lack of sleep, adorable puppies, you name it. During the 2017 Super Bowl, for example, I cried at eight different commercials before halftime alone. I think one of them was a Volvo ad. Really. But here, my propensity toward tears was paired with utter exhaustion and an emotionally charged moment. Emotionally charged for the campaign staff I'd come to respect, for the supporters whose dreams were dashed, but also for me personally. I've covered campaigns long enough to know that you've gotta brace for the comedown that follows the adrenaline rush of a campaign ending. Those of us who do this work talk about it as a kind of post-campaign depression. And for someone like me with general anxiety and depression already, I steeled myself for the looming negative impact that big moments of change—like a campaign ending—would have on my mental health. I had anxiety about the anxiety; a bad habit of taking my pain in advance.

All this lent to the unspoken words between Molly and me: *Please God, don't let Ali cry on TV.*

We both silently imagined the headlines: "Female NBC News Reporter Sobs Over Warren Drop." Or the potential Trump tweet: "Sad!

MSDNC Hack @alivitali Pulls A Cryin' Chuck Over Warren." The tears stayed at bay. *Don't cry, just talk.*

Craig asked me what else I could tell viewers about Warren's decision to leave the race and the kind of campaign she ran.

"The leading force of this campaign was all of her policy plans that she leaned into, but I just want to take a step back, as the person who has covered her campaign for this network for over a year at this point. This campaign was unabashedly feminist every single day that we were out here on the campaign trail." *Just talk.* "Elizabeth Warren was the last woman . . . in this race." Klobuchar had dropped out to little fanfare and with little time to unpack her own bid in the press given that she immediately endorsed Biden because it was "what is best for our country right now."

"We have two, septuagenarian, white men now left for Democratic voters to choose from . . ."

"Was that okay?" I asked Molly when I finished.

"That was great," she said in a way that I could really tell she meant it.

She was struggling, too. Her daily normal was being upended as well, not to mention the last few weeks had tested Molly and me as female journalists who couldn't help but see gender bias seeping into which campaigns got important airtime, which candidates were deemed plausible, which candidates' people still felt they had potential versus the ones people were impatiently finger-tapping to drop out. After her fourth-place finish in New Hampshire, an NBC colleague angrily asked me, *When was Warren just going to end it already? Didn't she see it was over?* I was confused about what they were so annoyed about, given that there were so many states left to vote and candidates in contention. Plus, what was I supposed to do about it? I don't run her campaign; I just follow them around. "I just work here," I shrugged.

Molly and I resolved that all we could control was the 90 to 120 seconds that I got on air every hour or two. So, we mind-melded and crafted hits in bullet-point form, trying to cap off each report with a final, overarching contextual point. "What's the larger politics point?" I'd ask Molly, sometimes hourly. It was an exercise that forced us to step back, to take stock of what we were seeing, and why viewers should care.

Today, the larger politics point was evident: there were no more viable women left in the race. After a cycle where more women than ever had run for the office, 2020 would not be the year of America's first female president. The reasons were obvious, in some ways. Biden. Trump. Fear. In others, they were more complicated. Electability. Likability. Lack of historical precedent. With Klobuchar dropping out just three days before Super Tuesday and immediately endorsing Biden to give him an edge in her home state of Minnesota, with Gabbard still in but clearly not going the distance, and with Warren leaving the race now, the most female field ever had dwindled down to . . . none.

I began to hear about Warren's final staff call from people on it. "She was just her inspirational self," one person told me. Emotions were high— including Warren's, who promised to "carry you in my heart for the rest of my life."

"Some of you may remember that long before I got into electoral politics, I was asked if I would accept a Consumer Financial Protection Bureau that was weak and toothless," she told her staff. "And I replied that my first choice was a consumer agency that could get real stuff done, and my second choice was no agency and lots of blood and teeth left on the floor." That quote had inspired memes, embroidered pillows, and even tattoos. It was now about to inspire the rest of this campaign, and those to come.

"And in this campaign, we have been willing to fight, and, when necessary, we left plenty of blood and teeth on the floor. And I can think of one billionaire who has been denied the chance to buy this election." CC: Michael Bloomberg.

"If you leave with only one thing, it must be this: choose to fight only righteous fights, because then when things get tough—and they will—you will know that there is only one option ahead of you: nevertheless, you must persist." I know dozens of staffers who, in announcing next jobs after this point, called them their next "righteous fight."

"One last story, one last story," Warren promised, closing the call. "When I voted yesterday at the elementary school down the street, a mom came up to me. And she said she has two small children, and they have a nightly ritual. After the kids have brushed their teeth and read books and gotten that last sip of water and done all the other bedtime routines, they do one last thing before the two little ones go to sleep. Mama leans over to them and whispers, 'Dream big,' and the children together reply, 'Fight hard.' " Warren's campaign slogan, called out at hundreds of rallies; an audible pinky promise with her supporters. "Our work continues, the fight goes on, and big dreams never die."

I furiously texted sources for more quotes, while also fielding texts from my mom—who had a knack for texting me to ask what more I knew, as if she were the only person asking me and the only one truly entitled to the answers. Whatever I emailed to our network, I pasted into texts just for her, even though I knew she was watching my every hit, just like always.

Between texts and live shots, we shuffled toward the side door to Warren's house. The local supporters were back, in smaller numbers this time and in a more somber mood. But the media's numbers had multiplied to more than fifty. Photographers, photojournalists, correspondents, producers, reporters, embeds, all jockeying to get a good spot for the last time. No taped-down semicircles on the concrete, not that they would've constrained us anyway. When a reporter I'd never seen before tried to edge me out of my position in the front, I planted my feet more firmly. After a year of not seeing my own bed, of nonstop travel, of living for this story, I wasn't about to let someone new get a better seat for its finish. She glared back and scoffed about needing a space, but eventually receded to the back of the scrum.

Staff, many wearing sunglasses to hide their red-from-crying eyes, sought to make sense of the chaos. A half dozen fuzzy boom microphones bobbled overhead, sometimes dipping low enough to graze someone's head, and twice as many handheld mics were balanced in the limited slots of the microphone stand that served as a podium. Reporters held up iPhones; some cameramen even hoisted their tripods overhead to get the shot.

Molly, Deepa, and I had prepped for this final gaggle hours before it started, ping-ponging potential questions in our group chat. "What's your message to women and girls who are feeling frustrated by their options of two old white men now/feeling frustrated by another election where a woman won't break the glass ceiling," Deepa wrote. Why drop out now? Who will you endorse? Do you prefer Biden or Sanders? There were more questions than we would ever have time to ask, but Deepa was still the best at distilling the perfect question for the moment.

Gabrielle flashed us a sign: two-minute warning. She contorted herself into a crouched position under the microphone stand, as she had hundreds of times before, holding a recorder to capture her boss's quotes.

I crouched down so my head wouldn't block our camera's shot and with the bonus that this increasingly painful squat was as close to a workout as I'd gotten in weeks. "Two minutes," I said in my mic, waving in front of the camera so the control room knew the latest. I stayed dialed in to New York, listening to Andrea Mitchell's show in my ear. It was sometime in the noon hour. I told the time based on the anchor's voice in my ear and MSNBC's daytime lineup.

Warren walked out of her house, clad in the same purple jewel-toned puffer she'd worn just two days before, followed down the few steps out front by Bruce and their dog, Bailey. From the studio, I heard Andrea begin to narrate the scene in which I was standing. Warren, meanwhile, was thinking about the staff she'd just informed that the end had come— the twenty- and thirty-somethings who were now tasked with boxing up their belongings and scattering to the winds for whatever righteous fight was next.

As Warren drew closer, I took my earpiece out to fully live in this moment.

"So, I announced this morning that I am suspending my campaign for president," Warren said. "I say this with a deep sense of gratitude for every single person who got in this fight, every single person who tried on a new idea, every single person who just moved a little in their notion of what a president of the United States should look like."

That last thank-you sticks in my mind, even now: *to those who moved their notion of what a president should look like, even just a little.*

It was the ultimate answer to electability, one that Warren and her campaign never found in numbers large enough to matter while she was in the race. Neither they—nor Klobuchar, nor Harris, nor Gillibrand, nor Gabbard, nor Williamson—ever got Democratic primary voters to imagine what they'd never seen before enough to vote for it. They never successfully convinced people to believe that "women win" just as often as men in a post-Trump era when they run. Or that it was proof enough for the last two female senators left in the race to *have* won all their races, where the men they stood next to had certainly *not*.

The skittishness, the risk-averseness, and perhaps most of all the *fear* of four more years of Trump had pushed Democratic voters toward what they'd seen forty-four times already: a white male politician who Everyone-That-Knew-Anything said could win. A man who ran twice for president before and won no primaries in 1988 and 2008; who suffered through three bruising losses in the Democratic primaries this time around, but won once, when it mattered, and never looked back.

"I will not be running for president in 2020 but I guarantee I will stay in the fight for the hardworking folks across this country who have gotten the short end of the stick over and over. That's been the fight of my life and it will continue to be so," Warren said.

The familiar, cacophonous chorus of "Senator Warren" rang out as soon as she finished speaking, heralding the last time we'd gaggle with the Massachusetts Senator Who Wanted to Be President. Warren immediately flicked her eyes toward me, locking in and signaling I had her attention.

"Senator, what guidance would you give to your supporters who don't know who to support now?"

"Well, let's take a deep breath and spend a little time on that. We don't have to decide that this minute."

I spoke quickly, trying to draft onto the end of her words before the group sang out again so I could get to my second question—the one I really wanted to ask.

"I wonder what your message would be to the women and girls who feel like [they] are left with two white men to decide between?"

"I know," she responded, her voice cracking just a little as a thin glaze came over her eyes. "One of the hardest parts of this is all those pinky promises and all those little girls who are going to have to wait four more years. That's going to be hard."

In those moments of pinky promises at a toddler's eye level she wasn't campaigning for votes; she was telling the next generation of women that they could run and they could win—even if she didn't.

Minutes later, *The Washington Post*'s Annie Linskey asked Warren about gender and the role it played in this race. A question they'd all been asked to grapple with in real time, now answered with a new freedom.

"That is the trap question for every woman," Warren replied. "If you say, yeah, there was sexism in this race, everyone says 'whiner.' And if you say, no, there was no sexism, about a bazillion women think, 'What planet do you live on?' "

I felt the women around me silently nod. We all knew exactly what she meant. These were questions only female reporters would prioritize asking, and answers that only female reporters could contextualize correctly. It was refreshing and important. A sign of the kind of depth of coverage that more diversified press corps and newsrooms can bring to previously male- and white-dominated spaces.

But I also wondered afterward if maybe we were part of the issue. How we, as a nation and as a press corps, regularly ask women to beat the odds and the sexist barriers that are built into the presidential process, and then ask them how they managed to do it. Or we ask them why they lost but downplay the intangible magnitude of gender bias as part—not all, but part!—of the explanation. It's almost like because gender's impact is often unquantifiable, we shy away from talking about it in a meaningful way when diagnosing what went wrong. That Warren would engage with it here made sexism a thing we had to talk about as we mulled her exit from the race.

As soon as the gaggle ended outside Warren's house, I pushed my earpiece back in. "Stand by. Coming to you," the control room warned. I gave my updated report, wrapping in all that we'd just heard from Warren: the blunt acknowledgment of sexism in the race, the significance of pinky promises, analyzing the explanation that a candidate in a third "lane"—not progressive, not moderate, but some amalgam of the two—could win was wrong.

The gaggle was emotional, and I was ready for a chance to catch my breath and organize my thoughts. Then Andrea Mitchell tested my ability not to cry on national TV more than Elizabeth Warren, or my mother, or the exhaustion of the last week, ever could.

"Ali Vitali," she said. "I mean, the virtue of having someone, a Road Warrior, with the candidate for so long is just so displayed with your sense—your knowledge of her, the way you got that question in, and the way you've framed all of your reporting. And I just want to thank you. And it continues. Just to see you out there is just a great thing."

Don't cry. "Thank you, Andrea."

Those who knew me best texted immediately. "That was so sweet from Andrea," my boyfriend at the time said. "How close were you to tears?" After years of counting Super Bowl Commercial Cries, he knew me all too well.

While Warren went to her campaign headquarters to share the day with staff, my live shots barreled on for several more hours. Between my MSNBC appearances, Molly, Deepa, and I took photos to memorialize our teamwork. We thought about "the larger politics points" to move the story forward. We took a run up the block for much-needed coffee. And we watched as the public started to say thank you to Elizabeth Warren.

"We are so proud of you," was freshly scrawled in blue chalk on the sidewalk where Warren had just walked hours before. I snapped a photo and tweeted the image. Followers replied, "I needed that. Like countless women throughout the country, I am sad with today's news." And another:

"I second that. I needed a big cry last night. I'm so done with this coun-try's stupidity and misogyny, and utter dismissal of female brilliance."

Fourteen-year-old Alice MacGarvie Thompson, with her mother and younger brother, slipped flowers and a card through a slat in Warren's front gate, a last show of gratitude, even as the high school freshman fought off her disappointment of seeing the field's last viable female can-didate drop out.

"That's hard to see," she told Molly, searching for a silver lining. "It's hard to see such a strong woman and know how good her policies are . . . but you just have to remember how hard she worked, how great her cam-paign was, and how important that is. And just remember that, even when sometimes it's dispiriting."

None of the women who ran in 2020 lost solely because of sexism. And none of them blamed sexism outright, either. That explanation wouldn't have been true. But they all agree that it was *part* of what ultimately caused their campaigns to fail. And any explanation without that would be sorely lacking.

Hillary Clinton, for one, after 2016 cited extraordinary circumstances—Russian interference, unprecedented publicity from the FBI around ongoing investigations into her and people close to her, and the Donald Trump of it all—but the media demanded that she take the blame unto herself. When she did, there was a sense from some that she wasn't remorseful or self-reflective enough. That in blaming those ex-ternal factors, she didn't also sufficiently accept responsibility. So, they settled on the explanation that one of the best-qualified *people* to ever run for this office may have also just been a bad candidate: unlikable, with too much polarizing baggage, and unable to excite the base. The explanation didn't consider *how* she became one of the most polarizing candidates in modern political history. And how that probably had something to do with the fact that she was an ambitious, outwardly intelligent woman in the political spotlight for decades, before it was "boss" or "badass" to be one. How the hyper-scrutiny of "her emails" and Benghazi were both the outcomes of valid, sustained media vetting of the candidate, but also dragged out because they were steeped in a deep mistrust of a politician that both the right and some in her own party had cast skepticism on for decades. Or that she was regularly forced to reckon with not just her own political decisions, but those of her husband, in ways that male candidates never were required.

When Warren looked back with me on the end of her candidacy, she didn't lay blame with her issues or her team or the way she ran. By contrast, she seemed to lay the bulk of the blame with herself.

"I felt so bad for them," Warren told me of her staff, punctuating each word with a pause. "I felt like *I* failed . . . So how do I say [to all these people on a staff call] 'this is not our time, this is not what America wants'—at least, as *I* carry it." Each "*I*" was pregnant and heavy.

It struck me, talking to her now, that as Warren heaped the blame on herself, she took little of the comfort of what she had accomplished. She worried about the way the campaign's failure would manifest in the minds of idealistic staffers, but I wondered how it changed her.

"Did it make you doubt, like maybe 'I thought the country was ready for something that they weren't ready for, on policy or on personality'?"

"On policy, no," she answered quickly. "I believe, I really do, about what's broken and what we need to do to fix it. *I* was the imperfect messenger. I couldn't get it there."

Climate change, systemic inequality, unequal access to opportunity. These, she told me in a much-truncated version of the speech I'd heard her give hundreds of times, were the issues that needed fixing and needed fixing now. "I felt this urgency around it. These are the things we need to do. If I couldn't explain it well enough or get people engaged enough, that's on me."

She hadn't thought about this similarity until I'd asked, she said, "But it's like teaching in this sense . . .

"When a class was having trouble understanding a really difficult concept, I never blamed them. I knew that I wasn't getting it across the right way. So, it was my job to back up and find another way. And that's what it is now. Remember, Ali, I've been doing the same thing for twenty years now. It's really the same core vision of how our country has been captured by the wealthy and well-connected . . . I got in the fight expecting someone else would be the public face of it, expecting it'd be [Massachusetts senator] Ted Kennedy and other folks in the Senate. I hoped it would be someone who would run for president. I didn't get in it because I said, 'Here's an opportunity for me.' I got in it because I was in that fight."

I buy that Warren never entered politics with the goal of being the consummate, principal, presidential messenger for progressive ideas. She declined, for instance, a presidential run in 2016 despite efforts to draft her in, telling people she wasn't ready then. And after Trump took office in 2017, she was asked to run in 2020. In one closed-door meeting with Progressive Change Campaign Committee cofounders Adam Green and Stephanie Taylor in August 2017, they told her they wanted her to run in 2020. That if she did, they'd help to leverage their grassroots coalition to support her. She seemed interested, but hardly ready to commit; not wanting to jump in without knowing if she was the candidate the moment required. We don't know yet what the world looks like after the 2018 midterms, she said, and we want to be able to freely assess then if we—or someone else—meet "the zeitgeist of the moment."

Plus, she had a Senate reelect to think about first. Some advisors told her to focus on that, to keep her head down in the meantime so she could win reelection in Massachusetts. The PCCC cofounders recalled Warren calling that "terrible advice," especially given that "the house is on fire." She came to Washington to do the work, to use her seat to advocate on her issues.

She thought about the 2018 electorate the same way she thought about the 2020 electorate. "If they really want a fighter, there's nobody better at that than me," she said, speaking among friends and connecting her next fight to her potential future one. If not, so it goes. But her 2018 race would either illuminate a presidential path or close it.

That's a careful way of running for president from someone who says she never saw herself as the ultimate standard-bearer. But I also know that there's no job in the world that requires a stronger sense of ego, self, and, frankly, chutzpah than that of president of the United States. Anyone who runs believes, at a fundamental level, that they are the best person to be the most powerful leader in the world. Warren may not have seen herself as that person at first, but she certainly came to see herself as such by the time she decided to run. You can't run without that deep, abiding belief. And she had it—if not wholly in herself, then at least in her ideas.

In the aftermath of the Warren exit, it wasn't just the candidate, or her staff, or the fourteen-year-old Thompson laying a card outside her house searching for a bright side. Many voters, especially women, were fighting against that crushing feeling of disappointment they had come to know all too well.

For many—those who supported Warren and those who didn't—the Thursday afternoon that Warren dropped out felt like November 2016 all over again: a gut punch of a reminder that it would be another four years before another woman could have a shot at the White House. In some cases, the "heartbreak" was about Warren herself: the loss of an outspoken progressive with a pragmatic streak who really felt like she could get there. In others, it seemed like people realized in the moment she left that they were, in fact, thirsty for female leadership—if only once they lost the chance.

But one Warren supporter and operative, Adam Jentleson, explained it this way on Twitter that night: "Everyone loves the woman once she's not trying to take power away from men anymore."

11

<hr>

"It's Just Time"
Female VP Candidates and the Mystical Gender Gap

SPRING 2020

No sooner had the dust settled in Cambridge than I was sent to Cleveland, Ohio, to begin my coverage of former VP Joe Biden. He was set to rally in the Buckeye State while post–Super Tuesday states, like Michigan, cast their votes. Senator Bernie Sanders would be rallying there, too, as luck would have it, making chilly Cleveland the political place to be for reporters staying with, or now joining, the last two Democratic campaigns' traveling press corps.

Almost as soon as Molly and I dropped our bags in the community college gymnasium, Biden's event was canceled. His plane touched down in Cleveland only to fly right back to Philadelphia, where he'd give a speech from a purposefully sparsely attended room. Sanders's team also canceled. It was the first time campaigns would cancel their events in the name of COVID concerns, the clear beginning of the end of campaigning as we'd always known it: events as big as possible, maskless thousands, with no concern that taking a breath to cheer or raising a hand to high-five a stranger could put you on a path to a ventilator and your last breath. How well-worn and palpable that feeling of fear is now.

But in early March 2020, my biggest fear was not knowing my next assignment. The virus still felt theoretical, far away, and untethered from the political sprint to the finish we were covering, despite my bizarre illness just a few weeks prior that just so happened to mirror all the symptoms we now associate with COVID-19.

After the Biden and Sanders events were canceled, Molly moved our camera setup outside and I reported to Brian Williams and Rachel Maddow that the Democratic National Committee would no longer hold the next scheduled debate in Arizona, as planned, but instead move to CNN's Washington, D.C., bureau—no audience, only anchors and the two candidates.

So, we headed back to Washington. On the plane we were joined by various members of the Biden and Bernie Traveling Press Circus who had all also fruitlessly flocked to Cleveland. "It'll be a week or two of badly needed rest," I joked with Jennifer Palmieri, the former Hillary Clinton advisor who had since hung up her Democratic operative hat to follow this presidential circus as a quasi-media member, as we settled into our seats. If nothing else, at least it was a chance to get some time in my own bed.

We truly thought this would be a much-needed week or two of forced rest. That we'd be back out on shared flights and crowded into the high school gymnasiums of battleground states in no time. Can you blame us? Who could've known what was ahead? That the virus would not just disrupt the entire political calendar and way of campaigning for office, but that it would do much, much worse. Kill an unfathomable hundreds of thousands of Americans. Force all of us inside our homes and away from our loved ones. Expose deep ineptitude in government leadership and response. Deepen the divide between those who believe the science and those who so badly don't want to accept this bleak reality that they'll call it "fake" and ignore all public health guidelines, risking their own health and—worse—the health of those around them.

We didn't know any of that pain, yet. Settling in to watch this very weird debate, I was just happy to be on my couch. The debate opened on the virus and what these candidates would do to keep it from ravaging

America. That gave way to a conversation on health care. I couldn't help but think of the plan that Warren had rolled out in January—January!—for combating a public health epidemic like this one. Some texts came in from sources and fellow reporters that wondered what it would be like to have her on stage. The topics ticked on. Then Biden made news.

It was as simple as just saying it.

"If elected president, my cabinet—my *administration*—will look like the country," Joe Biden vowed. "And I commit that I will, in fact, appoint a—I'll pick a woman to be vice president. There are a number of women who are qualified to be president tomorrow. I would pick a woman to be my vice president."

Not perfect. But it didn't need to be.

Biden's promise was historic. No other major presidential candidate had ever before laid that demographic line in the sand. He'd done the same just a few short weeks before, while fighting for his political life, when he vowed to appoint a Black woman to the Supreme Court should he have the chance. (In early 2022, he got that chance—and made good.) In both cases, some wished he hadn't been so specific about cutting men out of the equation, as others saw great power in him doing so.

"You don't have to talk about it, because then it gives someone else a bad faith argument about identity politics," said Amanda Litman, a former Clinton staffer who now runs the organization Run for Something, geared toward helping young people, including women, run for office. "Kamala was the right choice and a good choice and, obviously, a qualified choice. He should've just picked her. And been like 'I'm picking her not because she's better than all the other women but because she's better than all the other people.' Full stop."

But other Democrats found empowerment in the way Biden's promise structured the process. "There's something kind of fulfilling in 'You know what, guys? Sit down,' " a senior Biden aide said. "There was something awesome about being like 'Yeah, no.' "

Biden's team was aware they had to mobilize in advance to avoid the tropes and biases that had dinged past women cast in this vice-presidential role. They prepared ways to protect this Unknown Veep in advance of her rollout that would help to address any subconscious or conscious biases around women in executive leadership roles and in the presidency. The considerations, advisors involved told me, were more than just "hair and makeup and where your voices are on the register"—which were unfortunately still important—but ensuring that there was a foundation in the larger progressive party apparatus that would lift this woman up.

Biden's team wanted an ecosystem primed favorably toward a female candidate—something none of the rest of the women who'd come before had, in fact something few female candidates for any office had ever truly had—so they engaged allies outside the campaign to make it so. Those allies ranged from the party's top, respected female strategists like former top Obama aide Valerie Jarrett to outside groups like UltraViolet, EMILY's List, and Times Up that exist to bolster female candidates in myriad ways, from financial backing to fighting sexism. They all banded together—united by their determination not to let sexism derail another qualified female candidate from one of the most powerful positions in elected politics.

"We've all been to this movie before," Tina Tchen, then-president and CEO of Times Up, told me in the midst of the veepstakes, referencing 2016 and Hillary Clinton. "We knew what was going to happen and then, lo and behold, it's unfolding before us."

The group drafted open letters to network news organizations, political directors, and reporters, putting them on notice: "A woman VP candidate, possibly a Black or Brown woman candidate, requires the same kind of internal consideration about systemic inequality as you undertook earlier this year" around the killing of George Floyd and the civil unrest that followed, the collective group, called We Have Her Back, wrote, including guidance for news orgs on how to correctly frame sexist claims without giving them credence and tips for how not to talk about female candidates.

"We're not saying any attack on a woman is sexist. We're not saying that any criticism of a woman is unfair," Christina Reynolds, vice president of communications at EMILY's List, told me at the start of their effort. "What we're saying is there are ways in which we make women seem different, seem like they don't belong here, particularly women of color, and that we want to call that out, so people are aware of it, and they look for it and they don't accept it as the facts."

When female party leaders and operatives were booked on television, they purposefully turned questions about a potential veep's drawbacks into opportunities to highlight the diversities in their resumés, determined not to pit woman against woman or elevate one to the detriment of another. The groups mobilized war rooms and sought to disrupt any negative news narratives steeped in sexism, racism, and disinformation before they began. This was an unprecedented groundswell of disruption that could only come from women who had seen what unchecked sexism could do to female candidates. But it also required a media that was willing to reconsider past flaws in its coverage and would not have been possible without diverse newsrooms that empowered women. That's not to say women were the only ones. Plenty of men, in my newsroom and others, led the charge to ensure that the female veep, whoever Biden chose, got a fair shake.

But it's easier to recognize othering—especially the subtle kind—when you yourself have been othered. You know the signs because you've been on the receiving end of them. For a reporting class that was still becoming more racially diverse and more female, having had our own ambition thrown in our faces many times helped us identify these storylines in ways we weren't empowered to, or prepared for, in past elections (especially since so few of those past elections had included female candidates). It empowered us to see the euphemisms that sound like compliments but could be like slow-acting venom if not sucked out. To call out attempts to delegitimize Black women—from Stacey Abrams to Kamala Harris to Karen Bass—as "misogynoir." To be part of equalizing the playing field, which is to say, making it the same to run while female as it is to run while male. No commentary on appearance, no hyper-scrutiny of motive, just a focus on the policy and the resumé and the values. This all added up to a hyperawareness from the female members of the media when it came time to cover the 2020 veepstakes. No gendered reporting, and certainly no woman-on-woman crime allowed. At least, ideally and theoretically.

The campaign's VP search co-chairs, as well as top Biden camp advisors, underwent what one likened to a crash course in "Women Candidates 101." Among the co-chairs was Delaware congresswoman Lisa Blunt Rochester. After one team briefing with the Barbara Lee Family Foundation about the perils of sexism that women running for office face, another female colleague remembers Rochester remarking to her, "It's like they're telling me about my own campaign."

That's because, for many involved in the selection process, each new churn of the veepstakes felt new but also entirely familiar. Because in Biden vowing to nominate a woman and holding forth with a process designed to choose one, he wasn't necessarily treading brand-new ground—only in his deliberateness about it.

Congresswoman Geraldine Ferraro first broke the running-mate glass ceiling in 1984 when tapped by former vice president Walter Mondale to team up on the Democratic ticket against President Ronald Reagan and Vice President George H. W. Bush. Alaska governor Sarah Palin joined Arizona senator John McCain on the Republican ticket in 2008. And technically, Texas senator Ted Cruz selected former Hewlett-Packard CEO (a 2016 presidential contender herself) Carly Fiorina to be his would-be running mate, a move born of desperation in a last ditch-effort to snatch Trump's all-but-sealed path to the Republican nomination. (*The New York Times* called the move "the political equivalent of a student pulling a fire alarm to avoid an exam: It was certain to draw attention and carried the possibility of meeting its immediate goal, but seemed unlikely to forestall the eventual reckoning.") Hillary Clinton contemplated an all-female ticket in 2016, seeing it as "an upside-downside": "I mean, you would be asking a lot for the electorate to elect two women. That would be a huge step. On the other hand, it would be history making and let's roll the dice." She did not and Senator Elizabeth Warren, the woman she was considering, would not get the pick.

Warren's experience in 2016 would, however, be a harbinger of things to come on a larger scale in 2020. Former Pennsylvania governor and DNC chair Ed Rendell openly questioned her qualifications on a local radio show, telling the host Warren was "wonderful" and "bright . . . but with no experience in foreign affairs and not in any way, shape or form ready to be commander-in-chief." On *The Rachel Maddow Show* afterward, Warren was asked to respond.

"The most important job of being a vice president is to be ready to be president if, God forbid, something happened to the commander-in-chief," Maddow said. "Do you believe you would be capable of stepping into that job and doing that job . . ." Warren was already subtly nodding with her body, like a cat ready to pounce. "And I ask you because Ed Rendell . . . said recently that you were not in any way, shape or form ready to be commander-in-chief. I wanna know if you think you could be."

"Yes, I do," Warren replied. She pursed her lips. If you close your eyes and listen to the video, you almost hear each word drip with Warren's disdain that she should even have to be asked the question. She was a sitting senator who'd won a hotly contested seat, a former Harvard professor, an expert at bankruptcy and the economy, an author, and a mother of two. But somehow, she had to press her qualifications, again, and in a way the male candidates being considered did not.

Rendell would be at it again in 2020, but in a new and different landscape. Biden's pool of potential VPs was now No Boys Allowed. Which meant there was no explicit battle of the sexes, but not that sexism didn't fester anyway. And we'll get to that.

But while Biden's choosing a woman wasn't *new* ground, being a vice-presidential running mate wasn't a well-trod path for women, either—and it wasn't one that had ever yielded success. Mondale-Ferraro failed to stop Reagan-Bush's second term and McCain-Palin's loss ushered in the first term of Barack Obama and Joe Biden. And Cruz-Fiorina? Well . . . they barely even lasted a month.

The goal for Biden—and every other politician looking for a VP—was a "jolt." A way to generate excitement among the base and expand the campaign's coalition. That's the hope for *any* campaign with *any* vice-presidential pick. In the first two—okay, technically three—instances of picking a woman, that excitement was badly needed by the campaigns in question. And Ferraro herself, a congresswoman and women's rights advocate, knew it would take a particularly bad political landscape for a woman to be called in as the choice.

"There's no way any presidential candidate is going to choose a woman as a running mate unless he's 15 points behind in the polls," she once said at a closed meeting of the National Women's Caucus, prior to being tapped by Mondale. She wasn't far off.

Mondale's selection of Ferraro came while he was down double digits to Reagan and Bush. At the time that McCain stunned the political world by picking Palin (the only woman on his VP short list and a barely nationally known one at that), polls showed him trailing Obama and badly in need of an adrenaline shot. And Cruz's campaign was basically already dead when it tapped Fiorina, who had herself also admitted defeat at the hands of Trump.

By contrast, Biden—after long, hard months spent in the political gallows—was now at the height of his political power after a bruising primary. That he was the field's fore-runner was a foregone conclusion. Rivals, from Buttigieg to Klobuchar to the long-since-gone Beto O'Rourke, all fell in behind him in advance of Super Tuesday, a coalescing that came as each of the latter campaigns realized they had no track left on the trail and no cash in their coffers from which to build more. Once Warren dropped out, Kamala Harris—out of the race and the campaign trail's limelight since before most Americans hung Christmas ornaments on their trees in 2019—added her endorsement to Biden's list.

It all made the March 2019 debate between Bernie and Biden, in the minds of most Democrats, a formality. For the Biden campaign, it presented an opportunity. To try to win some skeptical or less-than-enthused backers of vanquished candidates to his cause and begin the unifying process. To finally be unequivocal about that which he had mused about publicly on the campaign trail. To say publicly what he had been emphatic about in private with advisors as far back as the 2018 midterms: *of course, we should elevate a woman.* "It's time."

"Women in particular were excited, but a lot of men were excited too, because they felt it was time as well," a top Biden advisor told me of the promise to tap a woman VP. "People within the party felt it was time. Of course, the disappointment of 2016 and not electing the first woman president" played a role. So did the multiple, inspiring female candidacies showcased during the Democratic primary in 2020. And Biden wanted to build a generational bridge within his party.

"We wanted to use the process to raise the profiles of a lot of these women, because even being considered leaves you in a better spot for next time," another Biden advisor involved in the VP process said. "If you were seen as a potential vice president once, then whether it's for Senate or governor or the presidency at some point, you would've already been elevated."

And they had options. Lots of them, thanks to Democrats' investments in filling their candidate pipeline with more women. Biden could offer a new chapter of that investment.

"Biden understands the political pipeline as well as anyone," the first advisor said. "He understands the history of vice presidents and the advantage they have in terms of being positioned for their party's nomination and to be president. All of those factors played into his decision to just go ahead and say, 'This is who it's going to be.' "

Not to mention, the campaign's top brass would joke, "it'll make the search easier because we've already ruled out half the people!"

But it was also an opportunity for Biden to once again align with most members of his party who believed that nominating a woman was essential, from the perspective of showcasing party ideals but also as a matter of good politics. For while a woman did not win the 2020 Democratic nomination, data still showed the landscape was favorable for female candidates and the base was clamoring for reflectiveness in their ticket.

All this factored into the Biden team's selection process. A process happening against the backdrop of a candidate who'd locked up his party's nomination without convincing the party writ large that there was wide-spread, screaming-in-the-street excitement about him. That kind of shrugging support put Biden parallel with another man who'd been in this position, although in a very different political and cultural time.

Former vice president Walter Mondale's 1984 campaign was often described as "dull" and unexciting. But the 1980s brought with them not just the power of Ronald Reagan's brand of Republicanism, but a focus on gender—and the way it was shaping the outcome of national elections. Prior to 1980, men and women voted for Republicans and Democrats in roughly equal numbers; there was negligible difference between the genders in their partisan split. But since 1980's match-up of Reagan versus Jimmy Carter, there's been a divergence—a "gender gap." One where, generally and over time, women were more likely to vote for Democrats and where men have participated in a rightward pull.

By the time Mondale was facing the incumbent Reagan–H.W. Bush ticket four years later, women's groups had seized on the data—specifically that Reagan bested Jimmy Carter by only 2 points among women—to press the case for a woman to finally be on the presidential ticket, to excite women who had drifted from the party back to it. Never mind that Reagan's success was also driven by winning *men* by 19 points, spurring a gap in gender "not by the movement of women away from 'that evil Reagan,'" as University of Virginia's Center for Politics wrote, "but by the movement of men toward 'that appealing Reagan.' Most women stayed firmly with the Democrats and many men joined and stayed with the Republicans."

When it came time for Mondale to vet and consider potential VPs, the women he considered were Congresswoman Geraldine "Gerry" Ferraro and then–San Francisco mayor (now California senior senator) Dianne Feinstein. Ferraro was a prominent voice in feminist circles and a well-known Democrat in D.C. She represented Queens and was close to House Speaker Tip O'Neill, who endorsed her for the VP job. But in the summer of 1984, she was being introduced anew on the national stage with all the attention that comes with running-mate buzz, as Americans and the media grappled with the potential for history ahead.

"The arguments 'for' [a female running mate] are that a woman would make history, add excitement to an otherwise dull ticket, produce a big turnout of women voters—which many consider the key to victory in November," NBC News correspondent Lisa Myers explained during her *Nightly News* package on July 2, 1984, shortly before Ferraro was announced. "The arguments against are that picking a woman is a gamble that could hurt more among men than it helps with women, that none of the women are qualified, and that Mondale could be accused of tokenism and giving in to another special interest." That "none of the women are qualified" was a sexist trope that would persist against female candidates long after Ferraro and Feinstein.

Once she was picked, Mondale extolled Ferraro as "an exciting choice" for a campaign and a candidate that hadn't been known much for excitement so far. Ferraro, hand raised mid-wave and wearing a string of pearls that cascaded over a red polka-dot dress, graced the cover of *TIME* magazine. "A Historic Choice," the bold white type declared. Inside, after readers leafed through ads for Newport cigarettes and Gold Rum, they found stories that all agreed: she *was* a historic choice. She was also a long shot, unlikely, and in need of deep scrutiny (as if others in her position weren't, regardless of gender). Her margin for error, it was noted in the press, would be "slimmer than ever; the slightest hesitancy or over-aggressiveness in manner, any fumbled response to a question or verbal gaffe will be enormously magnified."

"The selection of Ferraro will affect not only the woman in the voting booth," Roger Rosenblatt wrote for *TIME*. "It will be equally felt by the man who—today, next month, next year—stares across his desk, dining-room table or bed sheets and sees someone as if for the first time. There is no analogue to lean on, no sentimentalization to rely on, nothing Americans can do now but work the matter out for themselves and see where the rejiggled republic stands. The world's most powerful nation may be ready to be led by a woman, and any woman at all may prepare herself to lead it."

Much of the press excitement around Ferraro was founded on gender and history alone—traits that could inspire lofty sentences about what could be, followed quickly by hefty doses of reality checks and disqualification—and only spoke to a small part of what Ferraro brought to the table.

After Ferraro was picked, CBS/NYT polling found that one candidate with two X chromosomes may not necessarily beget all the other voters who also had two X chromosomes. Fifty-four percent of women and 62 percent of men gave Mondale's pick of Ferraro a "blah, 'all right' rating." While 22 percent of women polled were excited by it, 18 percent thought it was a "bad idea." But more than anything, it was clear they thought her gender, not her qualifications or leadership potential, was the reason she was chosen. Elsewhere in the pages of *TIME* her elevation was credited to "fate and gender, not her resume," bolstering the perception. Sixty percent of those polled by *The New York Times* and CBS thought Mondale chose her due to pressure from women's groups. Only 22 percent believed Ferraro was chosen because she was the best candidate for the job.

"One question which Mr. Mondale and Mrs. Ferraro will be asked often is whether she would be the choice if her first name was Gerald, rather than Geraldine," offered NBC's Lisa Myers in another 1984 report for the *Today* show.

So it was, both before she was nominated and certainly after. In San Francisco just before being selected, Ferraro responded to a question about whether voters shouldn't be more concerned with a VP's qualifications than their gender. "Who's kidding who?" Ferraro leveled with the press, the lighthearted tone she used to tell this truth made harder to suss out by her heavy New York accent. "You know, someone said to me: don't you feel badly about all this stuff—the attention you're getting? And, you know, would you get it if you were not female? I don't feel the least bit badly about it. Not at all." Applause rang out and women's cheers could be heard. "And I'm *duh*-lighted," Ferraro went on, "that there is no longer that big sign outside that door of the Office for Vice President that says white male only need apply. It's our turn, folks."

A turn where the odds were "firmly against Geraldine Ferraro," as reporters wrote in that same issue of *TIME*. "But the point was, no one could be sure. A thousand calculations—the effect of a woman national candidate on the female vote, the male vote, the South, the West, urban– blue collar workers, black and Hispanic voters—have to be done for the very first time."

One woman to represent them all. No pressure. And Ferraro did seek to represent them. She cast herself on the campaign trail as an example of what women could achieve outside the home, while not alienating those who chose to stay within it, speaking directly to female voters without hy- perfocusing on them, a point of reported contention within the campaign and Democratic Party apparatus at the time.

"For the first fourteen years of my married life," she said, at a Novem- ber 1984 rally, "I worked at home as a mother and wife. That was a fine profession. Then I decided to work outside the home, and that was also the right decision for me. Not every woman would agree with the decisions I have made. But the point is, the choice was mine and we can each make our own decisions."

There was opportunity in being the woman to set the tone for women in power. But the darker side to accepting this historic nomination was the historic potential to be blamed if, and when, it went wrong. Americans knew men won, and lost, races; we'd never had to react when women were put in the same position at the highest level of the political game.

What's more, it's hard—even today—to gauge and chart the exact, specific, individual impact of a running mate. They're half of the ticket, but the less powerful half. Most experts agree their impact is probably a point or two in terms of actual votes earned or lost, both negligible and make-or-break depending on how tight the margins are. Running mates can bring coverage bounces and be cited by voters as factors in their choice, but they're cloaked in the political brand of the name that's printed at the top of the ticket and in bigger, bolder lettering on campaign stickers than their own. They're inextricably linked with The Guy at the Top. Which makes it both harder and easier to blame VPs for things going wrong.

Plus, for female running mates, much of the gender-based excitement around people like Ferraro presupposed something never tested at these highest political echelons: that a female candidate would almost automatically usher female voters into coming on board.

In Rosenblatt's words, "More women, more votes." In 1984, operatives on both sides of the political spectrum agreed that Ferraro's ability to attract, or repel, female voters was subjective, untested, and thus a gut feeling rather than one steeped in data. The same novelty that spurred excitement also spurred warranted skepticism.

For all her political skill and blunt assessments of gender in politics, Ferraro on the Mondale ticket wasn't enough to stop the campaign's electoral bleeding. Nor was the premise upon which she was brought in, that women were monolithic and would vote based on sex above all else. That previously untested thinking ignored the reality: that women, like men, don't all vote the same way. Nor do they all count gender as a chief and explicit deciding factor for their vote, especially not in presidential general elections.

"Thinking about politics only through the lens of the things we can see is what causes dumb voters to say things like 'women won't vote for her, why should I?' The expectation that women vote for women because they vote for women is absurd," Kathleen Dolan, a professor of political science at the University of Wisconsin–Milwaukee and expert on the connection between gender and electoral results, told me, calling these narratives on gender "oversimplified." "Any notion that women should or do support women candidates at higher rates than do men is nonsense."

And yet, with each woman who throws her hat in the ring or runs alongside a man, the first voting bloc we look to are women. *How will they react? Will they flock to the ticket in some surprising way now?* And this expectation has become a lazy way to explain away the failures of female candidates at the ballot box when we chalk up those losses to "well, women didn't vote for her."

In 1984, Mondale-Ferraro lost, overall and by 12 points with female voters, to Reagan and Bush. The Republican incumbents netted 62 percent of men, according to exit polls from *The New York Times*, as well as 56 percent of women, bettering their standing among women from the election cycle before. That should have shredded the narrative that a female running mate would automatically bring a substantial number of women with her. (It didn't.)

The same thinking would once again pervade around Alaska governor Sarah Palin when she was chosen in 2008 as John McCain's running mate. There, at least, the theory matched with relevant data points—specifically that white women tended then, and now, to vote Republican, even as women overall trended more Democratic. But Hillary Clinton's near-miss for the Democratic nomination in 2008 gave the McCain campaign reason to believe they could leverage history and gender in their favor.

At a rally accepting McCain's tap, Palin invoked Clinton's '08 campaign and made an overture to the women who'd backed her. "Hillary left 18 million cracks in the highest, hardest glass ceiling in America," Palin said. "But it turns out the women of America aren't finished yet, and we can shatter that glass ceiling once and for all."

When McCain picked Palin as his second on his maverick, buck-the-party-style campaign it was for many of the same reasons as Mondale—the thinking that they could attract female voters who had been engaged politically already by Clinton and that the pick would recharge McCain's campaign and recast the presidential race. The McCain team had a slate of male potentials before them—well-known party names like Mitt Romney, Tim Pawlenty, and Joe Lieberman—the latter who, though not a Republican, was a candidate favorite and the man McCain later said he regretted not going with. Governor Palin was the lone woman on the list. The Republican bench of qualified, viable female known entities was thin at that time, to say the least. What won her the prize was the thinking that her novelty and historic potential, paired with a political "no bullshit" conservative brand in Alaska that mirrored McCain's, would rouse dormant parts of the GOP base and persuade wavering women to their cause.

The pick caught nearly everyone but McCain's closest aides off guard and forced a gender reckoning from both parties. Obama's advisors, *The*

New York Times reported, struggled "to figure out how to challenge the credentials and the ideology of a woman whose candidacy could be embraced by many women as a historic milestone."

"That very first day, the Obama campaign said, 'Well, we want you to go out there and criticize her,' " Clinton recalled in her book *Hard Choices* of conversations she had after the Palin announcement. "And I said 'For what? For being a woman? No, let's wait until we know where she stands, I don't know anything about her. Do you know anything about her?' " Obama officials argued at the time that they wanted Clinton to say the GOP's platform was inconsistent with the values Palin ran on, not attack her for being a woman. The Obama-Biden campaign, for their part, put out this statement on the day Palin was announced, seizing on the experience issue that McCain had been hammering Obama on for months: "Today, John McCain put the former mayor of a town of 9,000, with zero foreign policy experience, a heartbeat away from the Presidency."

Aides viewed the statement as "so clear cut," according to Obama campaign manager David Plouffe, that they didn't even run it by the candidate first. "We shouldn't have put out the first part of that statement," Obama said, seeing it. The campaign, recognizing a potential misfire by failing to acknowledge the historic nature of the first female Republican vice-presidential candidate, soon put out another statement doing just that.

And though Palin's gender presented a potential trap and complication for Obama and his team, Palin herself carried legitimate risks for McCain, too. Chief among them was that she'd served only two years as governor. Typically, that kind of executive leadership—paired with her two terms as mayor of Wasilla, Alaska—is welcomed onto the presidential stage. She'd been elected locally and statewide. While Wasilla's size was dwarfed by South Bend's, Palin *had* been successful on a statewide ballot more times than Mayor Buttigieg would be able to boast during his presidential run eleven years later.

But as with Ferraro ("only six years' " experience in the House), Palin's experience was called into question from the start, mentioned in the first three paragraphs of almost every major newspaper's report on her selection well before her now-well-known media screwups lent credence to the novice image. *The Wall Street Journal* wrote in its lede that the "surprise stroke aimed at attracting Hillary Clinton supporters . . . could undercut the campaign's key theme of experience." And *The New York Times*: "Senator John McCain astonished the political world on Friday by naming Sarah Palin, a little-known governor of Alaska and self-described 'hockey mom' with almost no foreign policy experience, as his running mate on the Republican presidential ticket."

The skepticism about her qualifications was swift and palpable. And the slapdash nature of the last-minute Palin pick was particularly lethal in that it looked cravenly political, undercutting McCain's key selling point as a steady, experienced statesman whose age and medical history also forced voters to consider whether Palin truly had what it takes to assume the office. Palin had spent fewer years in the Alaska Governor's Mansion than Obama had spent in the Senate. And even in an executive role, Alaska doesn't scream "booming economic epicenter" to most Americans.

Her obvious inexperience on the national media stage—as well as the already-higher threshold for women to be taken seriously and seen as qualified in national politics—was easily exploited by rivals. The experience she did have that should have lent credibility to her qualifications was overshadowed by being tagged with the ability to "see Russia from my house" (even though Palin never exactly said that) and her evolution toward racially inflaming comments against Obama, whom she regularly called by his middle name, "Hussein."

McCain and Palin lost the election, leaving the glass ceiling still intact and once again disrupting the idea that female candidates automatically beget female voters. The gender gap—the difference in proportion of women and men voting for the winning candidate—was 7 percent, according to exit polls, consistent with other presidential elections and mirroring 2004's spread. But Obama did better with female voters overall than John Kerry had in 2004, while McCain performed 5 points worse with them than George W. Bush that same cycle. Obama also made inroads with white women—46 percent compared to Kerry's 44—and benefited from record turnout of Black women.

Moreover, a 2010 study from Stanford estimated Palin cost McCain 1.6 percentage points. "The Palin Effect," as these researchers termed it, came out to roughly 2.1 million votes lost. That's a big swing to attribute to a running mate, one that researchers assess blossomed as voters got to know Palin over time, but also potentially from the reflection on McCain's judgment for choosing her in the first place. Given Obama's winning 53 percent of the popular vote, they concluded Palin's campaign performance did not necessarily change the election outcome but was certainly large enough to be substantively meaningful. Every vote counts, after all.

McCain strategists later deemed the pick "a story of when cynicism and idealism collide." During a scathing monologue on MSNBC's *Morning Joe*, top McCain strategist Steve Schmidt said: "I think when you look back at that race, you see this person who is just so phenomenally talented at so many levels . . . But also, someone who had a lot of flaws as someone running to be in the national command authority who clearly wasn't prepared."

Still, Palin—who didn't respond to my request to talk for this project—went on to become a key voice and kingmaker in some parts of the party. And she stands as a prime example of the kind of conservative woman who tends to do well on the national stage and continues to thrive in the Republican Party today. Her appeal will be tested anew in 2022 as she vies for an Alaska House seat that, should she win, would put her back in the center of the national political conversation, albeit as part of a very different Republican Party that is more accepting of her firebrand type of politicking.

"Women Republicans have a harder time coming through primaries," Kathleen Dolan allowed, which tracked with what I'd found in my own reporting. Republicans, until very recently, lacked the same kind of infrastructure—and frankly, desire—as Democrats to bolster female candidates in the nascent phases of their candidacies (primaries) where gender tends to cut hardest against them. However, "where we've seen [conservative] women's success is as they've tacked hard right and followed the party." She pointed to Tennessee senator Marsha Blackburn, South Dakota governor Kristi Noem, and Palin as examples.

Republican Minnesota congresswoman Michele Bachmann, too, found success—however short-lived—during her 2012 campaign for president. A founder of the House Tea Party Caucus who came to Congress in 2006 as the first GOP woman elected from Minnesota to the House, she rose for a brief time as a front-runner in the 2012 Republican presidential field, buoyed by polling success in key early states, like Iowa. But her time as the front-runner ended by the summer of 2011, in part because then–Texas governor Rick Perry cut into her claim as the field's Tea Party darling, but also because polling at the time also pointed to an electorate struggling to see her as best positioned to handle the economy and lacking in the ever-present "electability" metric. A *Washington Post*/ABC News poll in September 2011 showed only 4 percent of voters saw her as the candidate with the best chance to beat President Obama, down 3 points from a month and a half earlier. But even at Bachmann's pinnacle—winning key straw polls in critical states like Iowa—some on her staff saw the double standards she was being subjected to.

They played out most memorably on the cover of *Newsweek* at the height of Bachmann's polling success with an unflattering picture of the candidate, yes, but also in other areas of the media. During a June 2011 interview on *Fox News Sunday* with Chris Wallace, he took her to task for past controversial statements—ranging from saying President Obama created a "gangster government" to calling fellow members of Congress "anti-America"—ultimately asking: "Are you a flake?"

"Well, I think that would be insulting to say something like that, because I'm a serious person," she said in response. Wallace later apologized. But to some who worked for Bachmann at the time, it was yet another example of the different level, and different type, of scrutiny female candidates are subjected to.

"He wouldn't have done that to a man, I don't think," Alice Stewart, who worked for Bachmann at the time, told me. "She powered on, she didn't 'oh, cry-me-an-I'm-a-woman river.' She realized that's part of the territory."

It reminded Stewart of another moment from the race, after the first debate when Bachmann "knocked it out of the park," that crystallized the need for female candidates to not just be good on policy, politics, and authentic personality—they had to look a certain way doing it, too. "I'll never forget after that evening, in my hotel, a reporter called and asked what suit she was wearing. I said, 'Are you kidding me?' They said my editors want to know who she was wearing and who did her hair. I said, 'When you call the men and ask that, you can call me back.' Needless to say, they didn't."

Despite these moments, though, neither Bachmann nor the campaign ever felt the need to speak directly to gender. "She never used that as a crutch or an excuse for how she was being treated," Stewart said. "She always just realized that as a woman she has to be the first one in, the last one to leave, and has to be more prepared than the rest of the field . . . She never played the gender card."

That speaks to the mindset on the conservative side that other Republican women who have run, including Fiorina, talked about with me. The idea that neither candidates nor electorate are looking to be overtly identity-based in their voting choices, the concept of merit somehow being diminished by infusing gender or racial identity. But where Republican and Democratic women are similar is that they both see the paths they're carving out in real time.

"When she would talk to moms and little girls" during retail politics stops, Stewart recalled, Bachmann would say, "Wow, they can see this is what they can do when they grow up. She saw that at the retail level" and could lean into it there, but "it's just different when you're dealing on the national stage."

But in recent years, at the non-presidential level, we've also seen the rise of that certain type of right-wing GOP woman thriving in the party. Women like representatives Marjorie Taylor Greene and Lauren Boebert, though not in official leadership roles within Congress (MTG was removed and barred from serving on any congressional committees in 2021), are thought leaders—and prolific fundraisers—to vocal swaths of the GOP base. And that they have former President Trump's backing only further strengthens their position, controversies be damned.

"The broader argument is that as we've seen GOP women become more successful, we've seen a certain *kind* of GOP woman become successful," Dolan, the political scientist, concluded. But the idea of expecting female candidates to have success with female voters also wrongly presumes that American women are the ones most likely to shift in their political views. The widening of the gender gap has actually been driven by *men*'s changing political behavior more than women's, with men becoming more Republican over time and women remaining, overall, more left leaning. A greater or fewer number of women on the ballot hasn't enticed or swayed them in major ways. It's inspired turn*out* but not turning *on* the parties they already trend to vote with.

In 2020's Biden/Trump matchup—despite polls that predicted the potential for the largest gender gap in history—women voters voted . . . pretty much how they always do. In fact, Biden won women by similar margins to his predecessors in 2016 (Clinton) and 2008/2012 (Obama), but Trump made notable gains among white women—boosting his support with the group 6 points in 2020, according to Pew Research Center, from where it was in 2016. White women breaking for Trump that way was, for some, a stunning metric, even though the majority of white women have always voted Republican in modern American elections, save for two (1964 for Lyndon Johnson and 1996 for Bill Clinton). Trump, even saddled with dozens of credible sexual misconduct allegations and a proven track record of publicly demeaning women, simply continued the established trend. It reemphasizes that general elections are, for voters, more often about party loyalty than identity of the candidates running. And that women didn't abandon Clinton, betray their gender, and tank her election. She won women; just not the ones she—or any other Democrat in a general election—was already unlikely to win.

What narrowed the gender gap in 2020 was Biden's ability to cut into

Trump's support with white *men*, shrinking the 11-point advantage Trump had over Clinton in 2016 with the group to just 2 points in 2020, according to post-2020 election data from Pew. In 2020, Biden and Trump split the male vote almost evenly, where Trump bested Clinton in this demographic by double digits.

Certainly, adherence to tribalism is true in general elections, where the oft talked-about (but not so easily found) "swing voter" represents a smaller and smaller piece of the electorate pie with each new cycle. When it's Republican versus Democrat, voters are more predictable. But in a primary, when it's Democrat versus Democrat or Republican versus Republican—then what? And assessing those primary races through racial and gender lenses, in addition to ideological and economic ones, is compelling and essential. In 2020, we saw Democrats' answer in the age of Trump. In 2024, we'll see Republicans and Democrats alike answer that question anew—unless Trump and Biden run again, potentially replicating the same constructs that governed 2020. But I'm getting ahead of myself . . .

Biden made good on the promise to run alongside a woman five months after he first swore it on the debate stage. And mere days before the announcement, the word ricocheting around the process was "ambition."

Ambition. If someone owned that word, they'd be rich given that the weeks of Biden VP-watch coverage revolved around just that notion. But ambition was embedded in the process. Always had been. From the moment Biden announced that he would choose a woman, female politicians were putting their names in the ring.

Most were names we'd heard for the last year: senators Elizabeth Warren, Amy Klobuchar, and Kamala Harris. Others were names Americans knew from four years earlier, like Ambassador Susan Rice. More were names Americans would come to know: Illinois senator Tammy Duckworth, Michigan governor Gretchen Whitmer, Florida congresswoman Val Demings, California representative Karen Bass, Atlanta mayor

Keisha Lance Bottoms, Georgia State Senate Democratic leader and activist Stacey Abrams, and former Deputy U.S. Attorney General Sally Yates, among them.

Tracking the movements, interviews, and non-answers from these women under the whimsical guise of "veepstakes" made the process sound far more fun than it was. Because this period on the campaign is possibly the most soul-sucking series of weeks (in this case, months) for any reporter, where the campaign is doing all it can to keep their pick a secret and where every reporter is tasked with teasing out ultimately meaningless nuggets about The Process—all the while knowing the pick will come out only when the campaign is good and ready to share it.

Because Biden wrapped up the nomination so early the former veep's timeline for picking his *own* veep was about three times longer than Hillary Clinton's roughly six-week period in 2016. That yawning gap meant lots of extra time for meaningless speculation as well as grimace-inducing sexism, both latent and blatant.

The process was also happening during a global pandemic, further shrouding it in mystery, while providing a built-in and mandatory distance for candidates from reporters. But even as the pandemic changed it, some traditions remained. Network embeds were still tasked, as ever, with staking out contenders' homes and apartments; charting coffee runs or walks with dogs; looking for any disruption of the ordinary that could tip off an impending pick. I warned some of the MSNBC team that no matter how diligent they were, no matter how many bathroom breaks they didn't take or how close to dawn they arrived for their stakeouts, this was a process structured to dupe them.

It had duped the best in previous races. Wisconsin congressman Paul Ryan escaped the NBC embed staking out his Janesville home in 2012 by leaving through his backyard and cutting a path through the woods to reach his getaway car. Virginia senator Tim Kaine dodged his embed press corps by sneaking off in a Volvo with top Clinton brass John Podesta, who picked him up after a fundraiser in Virginia. The embeds in both instances are still easily riled by memories of the evasions to this day.

But not all campaigns are so lucky to see their hijinks pay off.

In 2008, Obama's pick of Biden leaked to the media—negating a campaign promise that supporters who gave up their phone numbers would learn the pick first and forcing the campaign to scramble, sending a text message to backers about the pick at the prime-time hour of . . . 3 a.m. ET.

In July 2016, I showed up to fly from then-governor Mike Pence's home state of Indiana back to New York City only to find one of Pence's top campaign aides, Marc Lotter, also standing at the gate for DL3361. *Why was he there?* we all asked him, our voices laced with suspicion and skepticism. Lotter shrugged his shoulders and none-too-slyly pleaded "meetings," while seeming to relish the attention from top media figures, like CBS's Major Garrett, to the lowly network embeds, like NBC's Me. Once we boarded, took off, and ascended to a cruising altitude, every reporter on that plane ripped off their seat belt and brandished their phone, armed with the latest round of speculation that Pence was, indeed, The Pick.

"I can't confirm or deny," Lotter said from his window seat, the woman seated next to him understandably confused about what this man did to earn three phones in his face at 30,000 feet. When we landed, Lotter—who himself had once worked in local news—allowed us to deplane before him, slowly walking up the jet bridge so that we could bobble our cameras and our carry-ons while shooting b-roll footage of him, as benevolent a move as it was attention-earning. Once off the plane, another reporter surreptitiously followed Lotter's car from the airport to the hotel Pence would hole up in until the Trump campaign made it official . . . eventually leading all of us there with him.

But there were few staffers to ambush on flights or follow out of airports in 2020. Most of Biden's final-round meetings happened over Zoom, leaving no travel trail to follow. Michigan governor Gretchen Whitmer's flight from Lansing to Delaware for an in-person meeting was the lone bone thrown to the aviator geeks and VP-watchers of the D.C. press corps, who closely monitored flight tracker websites. That most of the Could-Be-Picks also lived in apartments in and around D.C.—with multiple entrances and out-of-sight garages—made the embeds' jobs even harder.

As for me—having graduated from embed stakeouts but still subjected to the pains of the veeps game—I exercised the patience I was not born with while keeping up with the gossip on who was up and who was down with my sources, all too nervous to talk on the record lest the Biden campaign view them as leaky but all wanting to talk in hushed tones while working from home so they could know . . . whatever there was to know. Restlessness on all sides set in when it became clear that Biden's self-imposed August 1st deadline to make his pick wasn't much of a deadline at all.

But the pandemic also meant that how the process transpired on TV—in our reporting, in the leaks from key staff, and in the way the potential picks presented themselves—mattered immensely, given TV and digital media were now the only safe ways to campaign and politically maneuver.

And so, the women made their ambitions and openness to being VP known both publicly on those platforms as well as in private. Not a new strategy, but novel in that we were seeing only women voice their interest—since only women were welcome to apply.

"That normalized the idea that women should say what they want and go after what they want," my friend and MSNBC colleague, Alicia Menendez, told me. "And the fact that there were so many of them doing it meant that nobody got individually dinged for self-promoting."

"Well, yes and no, right?" I replied, recounting for her the number of calls I had with operatives over those weeks who would say in hushed tones that *yes, all these women were great, but so-and-so or so-and-so was being "too much" in her public self-advocacy for the position.*

"Yes," Alicia allowed. "*And* I think most American women missed that sideshow and instead what they saw was a group of accomplished women who were comfortable saying, 'I have the qualifications, I will stand behind anyone you choose, but I believe I am the best.'"

Certainly, watching everyone from Elizabeth Warren to Stacey Abrams to Tammy Duckworth lay their qualifications down on the metaphorical table was a very public, very important embodiment of confident women confidently going after what they wanted and self-advocating. But there was also plenty to be concerned about. The way the news cycle fed off and ate up that same female ambition and confidence was, to me, the loudest part of the story.

It bubbled up the way most gossipy political tales do: in the web pages of *Politico*, sourced anonymously. In this case, from a donor relaying the comments of former senator Chris Dodd—a longtime Biden friend and member of the vice-presidential search committee who was in fact working against Kamala Harris's elevation. As the reporting goes, Dodd told donors he was stunned when he asked Harris, during vetting committee interviews, about the debate moment when she went after Joe on the busing issue. Harris laughed: "That's politics."

Dodd's views were coupled with those of another longtime Biden ally, Ed Rendell, who said that Harris could "rub people the wrong way," as well as some donors who told CNBC they were advising Biden against Harris because "she would be running for president the day of the inauguration" and "she seems not loyal at all and very opportunistic."

"I'm not speaking politically but, it's just so unfair," one of our anchors said to me on-air one Saturday morning in August as I rehashed the latest turn in the ambition story. "Because ya know, you have Joe Biden who had been running for president for twenty-seven years and when Barack Obama picked him nobody was saying, 'Oh he's ambitious, you can't pick him.' So gimme a break."

In fact, much of the coverage of Biden as Obama's chosen veep focused little on his two past presidential runs as a sign of how badly he wanted to be president and instead on how unthreatening he'd be to his future boss. "At his age," wrote *The New York Times*, "it appears unlikely that Mr. Biden would be in a position to run for president should Mr. Obama win and serve two terms. Shorn of any remaining ambition to run for president on his own, he could find himself in a less complex political relationship with Mr. Obama than most vice presidents have with their presidents."

After fellow Californian congresswoman Karen Bass was added to the veepstakes mix, the Kamala's-Too-Ambitious stories morphed from an indictment of Harris's character into a comparison of the two lawmakers. *Politico* deemed Bass "the anti–Kamala Harris," citing her work ethic and saying she "cringes at having her picture taken and is content to let others grab headlines." The outcry came quickly, both because these two Black women were being pitted against each other and for the insinuation that Bass wasn't ambitious or skilled in promoting her own political career (which she had to have been to rise as she had over her career in politics).

This was the louder part of the veepstakes news cycle, but there was plenty that never made it onto chyrons on cable. I'd heard similar whispers months earlier about another potential contender, Elizabeth Warren. The knock on her, these People Who Know would tell me, was that she didn't "go along to get along." Politically, it was baked into Warren's brand that she held her progressive ideals high—and held other Democrats who seemed to be falling short of them to account. That she could have sharp elbows, insanely high expectations, and too high a value placed on her own beliefs. But Warren had also been sharing her homework with Biden for months, strategizing on policy in phone calls since she dropped out and he became the presumptive standard bearer. He'd incorporated some of her policy goals, as well as those of Bernie Sanders, in attempts to show the left wing of the party he was listening and open to their ideas.

Warren was also raking in millions for Biden on the fundraising circuit, helping him tap into her massive network of grassroots, small-dollar donors while also shouldering the round of negative headlines that came as she began doing traditional closed-door fundraisers with high-dollar donors—the kinds she banned herself from doing during her own presidential run. Those close to Warren would point to these moves as those of a good soldier, committed to this "righteous fight" against Trump. But did having her own political and policy style mean she couldn't be the kind of "simpatico" governing partner that Biden desired?

Stacey Abrams also suffered the ambition catch-22. When she declined to run herself for president in 2019, rumors abounded on the trail that she would be Biden's vice president should he become the nominee. There was excitement around her prospects but grumbling when she forcefully came forward about wanting the VP job. In May of 2020, Abrams told *CBS Sunday Morning* that she "absolutely" held running for president among her future ambitions. "And even more importantly," she said, "when someone asks me if that's my ambition, I have a responsibility to say 'Yes.' For every young woman, every person of color, who sees me and decides what they're capable of based on what I think I'm capable of." Not the usual politician's method of dealing with these kinds of questions, but Abrams said, "It's about, you cannot have those things you refuse to dream."

As VP season wore on, Abrams fell lower down the list. Asked if she felt she'd been punished for being so open about her ambitions, she said in an interview, "I do think that there was some unnecessary critique, but I don't think it's unexpected. When you do something different, when you meet the standards that are normative for men, with the behavior that they don't expect from you either as a woman or a person of color, then you're going to get critiqued. But my responsibility is to hear it and not only hear what people are saying but understand what they mean."

Somehow during what should have been an empowering process, the thinking emerged from small circles with loud voices that because some of these women had openly campaigned for president themselves or cultivated strong and distinct political brands of their own, they would be too concerned with their own futures to be an effective partner to Biden. Or they would shine too brightly, or have too strong a political brand, or make decisions with their own political futures in mind. Overtly ambitious acts were deemed somehow too political, too beyond the pale, and too risky. Signs that betrayed how much they wanted to be president, as opposed to examples that they could successfully attack the opposing GOP ticket or defend the nominee during the upcoming general election battle. Yet if they hadn't advocated for themselves, they could have lost out on the opportunity to leverage an increased national profile and moment to spotlight their issues and political platform. The women were expected to simultaneously self-advocate and defend against criticisms for that self-advocacy.

Ambition was the perfect, loaded word with which to wreak havoc in this environment.

"You'd rarely, if ever, call a white man too ambitious. If you did, I've seen few examples where it would torpedo his career," my colleague Alicia said. "You use that word to describe a woman and it becomes 'she's ruthless, she'll do anything, there must be something inherently wrong with her to want what she wants so badly.' Ambitious is an indictment of a woman's character in a way it's not of a man."

All these snapshots lent to a feeling that the Biden campaign's talk about wanting the process to "elevate" the women's profiles wasn't exactly manifesting as such in the press, in part due to some of their own people inside the process. They talked about wanting a governing partner, but the women in contention for the role also seemed constrained in being able to tout their governing skills or policy chops or political prowess too publicly lest that mire them in a negative feedback loop among Biden advisors or in media circles. Or, as Deepa put it to me over text: "We want you to be ready but only in secret and only when we say you're allowed to be ready."

Meanwhile, in terms of making the actual pick, months of deliberation and vetting hadn't changed the fact that all roads seemed to lead back to Kamala. The man who'd been a VP for eight years reiterated his criteria multiple times during his months of deliberation: a governing partner, someone "simpatico" with him, who can have a similar relationship to the one he had with Barack Obama. Harris, despite "the busing moment" still sticking with some advisors, ticked all those boxes. At times, the search seemed to go on despite her unofficial status as the front-runner. And especially once the summer of 2020 became a reckoning on race after the murder of George Floyd by Minneapolis police officer Derek Chauvin and the police shooting of Breonna Taylor in her own home, the already vocal pleas from Black activists about the need to elevate a woman of color were nearly impossible to ignore.

In taking herself out of VP contention in June (when scrutiny of her time as Hennepin County Attorney was hitting a fever pitch), Senator Amy Klobuchar said: "America must seize on the moment, and I truly believe, as I actually told [Biden] last night when I called him, that I think this is a moment to put a woman of color on the ticket." Those of us reading the tea leaves saw the implications immediately, both in favor of women of color like Harris or Rice, but also cutting against Klobuchar's old 2020 rival, Warren. That felt, at least, like politics as usual at a time when little else did.

And maybe the ambition news cycle was familiar, too. The same version of what we'd seen before, but in a new spotlight and with a new answer.

Because to rise in politics, all candidates have to have it. Hell, to run for any office in the first place requires immense energy, intense focus, a lot of ambition, and, yes, the *ego* to believe that you're the best person for the job and willing to campaign that way. Politicians don't rise and climb on the national political stage by accident; they strive and campaign and scheme for it even as they work to build a policy and political resumé to bolster their case.

Congresswoman Karen Bass didn't just wake up one day as speaker of the California House during the governorship of celebrity-turned-GOP-politician Arnold Schwarzenegger. Senator Kamala Harris didn't accidentally chart a path that broke barriers from district attorney to attorney general to hotly anticipated presidential candidate. Senator Elizabeth Warren didn't walk out of a Harvard classroom one day and into one of the Senate's most competitive seats the next. Stacey Abrams didn't just show up to challenge Brian Kemp for Georgia governor not once, but twice, without first climbing the ladder of state politics in a traditionally red state. They set an intention to get into those roles, to insert themselves into these spaces, to campaign as prepared and qualified—in many cases, as the first of their kind. Call it chutzpah, guts, persistence—it's all a manifestation of ambition.

It's what made Kamala Harris stand up (or rather, sit down, on Zoom) at the pinnacle of the ambition news cycle and say that this was the kind of blowback she grew up being warned about. Quoting her mother, as she often did, Harris spoke plainly to a group of Black female leaders, all seated in their virtual chat boxes, as the moderator asked her about navigating the predominantly white male political space.

"It has happened my entire career. My entire career. You know, where people, they literally look at you like *how dare you* literally walk in a room, and challenge your very existence. And challenge you when you exercise your authority. Where people would like to go to a place of thinking that *you are out of your lane* or that *you're uppity* or *you need to go back to your place*. My mother, again, she had many sayings." Harris had the edge in her voice that came when she was speaking plainly, almost literally cutting through the noise.

"And one of them she told me years ago. She said, 'Honey'—and I'm saying this to all you young ladies—'people will be fine when you take what they give you. But oh, don't take more.' " She paused as one moderator silently snapped in appreciation of the point.

"I say that to say: there will be resistance to your ambition. There will be people who say you are out of your lane. 'Cause they are burdened by only having the capacity to see what has always been, instead of what can be. But don't you let that burden *you*."

Harris wasn't asked about the ambition news cycle directly that day, but it was hard to see her words as anything but a rare, strong rebuke of the political landscape she was at the center of. And the advice she offered was as much for the women receiving it as it told a story about how Kamala Harris overcame moments of sexism or racism before.

"When you walk in that room and you're the only one that looks like you—and you will have many, many times that happens. It has happened to me many, many times. When you walk in that conference room or boardroom, or courtroom, and you're the only person who looks like you, one of the things you must remember is we are all in that room with you."

On August 19th, Kamala Harris walked into a very quiet room in Wilmington, Delaware, with the aspirations of all the women of ambition who ever dared to try alongside her. The woman whose own presidential campaign logo nodded to Shirley Chisholm—the first Black woman who announced she was running for president only to have people laugh at her in response—was now stepping into uncharted territory; a woman of Black and South Asian descent, accepting the Democratic Party's nomination for vice president of the United States.

She made this history in a near-silent room with roughly two dozen reporters seated in front of her in socially distanced chairs separated by pylons with state names emblazoned on them. I was one of them, finding my place between Indiana, Oklahoma, Arkansas, and Northern Mariana Islands. At a normal, non-pandemic convention, these pylons would be foisted high above heads by raucous convention-goers who punctuated each point of Harris's speech with applause. Ferraro recalled this moment even decades later, "stunned by the reception" and remembering the women in the crowd who cried with her elevation. She told her daughters, "Whatever you do, don't cry, because we can't. Women can't cry over these things. It's too emotional and it's a tough job and you have to be tough to be vice president." When Ferraro announced herself, the convention center went wild, ushering her into the history books.

But now, there were no cheering crowds punctuating Harris's historic moment. There was only us: temperature-checked, COVID-tested three days in a row, and now settling into the heavy air thick with historic significance. My footsteps made no sound as I walked onto the plush blue carpeting, sat down, and arranged my various tech items on my lap, making sure anything that could make noise was silenced so that a rogue text from my excited parents wouldn't ding Harris's moment.

Hours earlier, I'd joked with friends that this was the week where all of Biden's decades of ambition had finally paid off. Now, I got to see Harris on full display and bearing fruit. Just like in South Carolina, I heard her before I could see her, the steady *click click click* of her heels announcing her to the stage.

They laughed at Shirley Chisholm so that Kamala Harris could be taken seriously. And now, she had to be.

12

"Just Not That Woman"

What Hillary Learned

SEPTEMBER 2020

Fifty days out from Election Day should've been an all-out sprint.

There should've been throngs of cheering people waiting shoulder to shoulder in the crisp fall air to hear the candidates give some variation of the same speech three or four or five times per day. There should've been the traditional get-out-the-vote efforts, volunteers fanning out over every neighborhood, in every swing district, in every battleground state. For reporters there should've been less *zzz*'s caught, less salad (or anything green, for that matter) munched, and definitely no time spent at home.

And yet, here I was. At my kitchen table, sporting my Evening Lulu-lemon Pants (not to be confused with my Workout Pants or my Daytime Lounge attire), I clicked my way into a night of virtual campaign coverage. Wine in hand, I balanced my laptop on my thighs and waited for some of the world's most powerful faces to assume their Zoom boxes.

VP-nominee Kamala Harris, former secretary of state Hillary Clinton, and their *Saturday Night Live* doppelgangers, Maya Rudolph and Amy Poehler, gathering with supporters on this mid-September evening for a virtual fundraiser only accessible with a donation of $1 or more. Taking a long sip of Syrah, I realized this was the most relaxing campaign event I'd ever covered.

But Hillary Clinton was here on a mission. Though she came armed with a witty joke to lighten the increasingly dire mood these kinds of events had taken on since the pandemic started, she was also here with a warning for Kamala Harris ahead of the first and only vice-presidential debate: *watch your back.* Few understood the dynamics of a debate stage—and the ways gender subconsciously manifested in each moment—as well as Clinton did. Among the indelible moments of 2016 was Donald Trump looming behind her, scowling, during an October town hall debate. The moment earned backlash for Trump, with former Republican operative Nicolle Wallace saying, "If a man did that to me on the street . . . I'd call 911."

But Trump's hypermasculinity cut both ways. I'd meet voters after the debate at Trump events who saw it as a moment of Clinton getting "owned" by Trump; a sign of his strength and power; a real-time embodiment of the buttons sold by vendors at Trump rallies that advertised "Trump that bitch."

But now, four years later, it wasn't the debate stage with Trump that Clinton was worried about. Harris versus Pence was simultaneously the most essential, critical, must-win night in politics and also the least consequential event of the entire campaign. Anything short of perfection would surely threaten to tank the entire presidential endeavor; and any perfect breakthrough moment would die on the vine within a few hours on Twitter, after first spiking small-dollar donations. Then, the sound bite would settle into its rightful place on the dusty shelf of VP Debate Zingers Past, alongside Lloyd Bentsen telling Dan Quayle, "You're no Jack Kennedy."

In a pre-debate-night story my colleagues and I crafted for NBCNews .com, presidential historian Michael Beschloss said, "Vice presidential debates oftentimes get a lot of attention at the moment, and then a few days later they're forgotten." But, he allowed, "this year it may be different."

The biggest differentiating factor in 2020 was that presidential fallibility was front and center, the pandemic and the age of both Trump and Biden thrusting the ever-present possibility that the VPOTUS could become the POTUS farther into the realm of reality. Unlike during the Obama years, or even the Bush years, it didn't require a lot of imagination to see this happening. For Pence, those stakes had risen the moment President Trump went into the hospital after getting COVID-19—a shocking, and simultaneously entirely predictable, twist to the election saga. For Harris, running alongside a man who would boast the title of Oldest Man to Ever Be Sworn In as President forced voters to imagine her as someone who could, at some point, also be sworn in as his replacement.

For both Pence and Harris, gender and race were guardrails they were prepped to make the most of and also primed to avoid. Over in Pence World, we reported that the VP's mostly white, mostly male inner circle broadened out the prep circle to include more female advisors. Those involved in the process told my White House colleagues at the time that there was an emphasis on the importance of a respectful tone. Or, put more bluntly by an ally: VP Pence was being cautioned "not to attack a woman."

Pence's concerns were not unlike those of the last Republican man tasked with taking on a female vice-presidential opponent. George H. W. Bush's 1984 debate with Geraldine Ferraro was the first time Americans saw a man and a woman spar on the debate stage. Bush knew he had to be careful, commanding the stage without looking "like he was beating up a woman," according to Peter Baker and Susan Glasser's book *The Man Who Ran Washington*. "If he pounded too hard, it might generate sympathy for her."

Despite this awareness, Bush did not tread lightly. Pushing back on a foreign policy point, he said, "Let me help you with the difference, Mrs. Ferraro, between Iran and the embassy in Lebanon." Nowadays we'd call that tone a mansplain. Back then, Ferraro just called it a "patronizing attitude." The day after the debate, Bush offered a review of his performance over a meeting with longshoremen in New Jersey. "We tried to kick a little ass last night," he said, unleashing a new round of criticism for sexism in the press. Years later, George W. Bush would write in his dad's biography that H.W. and Ferraro later became friends. In a letter toward the end of her life, the elder Bush wrote to her: "I often think of our strange and wonderful relationship, and I hope you know that I consider you a real friend."

That Pence and his team were even considering how his masculinity might cut against him on the stage marked a departure from Trump, well-known for trading in sexism and racism to attack his opponents. Belittling one-time 2016 primary opponent Carly Fiorina for her looks ("Can you imagine that, the face of our next president?"); declaring that Hillary Clinton lacked the "strength and stamina" to be president; and reviving the same birtherism lies he tried to weaponize against Barack Obama by saying Kamala Harris "doesn't qualify because she wasn't born in this country" even though she was very much born in California, USA.

Pence was different. The former Indiana governor had proven himself a loyal, if sometimes off-brand, messenger for his boss's agenda, sticking to the Trumpian line right up to the moment that line threatened to blow up the very democracy presidents swear to protect. Even after he narrowly escaped an angry mob of pro-Trump insurrectionists who stormed the Capitol and hoped for the chance to "hang Mike Pence" on January 6, 2021, it took the former VP more than a year to directly rebuke his old boss about that day. Prompted by Trump's January 2022 claim that "he could have overturned the election!" Pence responded, "President Trump is wrong."

Speaking at a gathering of the conservative Federalist Society in Florida in February 2022, he continued: "Under the Constitution, I had no right to change the outcome of our election, and Kamala Harris will have no right to overturn the election when we beat them in 2024." Though he'd defended his role on January 6th before and said he didn't think he and Trump would "ever see eye to eye on that day," it was a clear break on an issue that had become a litmus test in the Republican Party.

But over the years Pence had been at Trump's side, his personification of the America First agenda was radically different from his boss's—which is what the Harris team was concerned about. Pence, a skilled debater, preached the MAGA Gospel in dulcet monotones. And as a powerful, practiced white man in politics, it would take a lot for Americans to see him as *too shrill* or *too aggressive* or *too ambitious* on the debate stage. Even though it was well-known that he had presidential aspirations of his own.

Pence would work to "subtly undercut Kamala," Clinton predicted that night on Zoom. He'd try to "put her in the box of the inexperienced woman candidate. And she's not going to stand for that."

But even in not standing for it, there had to be a strategy. Harris would "have to modulate her responses," Clinton advised. "Because we know there's still a double standard alive and well when it comes to women in politics." Be "firm and effective," but "do it in a way that doesn't scare or alienate voters," she said.

This was already front of mind for Harris's team. Their top concern, a senior advisor told me, was that Pence would try to "make her into an angry Black woman." Toeing the line between calling Pence out on the actions of his boss and ensuring that he didn't look, in the words of this advisor, "like the victim or the martyr" was Harris's task. To do that, Harris practiced commanding the stage without being off-putting to voters while also cramming on binders full of Biden's record: three decades worth of policy positions that spanned the Senate, three presidential bids, and eight years in the White House. His record was hers to defend now, along with her own.

And historic potential loomed over it all, fueling Kamala as much as it could hurt her. She wasn't just defending politics and policy amid a seemingly insurmountable pandemic; she was also tasked with constructing the image of a biracial, female vice president in real time for voters' consideration. Clinton knew the power of being the first, but she also knew the drawbacks.

"We've never had a woman vice president. We've never had a Black or Asian vice president. She was really the one who was going to figure out how to navigate through this difficult time," Clinton told me months after that campaign Zoom. "And if you go online, there is so much vitriol filled about her, so many attacks directed against her, and they rarely, if ever, are rooted in anything other than misogyny, racism, and sexism."

Clinton's no stranger to vitriol and attacks—partisan and otherwise.

"I'm aware of how they insidiously undermine a person," she said. "And if it's a woman, that job is slightly easier because for whatever combination of biological or historic reasons people are slightly more inclined to believe lies about women. It goes back to the Salem Witch Trials and further back than that."

Hunkered down in prep, Harris workshopped responses to anticipated lines of attack and held mock sessions, always keeping the index cards she used for practice—an old habit from her law school years—close at hand. Opposite her in the mock debate sessions was former rival and South Bend mayor Pete Buttigieg, who assumed the role of his fellow Hoosier, Mike Pence, with an actor's skill that was ultimately described as so spot-on "it was kind of creepy, actually."

All of this lent credence to Clinton's biggest piece of advice to Harris that night on Zoom: "You've gotta have almost 360-degree awareness. As I found in 2016 with Trump, he could have cared less about answering the questions or even giving accurate information. He came prepared to insult, to bully, to loom over."

The 2016 election was not decided on gender above all else. Hillary Clinton isn't in the presidential annals of history only "because sexism." The 2016 results actually tell the story of a country where the majority of American voters *were* finally ready to elect a woman to that position, and voted that way. The reasons for her loss—from a lack of attention to Michigan and Wisconsin, to Trump's powerful harnessing of economic and social "populist" grievances, to Russia's meddling, to the timing of public statements and investigations by James Comey—have been well-litigated. But gender permeated all those explanations, too. Even the most widespread explanation—that Hillary was such a specific and special case—must consider that a good portion of the baggage she carried, that contributed to the mistrust and dislike of her, was *another* Clinton's. That's a yoke no male candidate has been asked to carry. Her gender is both the chicken and the egg; you cannot think or talk or report on or vote for

Hillary Clinton without acknowledging the role it has always played in branding and defining her.

"Constantly having to answer for her husband, I think, for an accomplished woman, is the ultimate dismissal," a Democratic strategist with ties to the Clintons told me. "Were there moments of sexism? . . . Sure. I actually believe the reason she lost is because people were more exhausted by the notion of Bill Clinton and the [Clinton] Foundation, and the problems and the connections that would be too much to bear." Those were, they said, "the essence of the Comey investigations." To this person, "had [Bill] not been in that situation, that would not have occurred."

Bill Clinton was, of course, an ever-present theme in the story of Hillary. As was the sexist undercurrent that dogged her as a part of his narrative. In 1978, during Bill's first run for governor of Arkansas, her decision not to take his last name "was in the forefront" of the campaign. In 1992, during her husband's first presidential run, she was pilloried by women's groups for an unartfully phrased comment that she "could have stayed home and baked cookies and had teas, but what I decided to do was fulfill my profession." Once in the White House, she was viewed skeptically for her role as both spouse and policy advisor.

Later, it was her decision to stay with her husband after his affair with Monica Lewinsky, though leaving would've brought with it its own criticisms. Throughout 2016, I met voters who couldn't forget—and who saw that very personal situation as a reflection of how she'd govern. "If she can't take care of her husband," I'll never forget being asked by several female voters, "how can she take care of the country?" And those comments were tame compared to the gross T-shirts sold by vendors outside Trump rallies that read, HILLARY SUCKS, BUT NOT LIKE MONICA.

All decisions made in public view have ramifications. There is always a damned-if-you-do, damned-if-you-don't aspect to politics, but this felt next level. Especially as her husband, the man who'd created this problem, was able to recover and go on as a force in Democratic politics—at least until the #MeToo movement forced a new reckoning over his past.

That's not to say there weren't also moments of triumph.

Clinton captured the world's attention by declaring at the September 1995 United Nations Conference on Women that "women's rights are human rights and human rights are women's rights." Her time in the Senate proved her bipartisan legislating chops. Her time leading the State Department solidified her brand as a competent diplomat and viral feminist icon, most notably through a blog called "texts with Hillary." Her doing the job brought with it some of the highest approval ratings of any other person in her party. That she'd accepted the role in the Obama administration in the first place showcased her ability to subsume her own political ambitions and ego to the man who'd beaten her for the nomination several months earlier.

Clinton watched the political world contend with complex female figures taking up space in powerful rooms firsthand, from the moment she arrived in Washington. The same 1992 election that heralded the first Clinton term was also the first "year of the woman"—four women were elected to the Senate in the same year, bringing the grand total to a mere six out of one hundred. Clinton saw the shift in real time then, hoping that we wouldn't need any more "years of the woman," but knowing better.

"Those of us who would like to retire that phrase know that we still have work to do," she told me. "That there's going to be a constant pressure needed to keep electing women."

Clinton noted the recent strides made within both parties, Republicans more slowly and still in smaller numbers than Democrats, while also expanding the bounds of what it means to be electable.

"There's a range of women now running for office, being elected to office, [who] I think have stretched the whole concept of 'electable,' " Clinton said. "A woman holding an assault rifle twenty years ago probably would not have been elected, but now, in certain parts of our country, that makes her more electable."

She was right, of course. Both about the expanding view of electability on the right, but also that the assault rifle might be a more powerful sell to a conservative electorate than the fact that it was a woman holding it.

It's essential to note that the permission structures at play in conservative circles around conservative women are different from those applied on the Democratic side, mostly due to the reluctance or, more often, downright distaste at playing "identity politics."

One 2020 psychology study entitled "When Racism and Sexism Benefit Black and Female Politicians" probed the ways conservative voters—who are less concerned than their Democratic counterparts with gender and race egalitarianism in politics—engage with minority and female candidates. The study found that while a conservative candidate's gender and race matter, a candidate's ideology trumps their demographics. "Ideology moderates prejudice's effect more than politician's demographic background," in the words of the study's author. For instance, using candidates from the 2016 Republican primary, they found "respondents who score high on racism and sexism measures are more likely to view conservative politicians favorably, even if the politicians are Black (i.e., [Ben] Carson) or female (i.e., [Carly] Fiorina)."

For minority and female candidates competing in the conservative space, there is less explicit focus on their gender and a bucking of "identity politics," but there's also an onus on them to assure voters that despite their gender or racial identity, they are still in line with the party's ideology on those issues. It's one possible explanation for why we see women and candidates of color on the extreme flanks of the GOP ascend to its highest positions of official and unofficial power. As if an essential part of their successful sell comes from showing they don't hold bias on issues like reproductive rights or equal pay or affirmative action.

Think, for instance, of Tennessee senator Marsha Blackburn, a "hard-right firebrand" who rose from state senate, to multiple terms in the U.S. House, and finally to a U.S. Senate seat by establishing herself as a mainstay on the rightmost wing of the party, campaigning on small-government ideology paired with the culture wars of the moment—from bolstering the birtherism conspiracy against Obama, to allying with Donald Trump, to incendiary statements about abortion that cemented her among both parties as a staunch anti-abortion advocate. During one congressional battle over funding Planned Parenthood, Blackburn charged that they were "selling baby body parts on demand" and alleged they tried to illegally profit from selling fetal tissue—which they denied. Interestingly, the fiery anti-abortion rhetoric dissipated when she ran for Senate in 2018 against a popular moderate Democrat to replace an otherwise moderate Republican retiring from the seat. She won the seat, one of the nation's most-watched contests that cycle, with a tempered conservative message built upon years of street cred with the party's hyper-conservative base.

It reshapes politics to have this range of paradigms. It gives the next wave of women looking to move into the House or Senate more examples of how. And moving into 2024, Republicans, just like Democrats, will continue remolding this space at the congressional, statewide, and yes, presidential level. Former South Carolina governor Nikki Haley and South Dakota governor Kristi Noem are both mulling potential bids. But if or when they make that decision, they'll—admit it, like it, mention it or not—follow in the footsteps of Hillary Clinton.

Clinton did more to begin reshaping what leaders can look like in America than almost any other figure in modern politics. In the same way that Ferraro cleared a path into presidential politics for female candidates, Clinton showed that path could lead to success. Or, fall just shy of it. Just as Julián Castro posited that "to be groundbreaking is usually to lose," Clinton did not get to fully reap the benefits of that work—at least not at the highest level. Women in the public eye still walk a tightrope, but when America was first truly forced to grapple with Hillary in the 1990s, as I was growing up, it seemed as if she fell off the high wire a lot. It took until I was older to realize she was being pushed off a lot, too.

By 2020, though, she was using all she'd learned and all we'd collectively seen to push back and hold other women steady.

"I wanted the audiences that I was talking to through my podcasts [in 2020], through the events that I did during the campaign, to be on guard so that they could speak up for [Kamala Harris]," Clinton told me after the 2020 election was all said and won. "So that they could be in alliance with her as she charted a path nobody's ever charted before."

But there were more lessons than just Hillary's. Americans had seen two women run for president in the decade prior to Clinton—Elizabeth Dole as a Republican in 2000 and Senator Carol Moseley Braun as a Democrat in 2004. Neither woman was a stranger to clearing new paths; both were the only women in their field of primary contenders. And both became stories of firsts falling short.

Elizabeth Dole announced her 2000 presidential bid against the backdrop of a Republican Party desperate to retake the White House after two terms of Bill Clinton and a country still roiled by the Lewinsky scandal. The GOP pitched a return to family values and to integrity. But Dole also came in at a supposedly prime moment for female candidates. A Gallup poll at the time found 92 percent of Americans would vote for "a well-qualified presidential candidate who happened to be a woman." (We should note that when the same poll asked, "Everything else being equal, who do you think would make the better president?" 42 percent said a man, 31 percent said a woman, and 22 percent said they did not care. "Those who said a man would be a better president most often cited the ability to control their emotions, the tradition of male presidents, and the ability to make decisions were factors in their choice," according to a CNN article at the time.)

Married to Bob Dole—who had, himself, run for president thrice and been nominated once by the GOP—the woman affectionately known as "Liddy" benefited from national name recognition and deep connections within the party. She'd served multiple presidents, from Federal Trade Commission member under President Richard Nixon to "a lieutenant in Ronald Reagan's army" as a White House staffer and later the first woman to head the Department of Transportation.

All that, plus a resumé of service and a tenure atop the American Red Cross, spurred *The Washington Post* to write of her bid: "Her well-known name and national reputation made her the most formidable woman ever to run for the White House."

When she entered the race, polls suggested she was a front-runner alongside then–Texas governor George W. Bush—also the beneficiary of a well-known political last name and an impressive resumé. Dole let her gender operate in the background, interweaving her identity as *part* of her narrative as opposed to a top selling point of her candidacy. In another *Washington Post* report from the campaign trail in 1999, this one entitled "Dole Crafts Strategy to Close Gender Gap," they wrote: "From her appearance (painted nails, high heels and pearl chokers) to her rhetoric ('What does a woman like me have to offer the country?') Dole is capitalizing on her most obvious asset: She is the only woman in a Republican lineup that currently includes nine men. With the weight of history upon her as the first truly viable female presidential candidate, Dole is taking a calculated risk. She is attempting to craft a political persona that exploits the advantages of her gender but does not rely solely on that fact to woo voters."

GOP pollster Tony Fabrizio described Dole's challenge and opportunity to the *Post* at the time. "There is a huge opportunity there for bridging the gender gap," he said. "Meeting the challenge of that opportunity is kind of tricky. The question is can you make it through the primaries without alienating those swing female voters who may be looking for a reason to vote for you?"

This is the needle oft threaded by female conservatives, speaking to what's visible while also not being co-opted by it with an electorate that isn't focused on identity politics first. Dole herself spoke to this in a 1999 interview, saying, "I'm not running because I'm a woman, and I don't expect people to vote for me because I'm a woman." Yet on the trail she celebrated taking over the male-dominated ("male bastion") Transportation Department or succeeding despite power structures not built for the success of ambitious, smart women.

Years later, former Hewlett-Packard CEO and 2016 presidential candidate Carly Fiorina picked up on this thread talking to me for this project: "I think the goal in our nation is a meritocracy. We're a long way from that goal. . . . but I've often said, if you want diversity then create a real meritocracy and diverse candidates will rise to the top." This conclusion stood side by side, and in competition with, her other summation of the experience of running as a qualified female candidate: "It's different when you're different."

"On the one hand, many think Republicans will be first to elect a woman president," she told me, echoing a theory that multiple Democrats, including Hillary Clinton, also lent credence to. "But polling shows they're not thinking about it like 'oh yeah, we wanna elect the first woman.' They're not hoping for it."

It's a key difference between the two major parties, both for candidates and their voters. Candidates in both parties need to meet ideological benchmarks to be taken seriously by their party's bases, but Republican hopefuls tend to subsume gender and identity to their larger platform while Democrats, and their voters, consider it at the foreground. Republican voters rarely, if ever, have expressed to me that they're making decisions based on a candidate's demographic profile, yet I met voters constantly while following Democrats who said they were drawn toward "the women" in the race. Those same Democratic voters also fretted about whether those same women in the race were electable—forcing one to question whether the downside to being "woke" to systemic gender and racial barriers also caused the electorate here to manifest them into continuity.

For Dole's campaign, the biggest difference ended up being a difference in dollars before voters could even have their say. Despite strong showings in the polls and at key points in the race, including a top-three finish in an August straw poll in Iowa that garnered attention, an inability to fundraise the cash she needed—as well as organizational issues—felled her bid, less than a year after it started.

But research later found another difference, one that we've seen before in these pages: that even though she was considered a front-runner—often in one of the field's top three positions—her media coverage lagged. Though she was consistently running second to George W. Bush, and polls also showed her beating Vice President Al Gore in general-election head-to-heads, a 2000 Rutgers study found Bush was mentioned in 72.9 percent of all the articles they examined that spanned the seven-month period she was in the race. John McCain earned mentions in 33 percent of the coverage. Dole was mentioned in only 19.7 percent, or one in five.

Among the explanations for that reality explored by the researchers was that media bias could be informed by the sex of the reporters. "Men and women may dial their telephones the same way, type on their word processors the same way, and organize their stories similarly," the study quoted, "but men and women often see different things while on assignment." News judgment requires the judgment that something, or someone, is important enough to be considered newsy, after all. Other studies show that female reporters were more likely than their male counterparts to cover female candidates, as well as more likely to rely on female sources.

Dole's presidential bid failed, but it further elevated her national profile. She went on to serve one term in the U.S. Senate, becoming the first woman elected from North Carolina in 2002, and remains steadfast in public service even now.

Carol Moseley Braun was a barrier-breaker, too: the first African American woman elected to the Senate in 1992's "year of the woman," focusing her candidacy then, just as other Democratic women running did, around the need for diversity in the body evidenced by the Anita Hill hearings in front of an all-white, all-male Judiciary Committee.

Upon being sworn in, Moseley Braun said, "I cannot escape the fact that I come to the Senate as a symbol of hope and change, nor would I want to. Because my presence in and of itself will change the U.S. Senate."

It did—in ways intended and accidental, it would turn out.

"I had no idea there was . . . an unwritten rule in the Senate about women not wearing pants," she recalled in a 2017 interview. "And I came to work one day. I thought I was all decked out in this nice pantsuit. You know? I thought I looked good. And everybody started whispering and whispering. I was like, 'What's going on here?' Well, it turned out this was a big deal and it actually made the newspapers that I had worn pants on the Senate floor . . . And that was shock. Shock! Oh, this is terrible. She broke protocol. But the good thing was that some of the Senate staffers then insisted on the right to wear pants to work, too. They said, 'Well, the senator is wearing pants, so why can't I?' And so, it was like, yes, this makes sense. This is a good thing."

Of her tenure in Congress, Moseley Braun recalled working across the aisle with other women—"we were forced into bipartisanship because we were such a minority"—carpooling to the Senate or gathering at Senator Barbara Mikulski's apartment to discuss issues, creating their own, small women's group within the nation's most impermeable Boys' Club. But she also saw a gender-based focus in the issues she was expected to take on, just as candidates like Gillibrand and Castro did.

"I mean, you're expected to have warm fuzzies on any issues having to do with children, any issue having to do with domestic concerns," she said in that same 2017 interview. "Even though we will say, you know, 'every issue is a women's issue,' which, of course, it is, if you act like you want to talk about taxes or financial matters or foreign policy, they look at you like, you know, what are you doing here? You know, it's like you just stepped out of your place, again."

Moseley Braun served only one term in the Senate but returned to the national stage in 2003 after a stint as ambassador to New Zealand during the Clinton administration. After months of exploring a run, she launched her presidential bid at the famed historically Black college Howard University in Washington, D.C., highlighting, among other things, her historic potential—just as Chisholm did before her and just as Harris would do after.

"Just last week, my little nine-year-old niece Claire called me into her room to show me her social studies book," Moseley Braun said. "Turning to the pages on which all of our Presidents were pictured, she looked at me and complained: 'But Auntie Carol, all the Presidents are boys!' "

It was hard not to draw a line between Moseley Braun's words then and Klobuchar's riff about not being able to play the game "name your favorite female president" in 2020.

"I want Claire, and your daughters and sons, to know that in America," she finished, "everyone has a chance to serve and contribute. I believe that America is ready to take the next great step in the direction of her most noble ideals of service and merit and equality."

Just as the media would surmise about Kamala Harris nearly twenty years later, Moseley Braun was talked about as someone who could do well in South Carolina—despite not having paid staff on the ground there when she announced—with reports citing her race and the heavily Black Democratic electorate there. If only she could make it to that point in the calendar. Her campaign struggled to fundraise and build out a long-lasting infrastructure, especially compared to the top-tier candidates in the race that season. She dropped out before votes were cast.

Though Dole and Moseley Braun expanded the space just by being in it, their short-lived candidacies that ended before any votes were cast also meant that when Hillary Clinton announced her presidential bid in 2007, Americans had gone twenty-four years—since 1984 with Mondale and Ferraro—without even having to *entertain* voting for a woman from one of the two major parties when they looked at their ballot. It wasn't even a question of if they *would*; they weren't even given the option.

In the 2008 cycle, Clinton was the lone woman in a field of Barack Obama, Joe Biden, John Edwards, Bill Richardson, and others, figuring out, as Dole had years earlier, what it meant to run as female and a front-runner from early on. What her campaign placed a premium on was a run that showcased masculine leadership metrics. The commander-in-chief test was consistently front and center: framing her candidacy around strength and experience, asking voters who they trusted to answer the phone at 3 a.m. in case of crisis, and highlighting her extensive D.C. know-how while also calling out Obama's relative lack thereof. But the campaign struggled over how to meet masculine ideals of presidential leadership in an authentic way that also allowed Hillary to showcase a wider range of emotion and softness. Because even with their framing of the race, the feminine still needed to be present somewhere.

Gail Sheehy, who chronicled Hillary for years, wrote of the 2008 Clinton campaign in *Vanity Fair*: "[Hillary's chief strategist Mark] Penn did not appreciate the strength of her character as a woman. He and Bill Clinton insisted that she not run as a woman. They ran her as tougher than any man. They also put her out in front as her own attack dog, never an appealing role for a candidate, and one that Senator Obama's surrogates played for him. In the losing rounds of the five-month primary season, Hillary loyalists repeatedly challenged Obama's manhood, openly proclaiming to reporters that she was 'the only candidate with the testicular fortitude to be president.' "

That's not to say the parts of her orbit who advocated a softer side didn't also get their moments—however spontaneous. After being bested by Obama in Iowa by a significant margin, Clinton decamped to New Hampshire. During a campaign stop at a coffee shop in Portsmouth, a woman asked Clinton how she remained upbeat in the face of a tough campaign. "It's not easy," Clinton admitted, her voice uncharacteristically shaky and tears coming to her eyes. "And I couldn't do it if I just didn't passionately believe it was the right thing to do. You know, I have so many opportunities from this country. I just don't wanna see us fall backwards. You know, so . . . this is very personal for me."

In the Obama camp, both the candidate and his top advisors saw the moment as humanizing, honest, and disarming. Which is to say: potentially troublesome for their prospects. Some in the media saw it that way, too, and praised it as "dignified." Others posited that it was all an act, a calculated cry to spur a massive shift in strategy for a campaign in need of a save. Some saw in it a modern version of Ed Muskie's tearful response to nasty commentary about him and his wife in the *Manchester Union Leader* in 1972—a moment widely believed to have ended his campaign, while also showcasing the unfair gender stereotypes projected onto male candidates (that have thankfully waned for men in recent years). Others feared it would be Clinton's Pat Schroeder moment, harkening back to the former Colorado congresswoman breaking down during a speech announcing she would not run for president in 1987. Schroeder was parodied and decades later, she was still plagued by that memory, telling *USA Today*: "I want to say, 'Wait a minute, we are talking about 20 years ago.' It's like I ruined their lives, 20 years ago, with three seconds of catching my breath." The danger of crying, especially while female and seeking power, was well-known. Even Clinton had warned of its political pitfalls, saying, "If you get too emotional, that undercuts you. A man can cry—but a woman, that's a different kind of dynamic."

On New Hampshire Primary Election Day, female voters swung to Clinton, helping her clinch a badly needed win. But all these years later, even some of her own aides still wondered about those tears.

Clinton, for her part, remembered 2008 to me as voters choosing between "one of two firsts": the first Black president in Barack Obama or the first female president in her. Where Obama leaned in to the generational and historic change his candidacy could offer—"Yes We Can" was both a cool slogan and a counteraction to those who thought America would not elect a Black man president—Clinton was more constrained in her presentation. Throughout the primary she faced cracks from pundits across television media, ranging from Republican Pat Buchanan saying on *Meet the Press* that "when she raises her voice, it reaches a point where every husband in America has heard it at one time or another" to longtime MSNBC host Chris Matthews saying the reason she was a senator, candidate, and front-runner "is because her husband messed around." And while it would've been warranted, leaning into pithy clap-backs or hyperfocusing on sexism was a risk Clinton and her campaign didn't, or wouldn't, take. At least not every time comments like these would come up.

Obama, meanwhile, was able to find ways—albeit reluctantly—to counteract the skepticism from the electorate that his race was a barrier to electoral success. Murmurs and dog whistles about his Blackness culminated in the "more perfect union" speech in Philadelphia, given against the backdrop of controversy around Obama's pastor, Jeremiah Wright, and controversial statements Wright had made about the United States. He spoke not just to how the deep wounds of slavery still were—with Confederate flags flying in the same states he won in the primary—but to the hope that those wounds could be stitched closed; that their scars could find a suitable salve in progress.

The speech by a preternaturally talented orator remains an inflection point for a major-party candidate taking on race. It was important and essential—both for the larger push toward progress but also for Obama to sufficiently answer one of the key questions about his own electability. It also came at a point where he'd proven he could win and was gaining momentum toward the nomination. Clinton, by contrast, struggled with her own different but parallel "ism" in need of a political answer. But in 2008, she was unable, unwilling, or both to give it.

In the end, 2008 pushed racial progress ahead of gender progress as it pertains to the presidency. Perhaps, as some posited to me in reporting this book, "systemic racism is very real, but we are more scared of being called racist than being called sexist." And certainly, Clinton aides harbored that notion even years after the loss to Obama.

"I think that we were not prepared," one former Clinton cohort said of the media and electorate writ large. "As groundbreaking and hard as it was for Obama, I'm not discounting that, a guy in a suit still kinda sounds like the guys we've always elected president. No part of Hillary did. No part of Hillary looked like that. It takes more for our brains to get there."

In 2016, Clinton and her team were still working that through.

"In 2016 the whole idea of that campaign for me was to make it clear that I would build on the progress that came before, but I would go further in a lot of areas and would be, I thought, a revolutionary candidate as a woman running for president," she told me. "And when people would say, 'Well, you know, you're part of the establishment,' I would just be gobsmacked because yeah? The establishment that does everything it can for 230-plus years to prevent women from becoming president? That establishment?"

It was a convenient answer for a woman who personified a Washington

Insider. But that didn't make it less true: power structures retain power for the people who create them. And the presidency certainly wasn't created with Hillary Clinton in mind.

At the outset of her presidential run in 2016, *The Washington Post* revived an old metric: likability. "Regardless of whether it's fair, it's a question that has followed Clinton. And even if it's a double standard, it's still a potentially real factor for her when it comes to getting people to vote for her—at least theoretically."

Lending to this idea was the way the coverage of her second bid was framed. ABC *World News*, the top-rated network nightly broadcast at the time, led off their program: "After months of dodging the question, *finally* saying she's running for president for a second time. But she didn't do it in person, instead the campaign kicked off with this video sent out on social media . . ."

Compare that to how Joe Biden's announcement four years later—also via a campaign video—was billed on my network, NBC: "The former vice president officially jumps in the race, polling as the front-runner in a crowded fight for the Democratic nomination," adding later in the broadcast that "the announcement was no surprise, but *how* Joe Biden entered the race for president today turned a lot of heads, taking on Donald Trump straight out of the gate" with a "sharp moral distinction."

When both Clinton and Biden made their respective (video) announcements, no one was surprised. But words matter. Her official bid was framed as the result of months of "dodging"—when that's what every candidate does until they're ready to officially announce so as not to trigger the Federal Election Commission—making it sound like there was something sinister in her avoidance. It's a subtlety that's hard to catch in real time, but one that would happen constantly in 2016, playing into the idea of someone who was lying or misleading or evading the truth. Something notoriously easy and commonplace to tag onto female candidates. And something that naturally fits as a tangible reason for why there's "just something about" that female candidate you don't like.

And *that* establishment Clinton talked about was alive and well throughout her race, too. Compared to the Democratic Socialist from Vermont, Bernie Sanders, who was challenging her from her left, she was emblematic of a return to a political dynasty that represented the entrenched wing of the Democratic Party. One that represented a time of economic prosperity, but also reminded voters of the cultural and ethical tumult that administration represented. Clinton once again entered 2016 as the presumed front-runner for the base of the party, lending further credibility to an already credible effort. Sanders pressed Clinton leftward on policy, dragging out the primary and laying down a deeply set fault line between Democrats that many saw as rooted in sexism for the ways the Sanders campaign allegedly cultivated and urged on its loyal digital fan base of #BernieBros.

More than Bernie or the bros, though, was the Trump of it all.

Trump raced to the proverbial bottom against every single opponent, man or woman, he'd ever faced. A true equal-opportunity offender. Having watched Trump gleefully brand Jeb Bush "low energy" or Marco Rubio "liddle Marco" or Ted Cruz "lyin' Ted," it was clear how much he enjoyed deploying this taunting tactic against his rivals.

But he seemed to especially enjoy going after Hillary Clinton. In 2016, Trump bashed Clinton as corrupt—"crooked Hillary"—and treacherous—so much so that to "lock her up" was the only way to have her answer for her undetermined crimes. At one rally he left it simply at: "She's the devil."

She was polarizing. She had so much baggage. Did anyone *really* even know *why* she wanted to be president anyway, other than the decades she spent laying the bricks that would form the foundation of her inevitable runs? The Clinton name was a problem. Bill was a problem. Their charitable foundation was an issue. *The emails.* Women hated her. Men hated her. Again, *the emails.* Of course, Trump piled on, giving Americans who wanted a woman—*just not Clinton*—the out voters needed so as not to feel so sexist ahead of Election Day. In July 2016 in Scranton, Pennsylvania, he told a packed and rowdy house it wasn't that he never wanted to hear "Madam President"—it's just that he doesn't want that said in reference to Clinton.

"They'll say, 'Madam President.' " Trump conjured the image for the crowd with his usual flourish. "Oh, I don't want to hear that. I do want to hear it eventually 'cause I want to see a woman become President. But it can't be her. She's a disaster. She's a disaster."

Not only that, he went on: "She'll set you back a long way, women, if that happens. It'll be a long way before it happens again. You better be careful what you wish for."

By the time the popular vote was won and the Electoral College lost, there was no shortage of well-documented excuses for why *this woman* was just the wrong woman. But before then, and despite the myriad barriers and causes for skepticism, Clinton still thought she was going to get there.

"I believed I was on my way to winning," she told me. "I believe that a combination of Jim Comey and the WikiLeaks that were dropped in the last weeks of the campaign fed into doubts that people had, particularly women in the suburbs, about whether they could take a chance on a woman, and particularly me . . . I think that my adversaries went to great lengths to derail my campaign and I think some of it was rooted in their opposition to my politics, some of it was playing off my being a woman."

Here, she makes a point that cannot be overlooked. White women as a demographic are already more prone to vote conservative, but suburban women—we know now—swung elections in the Trump era, specifically for Biden in 2020. In the same way "soccer moms" won it for Bill Clinton in 1996, female voters can change the tides of history. But in 2016, they didn't change their political stripes in meaningful ways—unsurprising given the way party politics controls general election results—and they did not come out for Hillary Clinton the way, or in the states, that history demanded. Philippe Reines, a longtime Clinton aide who rose to prominence in 2016 as "The Aide Who Played Trump" in Clinton's debate prep, put it simply: "the biggest problem women running for office have are women."

And yet. Had other, previously reliable voting groups, like Black men in Philadelphia or Milwaukee, come out in larger numbers, that could've turned the tide, too. We talk about female voters as the convenient excuse, but they're not the group who's seen the most change in voting patterns over time—it's men.

Though history can be a galvanizing and powerful force to turn out voters, after 2016 studies showed that gender is not as uniting a factor for women as race is for Black Americans. While Black voters already regularly vote Democrat, they did so in such high numbers for Obama in 2008 and 2012 due to "strong feelings of racial solidarity." That same sentiment didn't exist for Clinton because data shows gender does not inspire that same feeling of cohesion, of solidarity.

Even still, Clinton won women by 13 points—nearly the same as Barack Obama fared in 2008 and 2012 with 13- and 11-point wins among female voters, respectively. Biden's 2020 margin was similar with women, even as Trump made gains where his past fellow Republicans had struggled.

Clinton did win, though. Not the presidency, but the popular vote.

"Hillary's the only person in the '16 race who proved she could get more votes than Donald Trump. There were nineteen people who tried and she's the only one of all those people," her former communications director Jennifer Palmieri told me plainly. "It proved a woman can win."

Maybe, now in the name of Kamala Harris in 2020, that fact could be enough to prove that a woman could win again.

Who better to warn Harris—and the electorate—of sexism's potential to roil the inevitable than Clinton? Over her decades in the highest echelons of power she'd played many roles: barrier breaker, icon, disappointment; the wrong woman, the perfect woman, the most qualified woman, the woman we should be afraid of; the coldest, the shrillest, the emotionless, the calculating, the skilled, the battle-tested, the toughest, the weakest; the woman our parents warned us about and the woman our parents urged us to look up to.

She'd seen misogyny in all its forms: from the sneaky is-that-really-sexism that contributed, in whatever part, to the mistrust most Americans harbored about her, to the shout-it-from-the-rooftops sexism when Donald

Trump called her, among other things, a "nasty woman." That the last one would be wrested from the patriarchy's jaws and turned into a rally cry in the mouths of millions of women marching across the world was a sign of progress. That Clinton would lose anyway was a sign of how far we'd have left to go on the road to progress. And for Kamala Harris, Clinton's loss was a reminder that even if she did make history, the woman before her had notched her place in the history books and still had the scars to show for it.

"You have always been that person who not only has broken so many glass ceilings," Harris said to her. "You do it with such grace and you always do it in a way that's about creating a path for others to follow."

And then she said the thing that these women rarely talk about: "Breaking barriers [as Clinton has] involves breaking things." Sometimes, in the process of that breaking, "you get cut and it's painful."

13

Madam Vice President

How Kamala Navigates Being First

JANUARY 2021

On a sunny, cold day in January on the West Front of the Capitol, Kamala Harris stood in front of the world and took her own advice.

"Please raise your right hand and repeat after me," Supreme Court Justice Sonia Sotomayor intoned, her voice cascading over the speakers, each word bringing us closer to the precipice of making history.

Harris stood and removed her black cloth mask—a once-bizarre, now-ubiquitous hallmark of our times. She wore a deep purple coat, a nod to the suffrage movement and the women whose shoulders she stood upon. One of those women, Hillary Clinton, had also planned purple for a moment of triumph, only to don the color while commanding a hotel ballroom in Midtown Manhattan, graciously accepting a loss most people never saw coming. What a different mood this deep jewel tone sparked now for millions.

On the other side of Pennsylvania Avenue, Molly and I stood along an inaugural parade route that was eerily quiet and devoid of spectators. The city felt shell-shocked after the January 6th insurrection just weeks earlier. Every street we walked through in downtown D.C. was a fortress, bolstered by tanks and troops. But with each minute of the inaugural ceremony that went off without a security incident came a sense of relief and a continued hope for calm. Huddled around our crew's monitor, we watched Senator Harris raise her right hand.

The Soon-to-Be-Veep smiled tightly, inhaling a big gulp of icy January air that filled her chest as she threw back her shoulders and jutted out her chin. It was a normal enough gesture—but an important one if you'd been listening to Kamala Harris these last few years.

"There may have been nobody like you there before; that doesn't mean it's not your place," I'd heard Harris tell young, would-be leaders, an acknowledgment that the work of breaking new and historic ground could be as solitary as it was celebrated.

"Know that when you walk in that room and you're the only one that looks like you . . . you carry us with you," she'd say. "And we expect that when you're in that room, you sit shoulders back, chin up, and you use that voice."

Today, in the biggest "room" there was, Harris threw her shoulders back, thrust her chin up, and used her voice to repeat the oath of office— the same office that dozens of white men of a certain age had taken for hundreds of years before her. Vice president of the United States.

Finishing her oath and taking her place as second in line to the presidency, Harris embodied the start of a new era in Washington. From behind her, an "alright!" came from the soon-to-be-sworn-in president who'd just helped put one more crack in the nation's hardest glass ceiling.

Madam Vice President stood as one of the central figures in an historically diverse slate of cabinet members that made up President Biden's administration. While covering the Biden campaign's transition into power, I couldn't report on a single nomination without speaking to their history-making nature.

Twelve women, mostly of color, serving concurrently in one administration's cabinet—a new record. The wave that first began with Frances Perkins's elevation to Roosevelt's cabinet back in the 1930s was finally reaching its apex. Among the twelve, America's first female Treasury secretary and female director of National Intelligence. Biden's cabinet also boasts the first Latino Homeland Security and Health and Human Services secretary, second openly gay cabinet member heading up Transportation, first Black Pentagon chief, and first Native American woman atop the Interior Department. And with Harris's ascension also came the first second gentleman, forcing a reckoning over the expectations we have of spouses when they are men versus when they are women. Expanded paradigms of power and influence in a city where those are the only currencies that count.

But the sugar-high honeymoon of history-making rarely lasts long. No sooner was the Biden-Harris administration through the front door of 1600 Pennsylvania Avenue than they began to get their arms around a country shuddering under the weight of the COVID-19 pandemic, the economic slump that pandemic caused, and the emotional toll of death and chaos dominating nearly every corner of American life. And then there was also the all-too-dark and all-too-predictable end to the Trump presidency on January 6th.

Back in October 2016—as Trump dropped his earliest seeds of doubt about a "rigged" election system for a race he was likely to lose—I met his supporters who told me they were ready to march on Washington if that happened. As I watched the insurrection, I thought back to a man in Colorado who told me in the fall of 2016, "I have a saying. That by prayer, by peace, or by pitchfork we will get this country back one way or another. They can take it to the bank." His wife stood next to him, nodding. The threat of America's next civil war spoken to me as plainly as if he was telling me the next day's forecast.

I knew then that I was seeing the earliest ripples of a wave that could eventually wash over the country but pushed those thoughts aside. In the years that followed, other reporters who'd also covered Trump intimately would also joke that before the 2020 inauguration we'd first have to cover the next American civil war. It was the kind of gallows humor that often permeates the news business; almost an attempt at staving off the darkness of a story you hope to avoid but know will come anyway.

For Biden, devastation and a simmering unease was the national backdrop to his ascension, a landscape that also played to Biden's penchant to urge us to look for America's better angels. It was the kind of return to morality that he ran and won with. He promised to lead with empathy, tackle the pandemic with science, prioritize women and minorities most systematically disadvantaged by the pandemic's recession, and return a sense of calm to an institution that had been bent but thankfully, not broken by the last four years.

Biden's task, while tall, was also one that could easily be scored by the referees of Washington. Measured in shots in arms and schools reopened safely. But even beyond the pandemic, the Washington crowd knows what a successful presidency looks like. It's scored in approval ratings and legislative pushes signed into laws. In Supreme Court nominees confirmed, reactions to foreign crises, and the ability to keep a nation calm amid uncertain times. Biden's presidency has been—and will be—measured by the rush to vaccinate and save lives, by fluctuating COVID case rates, and by the rise and fall of inflation. He will be judged in troops lost, in infinite wars ended (like Afghanistan in August 2021), and alliances held together during the dark days of Russia's invasion of Ukraine in 2022. Eventually, Biden's presidency will be judged at the ballot box with the results of the 2022 midterm elections—referendums that are not often kind to the party that holds the White House. And ultimately, Biden's measure will be taken in the next presidential election—whether he's on the ballot again at the age of eighty-one or if his veep decides to run again herself, linked to the legacy of his administration (whether she chooses to run on it or not).

As of this writing, what Vice President Harris will do next is among the biggest open question in Democratic politics, while the GOP's shadow primary permeates ballrooms of conservatives gathered in key states. No explicit moves have been made on Harris's part, but that doesn't stop the speculation. For instance, on the September morning in 2021 that the powerful pro-Democratic women's group EMILY's List elevated a former member of Harris's campaign orbit, Laphonza Butler, as its new president, the texts started rolling in from tea-leaf-reading Democrats.

"Looks like Vice President Harris is running for President," one Democratic operative texted me. Every tiny move or moment viewed through the lens of whether it will help or hurt her chances. Each day a new window into a run that seems inevitable, but that remains constrained by the Man At The Top. "That bridge will be crossed when it comes," one person close to Harris said dismissively, clearly already tired of a question that I was far from the first, or last, to ask.

Still, she was already being sized up against other potentials. December 2021 brought with it multiple stories comparing how Harris and Transportation secretary Pete Buttigieg stack up. Could they run against each other? Could they run together?! As if their current roles were equivalent.

Even as Biden promised Harris would be his running mate in 2024, speculation ran rampant about her future on his ticket, especially after Democrats failed to pass the voting rights reforms that she was put in charge of. One January 2021 op-ed in *The New York Times* asked, "Biden-Cheney 2024?," musing about whether Biden would replace Harris with Republican representative Liz Cheney, after Cheney's role in investigating the January 6th insurrection and her condemnation of Donald Trump led to her ostracization from the GOP.

Asked about this a few days after the article appeared, Harris looked stunned by the question. "I mean, honestly, I—I know why you're asking the question because this is part of the punditry and the gossip around places like Washington, D.C. Let me just tell you something, we're focused on the things in front of us."

Pressed again, more specifically about the possibility of Biden-Cheney 2024: "I did not [read that article]. And I really could care less about the high-class gossip on these issues."

Some called the questions unfair or insulting. For what it's worth, if I were doing the interview, I would've asked them too.

But they underscored once again that it's through the lens of 2024 that the politicos and the national press have sought to make sense of the first year of Harris's vice presidency. Noting each policy triumph, waiting for it to be held up years from now on the campaign trail as an example of how

Harris made her imprint on Biden and the administration, and analyzing every misstep with an eye toward how she might explain or defend it in the campaign to come.

But most of the scrutiny came when Kamala herself was before the press. Among the most high-profile of Harris's snafus came on her first solo foray onto the world stage, a trip to Mexico and Guatemala to meet with heads of state and assess the "root causes" of the immigration crisis at the U.S.-Mexico border. My NBC News colleague Lester Holt got the exclusive with the VP on the ground.

Among the questions he asked was the one everyone knew would come: "Do you have any plans to visit the [U.S.-Mexico] border?"

"We are going to the border," she said, pointing out that they were having this conversation *across* the border "here in Guatemala." Her tone was defensive after being hounded by Republicans on this very issue for weeks prior to her trip. "We've been to the border. So, this whole thing about the border, we've been to the border. We've been to the border."

"*You* haven't been to the border," Lester clarified.

"And I haven't been to Europe," Harris replied. She followed with a wry laugh, but her frustration was palpable. "I don't understand the point that you're making. I'm not discounting the importance of the border." But it sounded to some like she was.

The episode sparked incredulity from supporters, glee from critics, and a cleanup by the Harris team. A day later, a reporter at a press conference in Guatemala asked if she could commit to visiting the U.S.-Mexico border soon and she offered a second prepared response.

"Yes, I will," she said, pointing out that she'd "spent a lot of time on the border, both going there physically and aware of the issues."

As a California lawmaker at the local (San Francisco district attorney), state (attorney general), and then federal (Senate) level, Harris was certainly not new to the crises at the border. Her home state is among those on the front lines of the immigration paradox this country faces. To that end, Harris had physically been to the U.S.-Mexico border numerous times, and her roles as both DA and AG required her to deal in real time with cases applying immigration law. As a presidential candidate she, along with most of the 2020 Democratic field, visited the Homestead detention center in South Florida, where more than two thousand teenagers sheltered while they awaited transfer to a family member or guardian living legally in the U.S.

What I wondered as I watched Harris's aides and advisors reeling from the blowback of this botched interview with Lester Holt was why the VP didn't immediately point to all the experience she already had on the border. Though she said "we've been to the border" three times in the interview, it barely grazed the depth of experience she brought. Even in her fuller, second response, she didn't talk about the real-world background or expertise she brought to the table. And while some in her orbit argue that the interview was not that bad, or the context was lost, those were the moments that everyone saw on TV, Twitter, and social media.

Before Harris even touched back down on U.S. soil, the D.C. consensus was that she had a problem. The classification of that problem varied from lack of media savvy to a proclivity toward gaffes to simply falling short of expectations—which were either understandably, or unfairly, high, depending on whom you talked to. That brow-knitting of concerned Democrats only worsened after it was reported that Harris had undergone "comprehensive" media training in April, ahead of the NBC interview and foreign trip—hardly an uncommon practice for anyone spending time in front of a camera, but interesting in that she'd already spent so much time in the public spotlight.

People wondered, here and since, if maybe Harris "just wasn't good at this." "This" being undefinable and unquantifiable, while also ignoring that she was *the elected vice president of the United States*. The take felt like Elle Woods getting into Harvard Law School and then asking, "What, like it's hard?" Yeah. Yeah, it is.

When I posed these criticisms to them, one former Harris aide deadpanned: "We elected Donald Trump president of the United States of America. Please . . . It's absolutely fucking ridiculous."

"My guess is if it was a man who was in her role," Democratic strategist Adrienne Elrod told CNN after the border dust-up, "he would not be nearly as scrutinized in terms of how he gave those answers as she was. When it's a woman, it's, all of a sudden, 'Oh God, she doesn't know what she's doing!' "

Others, though, saw legitimacy in the swell of negative stories because these were not new problems. Harris's short-lived presidential campaign failed in large part because of communications errors and mixed-messaging snafus. While the campaign obituaries laid the blame at the feet of her staffers, at least one of those involved admitted to me that those explanations were offered, in part, to preserve Harris's brand down the road. But those problems persisted even after one of her largest issues—a lack of distinct political identity—had been solved by coming under Biden's umbrella.

"It helped her," one former Harris aide allowed. "I think she's always better at articulating someone else's message than her own." Which can be a problem if *you* want to be president.

That the messaging woes continued now made the "border" issue among the most irresistible morsels in Washington: a problem that fits a larger pattern. And you could argue it did. There were clumsy messaging moments and interviews that sometimes spurred comparisons to the HBO comedy *Veep*, like in January 2022 when Harris was asked in an NBC News interview if it was time for a COVID strategy change and she replied: "It is time for us to do what we have been doing. And that time is every day. Every day it is time for us to agree that there are things and tools that are available to us to slow this thing down."

Amid the criticisms, though, was also a sense that many were looking for excuses to cast her down. She was hardly the first politician to step in it during media appearances, stumble over answers, or need some work to fine-tune their delivery. Plus, how many interviews had she done that we never picked apart because they were on message and struck the right tone? And the whole reason Harris was launched into the highest echelons of the Democratic stratosphere was because she'd successfully climbed, successfully run, and successfully won at multiple levels of the political game. It's not like she stumbled into the vice presidency by accident.

Issues with media interaction and interview style can be cosmetic, but the ability to command a news cycle by staying on message and grappling with tough questions is also the essence of the experience of *running* for office—especially running for president—and is one of the most important tools of championing causes while governing. And no, I don't just say that because I work in media.

Some experts and politicos I talked to for this book discarded this media savviness narrative as one of those empty-calorie stories that lawmakers and staff roll their eyes at and wait to pass. Viral moments and sound bites don't make a good president or a good leader, they'd argue. Yes, fair. But to become a leader, you've got to win elections. And the reality of modern politics is that most voters first "meet" could-be candidates through TV or the internet more than in person at their local diner or union hall. This makes the questions about Harris troublesome, if not valid. But she's also not the first person to endure this kind of scrutiny of her public image and messaging abilities.

Harris currently serves alongside a man as well known for his propensity to say things he shouldn't as for his policy positions. Fears of a classic Biden gaffe permeated his 2020 campaign and persist even now in the White House as aides weigh the pros and cons of the president speaking off the cuff or taking questions. But aides who worked on the Biden-Harris campaign recall that even as reporters asked questions about the potential for gaffes, they were never asked if Biden was being given more media training, unlike the reaction to Harris. And going back further, former vice president Al Gore was similarly vexed by media-related problems and derided as too stiff in front of cameras and reporters, a stark contrast to the charm and charisma of Bill Clinton.

But these problems were not, for Biden or Gore, disqualifiers from the presidency nor top of mind when assessing their ability to lead and govern. When as vice president, Joe Biden broke the cardinal rule of the vice presidency by getting ahead of his boss on gay marriage, no one wondered if the slip of tongue belied a flaw in his ability to *lead*. It was a reflection on Biden's inability to subjugate his own political beliefs to his boss's and a moment of political expediency, sure, but it wasn't a sign of a fundamental flaw in his ability to make tough decisions.

But with Harris, the negative conversation around the struggle to communicate a cogent and consistent message in the national press has felt like a deeper reflection on her ability to do the job of *governing*. And it's here that the difference feels stark and gendered. For Clinton, too, was often charged with an iciness and clear distance from the press. The fraught and distant vibe toward her traveling horde of campaign press was a constant conversation point and lent to a larger narrative about lack of transparency and overall trustworthiness. Those narratives, feasted upon on by cable news panels, ultimately fed into key questions that lingered over her entire 2016 presidential run and, in part, contributed to her loss. With Harris, though, the conversations around her inability to communicate on the border, or on her 2020 healthcare policy, or on who she *was* as a presidential candidate, were really ways of skirting the central question that Washington is still trying to figure out: *Is she ready to be president?*

The parameters of her current office will constrain her ability to answer that question directly, just as they did for nearly every other vice president who has hoped to go from Number 2 to Number 1. Namely because running for president requires an egocentric, selfish mindset, whereas being a good vice president means . . . exactly the opposite.

"You don't have an agenda anymore," a former top advisor to Vice President Al Gore, Mike Feldman, told me. "Your politics are your boss's politics. And in the end what matters is the person you're serving and their administration. Then, that will go to your benefit."

The key to success, according to presidential historian Michael Beschloss, is for a VP to have "a great relationship with the president they're serving under and, at the same time, telegraphing to the public that you're still an alpha leader. That's an extremely hard thing to do and very few people have been able to do that. And it's one reason why VPs tend to not get elected president."

Both George H. W. Bush and Gore are instructive in how they went about trying to make the jump—and both, Beschloss says, are important for Kamala Harris to keep in mind should she hope to do the same.

A popular president is essential. "If everyone wants [the president] gone, you're not going to win under any circumstances. If he's popular and strong, then the only route is to have a great relationship with him and seem to be his heir, or even his chosen heir, if possible." Being chosen is rare, with only a few presidents making their preference public until after their party's primary.

And, in these early days of 2022, Biden is facing some concerning approval numbers. Vice presidents are directly impacted by the polls of their presidents. But things were looking notably bad for Harris. In our January 2022 NBC News poll, 49 percent of respondents had a somewhat or very negative view of her—one that had gotten worse over her first year in office. Ours matched a larger trend. While she'd started her tenure as more favorably than unfavorably viewed, by June of 2021—the height of questions around her role on immigration and the border—unfavorables eclipsed favorables, with the gap between the two continuing to widen over time. According to a *Los Angeles Times* polling average in January 2022, Biden had a net favorability rating of minus 12 points. Harris's was 3 points lower than that. Compared to her vice-presidential predecessors from both parties at the one-year mark—Mike Pence, Joe Biden, Al Gore, and Dick Cheney—Harris is viewed considerably less favorably than all of them.

Already the job of vice president—when done right—puts her out of the spotlight. It also means taking on tough issues. That's governing, right? In Harris's case she was tasked off the bat with heralding the near-impossible-to-pass federal voting rights push through Congress, as well as dealing with the root causes behind illegal immigration from Latin America to the U.S. With each new assignment I'd get a new flurry of texts from sources that ranged from snide to delighted to downright concerned. All seemed to say, in that same range of tones, *can't wait to see how she handles this one.* The president certainly wasn't making it easy for her.

But some of Harris's issues are ones that Biden himself had when he was the veep, including the root causes of immigration in the Northern Triangle—part of why Harris was assigned the issue in the first place. "I'm building off of what the president, then Vice President Biden, did at that time," she told Lester Holt at another point in that border interview. "But also understanding that this—this moment is different in many ways." When some in her orbit grumbled about the tall task before them, some Biden allies would privately shoot back, *He did it and didn't complain.*

Still, for former members of the Obama-Biden administration, they see in Harris—at least publicly—the kind of partner that Biden was to Obama. "She is a VP in the way Biden was," one former Obama administration official described to me, noting the ways Obama leaned on Biden's relationships in the Senate to pass healthcare reform and how he was treated like an important part of the administration. "It's not like that was my impression of Mike Pence," the person quipped.

Certainly, under Obama, Biden was able to leverage his decades of relationships on the Hill to influence key legislative moments during his vice presidency, but that power seemed far diminished in the first year of his presidency as his party fell short of passing his signature Build Back Better spending bill to tackle climate change and reinforce America's social safety net, as well as voting reform. Most weren't expecting Harris to have the same pull in the Senate (after serving less than one term) as Biden did after serving for more than thirty years. But neither of them seems to be having success lobbying key senators, some in their own party, on their top priorities.

The players are new, but it's the same old politics.

Kamala isn't rewriting the VP role, but the perspective she brings is nevertheless reshaping the office.

"If the last person sitting talking to the president is someone who's never been in those rooms before—only once has a person of color and never a woman—if that's who's talking to him, I think that is amazing progress," veteran Democratic strategist Christina Reynolds told me.

This harkens back to a piece written right before Harris's inauguration—Kamala Harris knows things no vice president has ever known firsthand. "There is something profoundly moving about the fact that Kamala Harris has walked through the world as a woman," *Washington Post* columnist Monica Hesse wrote. "That she has thought, talked, purchased, exercised, sought medical care, sought justice, laughed and bitten her tongue as a woman. That she has thought about what laws would have made her feel safer and what policies would have made her life easier. This isn't because men can't be compassionate and sympathetic to women's issues. Of course they can. But in the entire history of the United States, we have only had presidents and vice presidents for whom the experiences of women are known and understood secondhand, if at all."

That lived experience allows her to keenly and deeply understand why the pandemic-spurred recession is so harmful to women, especially women of color, across the country. It's likely part of why abortion providers, for the first time, were invited to the White House to share their stories amid Texas passing one of the most restrictive abortion bills in the country with the sitting vice president and why Black maternal mortality has become a widely discussed issue in Washington. It informs the administration's focus on combating systemic racism from someone who has experienced it firsthand.

While I was reporting for both this book and for my day job, those who say Harris is doing a good job but getting a bad shake and those who say she's falling short of expectations all seemed to come at it from the same place: struggling for the metrics to assess her, in part because we expected that her "newness" would mean being tangibly different. Fundamentally unfair, because in theory each "new" vice president is new. But also, because it sets her up to fall short of expectations before she even begins. We didn't expect Pence or Biden or Cheney or Gore to reshape the office. Why, suddenly, is there an anxious foot-tapping for Kamala Harris to do so?

It's a pressure her office has keenly felt, too.

"People expect her to be making history every day," one former aide to the VP said. "They expect that she's out here, every single day, making news and creative policy. That is not the job. So, sometimes she is criticized because there's some people that don't understand the job and don't know where the bar is. They're measuring her against some unimaginable standards. And then there are other folks that fundamentally understand what the job is but they've never seen anybody *like her* do the job, right? Because every other vice president has been an old white man. She is . . . not an old white man. So, 'she' doing the job looks different."

And not just because she's a "she," either.

"If you look at Black women who have done jobs that old white men have done in any other sector—whether we're talking about business or education, other executive leadership roles in government, whether we can look at governorships, we can look at women in the United States Senate, women in leadership—all of a sudden, when a lady gets in there, the coverage looks a little different," this person told me.

Harris isn't undertaking an outright reimagining of the role of a vice president—nor should we expect her to. But there is, if subtly, a Harris-specific stamp being put on the office. How do we, in media and in politics, who regularly dole out wins and losses, assess this kind of subtle change? Is it success, is it failure, or is it just . . . different? What if being historic doesn't mean making sweeping change, but just means a subtle flexing of who we allow to lead and shape our national discourse?

"There are so many expectations of her, many of which conflict," Beschloss put it bluntly. "Any national figure who is an African American and Asian woman, unfortunately, in this society will be subjected to different standards."

But there also seems to be a fundamental lack of tangible scorecard metrics for vice presidents, broadly. What do they do and what should we expect of them? Beyond the obvious mantra of "don't fuck anything up," the role is largely one of support. Traveling messenger, advice-giver, presidential amplifier. Harris is doing all that. And as she does, the public is interpreting it through the lens of expectation (which has been infused and informed by gender and race) but also the future.

So, let's talk about Kamala Harris for President 2.0.

Her vice presidency may make it harder, sure. The high turnover in her office lends to criticisms of her leadership style. And the perception of her media savviness continues to cause problems. The scrutiny is constant, the high wire taller and narrower than anyone else's.

But being Madam Vice President also gives her more serious credentials for the job of president than anyone else who will run in the Democratic field against her. She will know what the pressure of the Situation Room feels like and the weight of a national crisis; she'll know what it means to win a legislative fight in the White House and how to bounce back from one she lost. She'll have been the vice president. Biden himself is proof of how much heft that can carry.

Add it all together—the pomp and circumstance, the access to national networks, *Air Force Two* versus a black car to Capitol Hill—and Mike Feldman asks me: "Would anybody out there who's thinking about running in 2024 *not* want to trade places with her?"

I know he's not looking for me to answer, so I wait.

"Of course, they would . . . She's the vice president."

14

"I'd Love to See It in My Lifetime"

MARCH 2022

I don't want to alarm you, but there are already people running for president in 2024. And there's kind of a lot of them.

Republicans, with their sort-of open (unless Trump runs) field, are fanning out across the country, seeking to make early friends with important party figures in key primary states and bolstering their credentials with the conservative faithful, one overly air-conditioned state party dinner and special-interest-group gathering at a time. Over the tinny cacophony of luncheons in Florida or dinners in North Carolina, they're making their veiled case for president as something else—a push for the Senate majority, a rallying cry to retake the House, a delicate dance around the forty-fifth president. Several of these could-be GOP candidates are women, notable for a party that has never boasted more than one woman running for president at one time, in one cycle.

Democrats, anxiously awaiting the possibility that *their* field also opens should Biden decline to run again, are quietly assessing what the 2024 list of hopefuls could look like. Harris and Buttigieg, sure, but there are more

Dems with their eyes on the Oval—including those who have run before, now older, wiser, and looking to give it another go.

It tees up the 2022 midterms but also the 2024 presidential race that will feature *more* women, *more* prominently. Because the answer—from everyone I've talked to in my reporting for this book—to getting women into the highest spaces of power, including the presidency, is just *more*.

The ceiling will not be broken in one shot. It will be chipped away at bit by bit, shattered crack by crack. The revolution will be televised in marches and strong campaigns and excellent debates. It'll look like voters going to the ballot box and just voting for the person they think will be best, without fear that their neighbors won't vote for that candidate too because of some subconscious electability bias. It will be based on women running in all the ideological lanes, from different parts of government (or outside of it!), with three of them campaigning on a Saturday across Iowa and reporters not even batting an eye.

This is what change looks like. It's evolving in real time and has already gone through multiple iterations—the election of Trump, the #MeToo movement, and two subsequent "years of the woman" in electoral politics, most recently—but it's a fight that's been brewing for more than one hundred years.

"Look what people said in 1920 around the [Equal Rights Amendment]," historian Michael Beschloss reminded me. "What they were saying then was the way you get a woman president is to give women the right to vote, legitimize the idea of women in the mainstream of the political profession, and very naturally you'll have more women in office as governor and members of Congress. It'll naturally flow."

It didn't. At least not exactly like that. The Equal Rights Amendment never happened. Neither has gender parity in elected government. The pipeline of candidates, of operatives, of reporters didn't automatically fill out in a more female fashion. Few reproductive protections and stigmas around motherhood made it that even when women wanted to run, they'd wait until later in life, by and large aging them out of the highest echelons of the political process for most of the middle and late decades of the

1900s. But soon culture caught up. More women were showcased in roles of power—both in the workplace and in made-for-TV White Houses. More women, albeit in small numbers at first, were elected to serve in Congress. Women started running for president. Pop culture and social norms quickened the normalization of women not as ancillary players, but as central decision-makers capable of wielding power. Getting comfortable with that was critical to getting us to where we are now, and where we will take it from here.

The process has not been perfect—far from it. Media must continue to learn in real time to buck the gender biases that often tilt against women. Americans have had to reconstruct their expectations of officeholders and executives, amending their view of roles that had always been hyper-masculine in presentation to accept the new, but not less powerful, ways that women lead. It's a slow, exhausting process, especially when we see backsliding in moments where we expected change. But even setbacks put bricks in the road to progress. There are more there now after 2020 that will further level the field for 2024.

Part of it, Julie Conway, who runs a conservative PAC backing qualified Republican women in primaries, points out, is simply making female electoral gains so normal they're not notable. "It has to stop being The Year of the Republican Woman, The Year of the Democratic Woman, The Year of the Blah Blah Blah. I think it just has to become 'this cycle we picked up five seats. This cycle we picked up seven seats.' "

On the Democratic side, Christina Reynolds, VP at EMILY's List and a former Hillary Clinton staffer, echoed that. "It turns out [women] are just good candidates. Maybe we stop assuming 'oh their networks aren't as good' or 'oh, they don't have the same experience' or 'oh whatever.' . . . We don't have to view them as candidates who are women, but just candidates, right? Which is exciting."

Thirty years out from the first Year of the Woman in 1992, we still aspire to retire the phrase. To do that, both party apparatuses must continue the work to engage women and diverse candidates so qualified female candidates permeate all rungs of government at consistent levels.

It took a while for the Republican Party to outright invest in and back female candidates, especially helping them get through primaries where gender dynamics are most in play. But after 2020's successes there is greater desire to keep winning. Because that's what GOP women in 2020 did.

Nancy Mace was one of them.

"We don't, as Republicans, typically focus on our gender or any of those things," the South Carolina congresswoman from a purple swing district that she flipped blue to red in 2020 told me. "We run on policy."

So she did, presenting a conservative, pro-business ideology embodied by her record as a mom, entrepreneur, and military daughter. Her tough-as-nails persona was predicated on her past experience as the first female graduate of the Citadel, who pushed through that hypermasculine military body and would apply that grit and conservative value structure to the House. She worked for Trump in South Carolina in 2016 (that's when I first met her) and remained close to him until the pandemic, once she was in office. The political break with the former president, and spats with his closest acolytes in Congress, is causing her trouble now in her 2022 reelect.

Nevertheless, Mace was one in a wave of more than two dozen GOP women to be sworn into the House in 2021, the GOP's answer to 2018's "blue wave" of female lawmakers on the Democratic side. In 2021, GOP women were responsible for flipping more than 75 percent of seats from blue to red. It made the power of female candidacies impossible to ignore, and impossible not to invest in. Which, for Conway, head of the Value In Electing Women (VIEW) PAC, is exactly what she'd been saying all along.

"This is where the rubber meets the road," Conway said. "Do the guys actually care? I don't know. They get it, because all of a sudden the women saved the guys' asses in not getting ours handed to us in 2020 . . . Once you convinced the guys that it was self-serving to help Republican women because they want to be in the majority, it sort of opened things up a little bit. Once they started realizing this is important and women are winning seats that guys couldn't have."

But in success there's also an emerging downside. If you're a proponent of simply having *more* women in the body, five of those GOP flipped seats in 2020—or more than one in three—were GOP women beating and replacing Democratic women.

"The sad part, and I really worry about this looking forward to 2022 and 2024, is that so many of our good Republican women took out good Democratic women," Conway said. "I'm a firm believer in parity and getting there . . . And if we now have these, let's say ten seats that are 'the girl seats,' where we just keep flipping back and forth, that doesn't help us get the parity."

Her fear may be borne out in the months to come. Of Democrats' thirty-two vulnerable "front-line" House lawmakers, sixteen are women. More than half of them could potentially see female Republican challengers once primaries shake out. The same trend is also likely to play out on the GOP side with their vulnerable members. Eleven of their twenty GOP House incumbents facing tough reelection campaigns are female, and it looks likely that at least several will see female challengers from the left. Which could mean fewer gains for women in the House body overall.

Another complicating factor that's GOP-specific, though, is the ideology and policy that they prefer to run on. Republicans can't seem to agree, of late, if their organizing platform is policy ideas or the personal preferences and vendettas of the forty-fifth president. Mace urges her party to "find and recruit candidates . . . that have our same principles and values, but also the principles and values of their district that they can win. A Republican in California might be different from a Republican in Ohio, or South Carolina, and even within my state, I'm a different brand of Republican than even my neighboring congressional districts that are Republican . . . If you want to continue to have a strong Republican Party, we've got to make sure that our faces reflect the rest of the country." But that's not so easy when Trump is playing kingmaker from Bedminster or Mar-a-Lago, rebuking lawmakers who've crossed him and backing primary challengers to purge the party of lawmakers who aren't loyal to him. And whatever headwinds Mace is facing, Representative Liz Cheney is facing in spades in her reelection bid in Wyoming.

The Trump-spurred ideology of culture wars over more traditional conservative values is a problem some pro-GOP women's groups were forced to grapple with, too, in the Trump years. Because electing women—of both parties, sure, but of late in the GOP—does not always mean positive returns.

"Out of all the [women] that were elected [in 2020], there are ten that are really exceptional, [but] no one can name them," Conway said. "Because they only know Marjorie Taylor Greene and Lauren Boebert. For me, that's horrible. [Of] these ten incredible Republican women, there will be a lot of Democratic women that say 'wow, they're pretty awesome.' It's like when we looked at a lot of the Democratic women that got elected in 2018. Those of us who weren't trying to paint everybody with a lunatic brush said really, there's a lot of really good Democratic women that got elected. It was women. That's awesome."

But in the post-Trump era, where the former president exercises his hold over the party through a hold on the base and abiding fear from lawmakers of his wrath, the question isn't just about recruiting reflective candidates who can win their districts after a primary; it's about whether the party apparatus can recruit for a GOP base that has a myopic view of the kind of candidate—demographically and ideologically—it is willing to support. And it's a party where Trump is still likely to get final say on who rises and who is cast out. The 2022 election will showcase, or buck, that theory. And the fear among many Republican operatives in Washington and beyond is that the Republican base won't know the difference, or worse, won't care, when it comes to electing strong conservative candidates versus just candidates who march in lockstep with Trump.

Conway, for her part, doesn't back these kinds of candidates, most prominently embodied in representatives Lauren Boebert and Marjorie Taylor Greene. And in response to the brand of Trumpian Republicanism that popularized them, VIEW PAC's website was amended to say they support only "credible, serious, electable Republican women running for federal office." For these kinds of stunt politicians, the lack of backing from VIEW PAC and other groups likely won't shake their standing. They do just fine with grassroots fundraising, and it's become clear that House GOP leadership refuses to rebuke or alienate them. But outside groups that bolster female candidates, especially in primaries, are critical for mainstream women trying to compete in a still male-dominated political structure.

And as conservative women seek to increase their ranks in congressional, state, and local governments, they'll also make future runs for the White House. South Dakota governor Kristi Noem, former U.S. ambassador to the United Nations Nikki Haley, Congresswoman Liz Cheney— all are names Republicans muse about as future presidential aspirants.

Haley served two terms as governor of South Carolina prior to joining Trump's cabinet and is widely seen as someone who could be a fierce competitor for the 2024 nomination due to her lengthy resumé, range of domestic and foreign policy experience, and proven political chops—that is, if Trump doesn't destroy her chances first. She's played both sides of the former president, calling him out and then walking those words back; continuously moving the goalposts to position herself for . . . whatever's next.

Cheney is currently in the political fight of her life, near, or at, the top of Trump's list of political blood matches for her House seat in 2022. The daughter of a former vice president who grew into the family's political business, she's fighting a lonely battle against most of her party, stemming from the January 6th insurrection and the role Trump played in fomenting it but playing out from there in continuous news cycles that show Cheney bucking her own party in Washington, rebuking both members and messaging as she tries to chart a path to a forgone brand of conservatism. Some wonder, as she rakes in cash for her reelection, whether the national attention and big dollars will roll her into a presidential bid—whether she keeps the House seat she currently holds or not.

There could be more. But the GOP has more work to do in terms of bolstering their pipeline with female candidates to eventually match their

Democratic sisters in presidential political arms. It's why the work they're doing at the congressional and gubernatorial level in 2022 is so important.

Governor Noem, for her part, has been road-testing her message over the last year.

In the sticky days of June 2021, I drove my rickety rental car through hours of Friday beach traffic and down to Greenville, North Carolina, for the state GOP's convention. Technically, NBC sent me to cover Trump, who was the headliner. But the silver lining to following Trump these days is the empty front row to the '24 shadow primary. Seeing these candidates as they workshop their stump speeches and figure out how to introduce themselves to audiences years before most of my colleagues would even start googling their legislative histories is a boon.

Governor Kristi Noem of South Dakota is one of those people. She spent 2021 bouncing from state party dinners to cattle calls in front of evangelical groups, even to backstage at Trump rallies due to her close ties to members of Trump's inner circle, including Corey Lewandowski, Trump's former campaign manager who served as Noem's political advisor until she severed ties with him in September 2021. Noem also denied having had an affair with Lewandowski, amplifying chatter in conservative media circles by tweeting, "These rumors are total garbage and a disgusting lie. These old, tired attacks on conservative women are based on a falsehood that we can't achieve anything without a man's help."

Still, the way she talks to audiences—like this one, feasting on a lunch of limp lettuce and "actually pretty good" chicken in Greenville—gripped my attention instantly. It was a standard stump speech, but it also anticipated many of the themes that we've talked about in this book that cut sideways for female presidential candidates.

For instance, during Noem's time in the South Dakota state legislature she ran for leadership—assistant majority leader—explaining that "if I was going to be away from all of my businesses, my husband, my kids, that I was going to be as effective as I possibly could. So, I decided to run for leadership." *Family values, but also a willingness to do the work.*

"I worked on policy that was important for our state [in the legislature] and then people kept asking me to run for Congress," she told the crowd. "I decided to run for Congress after people asked for two years. My husband and I finally said, 'You know what? Maybe we should just run. If we lose, they'll leave us alone.' " *Showing ambition but couching it in others' asking it of her.*

"When you get to Washington, D.C., and you're the only representative from your state, it's a little bit lonely," Noem explained of her time as a U.S. congresswoman. "So, I always was building a coalition on whatever issue I was working on." *Consensus building and problem solving.*

"By the way, there's no 'women's issues.' Okay? Can we just take that off the table right now? There's no 'women's issues' in this country. What there is, is a *woman's perspective* on *every* issue. On every single one," she said, a direct acknowledgment of gender without bashing anyone over the head with it. Not only that, but Kamala Harris and other female Democrats in 2020 regularly made the same point.

I didn't know what I expected from the governor of South Dakota, but a palpable undercurrent of female gender dynamics from a Republican woman testing the waters of a Republican primary—especially in the age of Trump, when all the conventional wisdom of what it takes to win has been turned on its head ten times over—wasn't it.

"For both parties, but specifically Republicans with Trump as a factor, we don't need to be telegraphing that we want a certain identity of a candidate, but more of the *ideology* of a candidate and the demeanor that's less toxic than Trump's," Alice Stewart, the GOP operative who worked for Michele Bachmann in 2012 and Ted Cruz in 2016, said as we looked at the presidential path ahead. "It's hard to look ahead until we see if the big elephant will stay in the room or go home."

And still, it's the best *candidate*, Stewart reminds us. Not *female candidate*.

"Will it be great, the day we see a woman sworn in as president?" Alice said. "Absolutely. But it needs to be the right woman at the right time instead of just a right now candidate."

Which is why groups meant to level that playing field, financially and with other resources, are so important—tilling political soil to ensure the right woman is ready at the right time.

Democratic groups, like EMILY's List and Higher Heights and Get Her Elected, have been in this fight for years—bolstering pro-choice and progressive female candidates' campaign coffers and lending their endorsements, amping up candidates' credibility and potential to get themselves elected. Republicans are playing catch-up on this front, and they cop to it. Political action committees like E-PAC, Congresswoman Elise Stefanik's political outfit, and Conway's VIEW are seeking to fill the gap on bringing women in and backing them early with political infrastructure and know-how. And they're finally getting buy-in from Republican leadership. In 2022, big GOP donors reportedly gave millions to the GOP House campaign arm specifically to bolster women and minority candidates in the Republican pipeline. Progress.

Moreover, one veteran GOP fundraiser explained to me that gender doesn't play as much of a role in fundraising as it used to when they started out decades ago. The big-money bunnies on the conservative side pick candidates to back like they pick stocks, they told me. "They don't care if it's man, woman, or beast if you can win."

But among voters, it's a different story. After decades of working races, watching trends, and trying to shape the party's sluggish pipeline of women, "none of [the grassroots] want to be identity driven at all," the fundraiser said. "It is deplored on the grassroots side."

I was pointed to a crowded 2019 House primary in North Carolina, where Dr. Joan Perry ran as one in a crowded field. An ob-gyn by trade who had "delivered half the babies in the district," Perry had deep ties to the community but lacked a political resumé and the kind of built-in voting base and campaign infrastructure that accompanies having run for office before. Post-race polling showed the leeriness GOP female candidates faced in this part of rural, conservative North Carolina.

"It was brutal," one person involved in that race told me. "They said things like 'women just shouldn't necessarily be going to Congress. It's just a big step for the ladies.'" Others, plural, said women were more likely to be "liberalized when they get to Congress," citing GOP senators like

Lisa Murkowski and Susan Collins. "Those names they know. And those things are cited again and again and again."

"Because all women are the same," I said. You could hear my eyes roll.

"Right," this person said back, sharing my incredulity. "If it can happen to Susan Collins, [Dr. Perry] was likely to be a liberal in sheep's clothing. So, the fight on all fronts is really to fight *that*."

Democrats, too, have their own fights to contend with.

The Senate, as it stands now in spring 2022, lacks any Black lawmakers and boasts only three women of color—senators Tammy Duckworth, Mazie Hirono, and Catherine Cortez Masto. Compared to the then-historic seven women serving after '93, twenty-four women serve now as senators—an addition of seventeen over thirty years. Or approximately 0.5 female senators added per year.

Governorships also remain a stubborn metric for female candidates of both parties. Nineteen states still haven't had a woman as their chief executive. New York only just made this history in August 2021 after Lieutenant Governor Kathy Hochul was elevated after Governor Andrew Cuomo resigned amid scandal. And the record number of women serving as governors at one time remains stuck at nine.

Mayoral races, however, have been bright spots for Democrats. For instance, in Tucson, Arizona, Regina Romero was the first woman elected mayor in 2019—a Latina leader in a state where Democrats hope to continue to capitalize on the changing demographics for cycles to come. Chicago mayor Lori Lightfoot and Atlanta mayor Keisha Lance Bottoms also mark women of color who ascended to lead major U.S. cities, with national profiles that boomed in 2020 because of both the pandemic and their handling of the Black Lives Matter rallies in their cities.

The expansion of the executive mold at the mayoral level could have an outsize impact on other executive roles farther up the ballot (i.e., governor's mansions) given how visible and consistently mayors are in front of the constituents of their cities. The pandemic only underscored the value of competent state and local leadership, and women were able to rise to the top of the national consciousness, for better and worse, because of their responses to the COVID-19 virus.

"I hope that that helps us, right?" Christina Reynolds said. "So, we don't just have to see women as just effective collaborators, but also as effective leaders. Nancy Pelosi helps that. Kamala Harris helps that."

While none of the gains in governorships or mayoralties or Senate and House races solve the direct question of how or when the U.S. will elect a female president, they're all part of the eventual solution. Executive leadership roles beget executive leadership experience begets . . . the highest executive office of all.

We can look around the globe and see the possibilities. England has been showing us for years. Through monarchy, sure. God Save the Queen. But also, and more relevantly, through female prime ministers who have risen within the ranks of their parties and been elected as leaders. And during the first year of the COVID pandemic, female leaders across Europe and Asia drew global attention. Angela Merkel in Germany, Mette Frederiksen in Denmark, Taiwan's Tsai Ing-wen, Jacinda Ardern in New Zealand, and Finland's Sanna Marin were all praised for their initial responses. Articles asked why female-led countries seemed to be doing better with COVID and studies answered that, in fact, they were. Data from the first six months of the pandemic showed countries with female leaders had lower COVID death rates than those run by men. Women locked down earlier and reacted more quickly, studies found.

Further, "[t]he leadership styles of women leaders in the COVID-19 response have been described as more collective than individual, more collaborative than competitive and more coaching than commanding," a 2020 UN Women policy brief stated. While executive leadership roles are associated with men, it was typically female leadership qualities in these heads of state that were arguably best suited for a crisis moment such as this one. The report points out the irony: "It is noteworthy that in 2019—prior to the pandemic—nearly half of the world's population (47 per cent) believed that men made better political leaders than women."

Still, the Council on Foreign Relations' 2021 "Women's Power Index" of 193 UN member states lists a mere twenty-two countries with a female head of state or government—a paltry 11 percent. Fewer have gender parity (50 percent or more women) in their cabinets, and even fewer have parity in the national legislature. The U.S. is hardly the only country with more work to do here, but leading on the world stage means doing so by example.

And in the next election wave, those examples will be shaped not just by party infrastructure and campaign mechanics, but in the media. Newsrooms must do their part in challenging assumptions and biases around female candidates and candidates of color. In the same way advocacy groups formed We Have Her Back during veepstakes to prime newsrooms and viewers alike to the sexism that often derails female-led campaigns, once you see the biases and slanted structures, it's hard to unsee them and harder not to call them out.

For reporters, myself included, who will spend their days speeding too fast down Iowa highways to catch as many candidate events as they can while surviving on oat milk lattes, we must reframe. To make sure we're reporting on the merits. Those can get pushed aside sometimes for Very Online, Very In-The-Beltway takes, until you meet someone in real life who is at a campaign event because they want to vote for the person who will prioritize health insurance because their daughter's preexisting condition will bankrupt them otherwise. And yes, most of these politicians we'll spend time with are spinning, and it's our job to call them out and cut through the noise. But it's also okay to allow that they might be real people with real ideas for this country. Both things can be true and we, as complex journalists with diverse lived histories ourselves, are allowed to showcase both the human and the political side to running for president— male and female. That doesn't make us less skeptical, less interested in the truth, less able to hold lawmakers to account; it allows us to give our audiences 360-degree views of the people they may vote for.

But it also requires us to understand the lived experiences of *all* candidates, which increasingly means looking outside the typical white male mindset. It requires understanding why it's powerful and meaningful for Kamala Harris to be an Alpha Kappa Alpha sorority member and why sisterhood is so deeply important. Or why Elizabeth Warren's experience with pregnancy discrimination as a young teacher can be easily fact-checked and then turned into a rallying cry for thousands of women who'd experienced the same. These are the life experiences that shape candidates in the same way they shape voters, and they deserve to be reported on seriously and with the right language. That requires preparation.

It also means being comfortable enough to call out the sexism of women being seen as "shrill" or "just too" and being cognizant of the ways we frame and phrase our questions. Electability is embedded in simply asking, "Can a woman win?" The presumption in that question is that they can't, when really, we just have no idea if they can yet.

If you're not sure, please check yourself. The number of times I asked my producer Molly, "Can I say that?" or "What's the best way to express this point?" are infinite. Men, this may mean you're checking yourself even more frequently. During the reporting of this book, one prominent female Democratic strategist told me she saw an uptick in calls from veteran Men In Media using her as a sort of sexism litmus test in 2020 once Kamala was on the ballot.

"Can I say Kamala looked great?" the callers—mostly men—would ask. "Ummm, okay," she'd reply. "If you can say that about Joe Biden, then go for it. If not, then no."

"Can I say she looked tired?" they'd inquire. "Okay," she'd say, "if you'll also say it about Trump."

It's hilarious when spelled out, but I'd also rather those conversations happen. They mark signs of progress. And so does just shutting up and listening when the women around your newsroom are bringing their perspective. You have expertise, but so do they. And as candidate pools become more diverse, it's entirely plausible that their expertise becomes more relevant than yours.

The same goes for white women, me included, who must unlearn some of the whitewashed feminism we've been taught and instead elevate, not speak for, our Black and brown sisters, colleagues, and friends. All these viewpoints, collectively, will make us stronger and lend to parity in the press corps that covers these presidential contenders, which will lend to a more holistic understanding of each candidate and less *otherizing* of that which we are not used to seeing in the mainstream. A flattening of the political playing field, built on merits. And really, that's all this is about. It's the job of the candidates to run, but it's on us to ensure the track is uniformly flat for all of them.

Because these female presidential candidates we cover, whoever they are, will eventually be *Electable*. They'll win—because women do when they run—and they'll inspire an entire generation of women to run in greater numbers after them. The immediate goal will be to be first, and then we should hope for the woman who comes second, and third, and fourth.

Until then, for the candidates, the rules of the arena . . . are what they are. That means strategizing to win within the reality that exists when you run. And all the advice on how to do that comes down to this: just do it.

"You just put your head down. You do the work," a former aide to Vice President Harris said when I asked the ethos of the office in the face of criticism—however unfair they feel it is. "Do the work and eventually people will recognize that you're doing the work."

So, what's left but to answer the nagging, pressing question that's followed us through these pages: *who will be first? And when?*

I don't know. I can't give you a name, time, or party affiliation.

Some, including Hillary Clinton, but also others on the Democratic and Republican sides of the aisle, have surmised that it could very well be a Republican woman who wins first, despite Democrats' longer-term investment into diversifying their party and premium placed on having women candidates at the forefront of the party.

"I thought it was possible," Clinton told me, "that the first woman president would be a Republican because if you look at women who became heads of government through a parliamentary system, by and large, they came from the center right or from the right of their political systems."

Many people I spoke to for this project were surprised Clinton would say that. And, before you are too, she made sure to tell me that just because it was historical precedent, "Obviously, I hope that's not the case."

But it does leave open the door to history in 2024 , or 2028, or 2032 . . .

I can't tell you *who* will be first, but I can tell you she's coming. With all the progress and milestones that we document in this book, she has to be.

As I was getting ready to hang up the phone with Secretary Clinton, she told me she was happy to help with this book in hopes it "dispels some of the myth and knocks down some of the stereotypes" around women seeking positions of power. At or near the end of her political career, it was hard to see it as anything other than tying up a dangling thread of what she'd dedicated her life to.

"You know," I said, "I feel like it's one of those things where once you say it and get people's attention, it's kind of hard to not think about it."

"I hope that's right," Clinton said, a little of that infamous laugh bursting from the other side of the line. "Because I would love to see it in my lifetime."

I laughed, too.

"And I would love to be able to stop saying that."

Acknowledgments

I wrote myself a note a few months into this process: *It's impossible for you to get this wrong.* And I really hope I didn't. But if I got it right, it's because of all the people who helped me—with this book and along the way. In fact, sitting down to thank all these people seems so overwhelming that it does feel possible to, at least, get *this* part wrong. But here it goes . . .

Thank you to Carrie Thornton and the team at Dey Street for having the vision to take my reporting and make it into something bigger, broader, and all-encompassing. I couldn't have done this without Albert Lee, Pilar Queen, Adam Liebner, and the United Talent team. And Mary Marge Locker, who kept me on the straight and narrow factually (and, sometimes, emotionally) speaking.

TV and reporting are team sports and NBC News has recruited the best of the best. To our amazing crews and producers—in the field, at the shows, across all our platforms, 24/7—I'm so grateful for your tireless work, passion, and friendship.

Thanks to Noah Oppenheim for the continued opportunities to keep telling stories—on the campaign trail, at the White House, on Capitol Hill, and soon on the campaign trail again. To Janelle Rodriguez for always keeping her door open to me and helping me find my voice as a reporter and correspondent. To Rashida Jones for a vision that prioritizes the kind of work we do in the field, following the story wherever it may take us.

To Betsy Korona for always finding a way to greenlight us to get there—and for asking me all those years ago what I wanted to be when I grew up. If you'd never mentioned the word "embed" to me back in 2014, I'm pretty sure I'd be a lawyer right now. But because you did that, Doug Adams hired me. He saw something in me before I found it in myself when he asked me to be an embed—and then to cover Trump—back in 2015.

I wouldn't have been on that path, or been able to stay on it, without Chuck Todd, who saw and kept seeing my "Vitality," and Dafna Linzer, who encouraged my interest in what it means to be powerful and female in this town.

Thank you to my fellow Road Warriors of 2020 and 2016. And to the NBC Capitol Hill team, who make the long hours fun and inspire me with their dedication every day. Thanks to my first NBC home in the 30 Rock mothership, to Ken Strickland and the Washington Bureau who adopted me as one of their own, and to the women whom I look up to here every day—led by the iconic Andrea Mitchell, who is as gracious as she is hard-working (which is to say, unquantifiably so).

Sue Kroll, Olivia Santini, and Erika Angulo, you poured your decades of knowledge into me, and I am forever grateful that I got to come of age on the air and as a reporter with you as my guides. Ben Mayer, thanks for teaching me, well, how to "correspondent" and being a real friend while doing it.

To Katy Tur, you wrote a whole book about the years me, you, and Anthony Terrell spent together following Trump and sometimes even I still don't believe it. To my Trump Embed crew whom I will always consider my family: thanks for being the best company in the Doghouse. I'm still mad about the wallet, though.

I'm so grateful to the candidates, staffers, and sources who were so generous with their time and insights—even (especially) in moments that were raw or painful—so that others may learn and build upon them.

Deepest thanks to my friends. How did I ever get so lucky? Alex Lemley,

Meghann Ambrose, Haley Talbot, Emily Gold, Deepa Shivaram, Kailani Koenig, Jackie Alemany, Stephanie Quintero, Elizabeth K. Harnik, Kristen Holmes, Noah Gray, Ben Perry, Molly Kadish, Shelby Coon, Shaq Brewster, Lauren Peikoff . . . for seeing these pages in their rawest forms and encouraging me to keep going, keep working, keep making it better, while plying me with an endless supply of Ted's Bulletin pop tarts and oat milk lattes. I love you all and feel so blessed to call you friends.

Molly Roecker, what can I say that I haven't already? Thanks will never be enough for what you gave to me.

My family, I love you so much. Pange, you showed me what a feminist was—even when I denied that I was one—by the way you lived and worked every day. In these pages, "the vaginal minority" finally wins. Lyss, thank you for being the best little sister I could ask for and growing into an even better friend. Someday, I'll prove to you I'm cool. Dad, I'm so proud of the allyship you've always shown and the ways you've lifted women up. Thanks for your unyielding support and for putting up with, well . . . all this.

Notes

3 "I will, I will, I will . . .": Fiona Apple, *Fetch the Bolt Cutters* (Epic Clean Slate, April 2020).

5 votes on Election Day: "Remembering Gracie Allen's White House Run," *All Things Considered*, NPR, November 4, 2008, audio, https://www.npr.org/transcripts/96588557.

5 Thirty-two women: "Women Presidential and Vice Presidential Candidates: A Selected List," Rutgers Center for American Women and Politics, accessed March 19, 2022, https://cawp.rutgers.edu/facts/levels-office/federal-executive/women-presidential-and-vice-presidential-candidates-selected.

7 "We are not a fad, a fancy, or a year": Marni Allen, "Senator Barbara Mikulski: Mentor, matriarch, movement maker," *Brookings,* March 3, 2015, https://www.brookings.edu/blog/fixgov/2015/03/03/senator-barbara-mikulski-mentor-matriarch-movement-maker/.

16 "moms in tennis shoes": Patty Murray, 1992.

17 America's Most Famous Parking Lot: IANS, "US election: The coronation of Vice President–elect Kamala Harris begins," *New York: Business Standard*, 2020.

18 "Stop the count": Donald Trump (@realDonaldTrump) Twitter, November 5, 2020.

20 More than 74 million Americans: NBC News Decision Desk, U.S. Presidential Election Results 2020: Biden wins, *NBC News*, 2020.

21 more women running at one time than ever before: Li Zhou, "Women running for president is the new normal," *Vox*, 2019.

22 "Amtrak Joe": Katherine J. Igoe, "Where Did 'Amtrak Joe,' Joe Biden's Nickname, Come From?" *Marie Claire*, 2020.

22 security concerns: Michael Crowley, "Biden will skip his planned Amtrak ride to the inauguration because of security concerns," *New York Times*, 2021.

23 Biden said: Joe Biden Pre-Inauguration Speech, January 19, 2021.

25 "not the last": Kamala Harris, Spelman Speech, October 23, 2020.

25 one in four Republicans: "She Votes: Women, the Workplace, and Pandemic Politics," *Gender on the Ballot*, March 16, 2021.

26 "audacity": Shefali Luthra, "Kamala Harris applauds Biden's 'audacity to choose a Black woman to be his running mate,'" *The 19th**, August 2020.

27 confirmations and elevations: Alisha Haridasani Gupta, "Fulfilling a Promise: A Cabinet That 'Looks Like America,'" *New York Times*, January 21, 2021.

27 throughout agencies: Kathryn Dunn Tenpas, "Tracking President Joe Biden's Cabinet and appointees," *Brookings*, November 2021.

27 "ignorant slut": Sen. John Kennedy, Neera Tanden's confirmation hearing for Director of Office of Management and Budget, *C-SPAN*, February 10, 2021.

28 "President of the United States": Kamala Harris (@KamalaHarris, November 7, 2020). https://twitter.com/kamalaharris/status/13251267 33482385409.

33 "backbone of our democracy": Kamala Harris Victory Speech, November 7, 2020.

34 "as his vice president": Kamala Harris Victory Speech, November 7, 2020.

36 The Democratic electorate was majority-Black: David Jackson, "Democrats Face a Crucial Primary Test in the South Carolina Primary: Can They Energize the African-American Vote," *USA Today*, February 29, 2020, https://www.usatoday.com/story/news/politics /2020/02/29/south-carolina-primary-african-american-voters-key -victory/4881243002/.

39 #CampaignFashionReport: Maeve Reston (@maevereston), Twitter, February 16, 2019. https://twitter.com/maevereston/status/1096806 779030290433?lang=en.

39 "of #campaignfashionreport fame": Ali Vitali (@alivitali), Twitter, February 16, 2019, https://mobile.twitter.com/alivitali/status/10968 04387685568512?lang=eu.

39 "overcoming hardship to succeed": Ali Vitali (@alivitali), Twitter, February 16, 2019, https://twitter.com/alivitali/status/10968084577584 82432.

40 "putting out glowing tweets about it": Brit Hume (@brithume), Twitter, April 16, 2019, https://twitter.com/brithume/status/1096821175 701983233?lang=en.

40 "she's supposed to be covering": James Taranto (@jamestaranto), Twitter, April 16, 2019, https://twitter.com/jamestaranto/status/109 6837036944826368?ref_src=twsrc%5Etfw%7Ctwcamp%5Etweet embed%7Ctwterm%5E1096837036944826368&ref_url=https %3A%2F%2Fthehill.com%2Fhomenews%2Fcampaign%2F430359 -kamala-harris-shopping-trip-stirs-twitter-controversy.

40 "the last time around": Robin Abcarian, "Column: On the Campaign Trail, Kamala Harris tries on a sequined jacket, and men go nuts," *Los Angeles Times*, February 22, 2019, https://www.latimes.com /local/abcarian/la-me-abcarian-jacket-20190222-story.html.

40 "eyes of many critics": Brian Flood, "Reporters pause political journalism to pick out clothing for Kamala Harris on campaign trail," Fox News, February 16, 2019, https://www.foxnews.com/entertainment /reporters-pause-political-journalism-to-pick-out-clothing-for-ka mala-harris-on-campaign-trail.

41 of the outing: Ashley Parker, "Skeet Shooting With Lindsey Graham— 'Katie Couric Is Coming!' " *New York Times*, July 9, 2015, https://www .nytimes.com/times-insider/2015/07/09/skeet-shooting-with-lindsey -graham-katie-couric-is-coming/.

41 facing the press and laughing: Geoff Earle, Lia Eustachewich, and Kate Sheehy, "Obama goes shopping at Gap for Michelle, Kids," *New York Post*, March 11, 2014, https://nypost.com/2014/03/11/obama -makes-stop-at-east-side-gap-store/.

45 "Is it workin'?": Hillary Clinton, interview with The Breakfast Club hosts, Power 105.1, April 18, 2016, https://www.youtube.com /watch?v=oRZd861Pog0.

55 "a mockery": Michael Brice-Saddler, "Sen. Elizabeth Warren called Cherokee Nation chief to apologize for DNA test, tribe says," *Washing-*

ton Post, February 1, 2019, https://www.washingtonpost.com/politics
/2019/02/01/sen-elizabeth-warren-called-cherokee-nation-chief
-apologize-dna-test-tribe-says/.

56 "seen it up close": Kirsten Gillibrand campaign event, May 25, 2019,
Iowa Falls, Iowa.

59 "points with his base": Julián Castro interview by Bill Maher, *Real
Time with Bill Maher*, HBO, April 5, 2019.

59 "wrong with white liberals": Julia Ricardo Varela (@julito77), Twitter,
April 5, 2019, https://twitter.com/julito77/status/111435622775938
6624.

63 "in front of us today": Amy Klobuchar campaign event, May 25,
2019, Iowa Falls, Iowa.

64 "could not be heard": Adam Nagourney and Jeff Zeleny, "Clinton
ends campaign with clear call to elect Obama," *New York Times*,
June 8, 2008, https://www.nytimes.com/2008/06/08/world/amer
icas/08iht-08clinton.13548782.html.

65 "talk about the economy!": Kamala Harris (@KamalaHarris), Twitter, February 21, 2019, https://twitter.com/kamalaharris/status/109
8681263014129664?lang=en.

66 "And that's going to matter": Amy Klobuchar interview with
EMILY's List, July 28, 2020, https://twitter.com/emilyslist/status
/1288238625080119303.

70 "each other anymore": Allan Smith and Doha Madani, "Biden dou-
bles down on segregationist comments, says critics like Cory Booker
'should apologize to him,'" NBC News, June 19, 2019, https://www
.nbcnews.com/politics/2020-election/biden-cites-segregationist-sen
ators-he-recalls-past-civility-senate-n1019211.

70 "#MeToo Era": Sheryl Gay Stolberg and Carl Hulse, "Joe Biden Ex-
presses Regret to Anita Hill, but She Says 'I'm Sorry' Is Not Enough,"
New York Times, April 2019, https://www.nytimes.com/2019/04/25
/us/politics/joe-biden-anita-hill.html.

71 "bring our country together": Scott Detrow, "Democrats Blast Biden
For Recalling 'Civil' Relationship With Segregationists," NPR, June
2019, https://www.npr.org/2019/06/19/734103488/democrats-blast
-biden-for-recalling-civil-relationship-with-segregationists.

71 "me. #DemDebate": Kamala Harris (@KamalaHarris), Twitter,
June 27, 2019.

71 it was not.): Kamala Harris (@kamalaharris, June 28, 2019, Instagram).

72 announcing her campaign: Stacey Solie, "Kamala Harris Kicks Off 2020 Campaign With Oakland Rally," *New York Times,* January 27, 2019, https://www.nytimes.com/2019/01/27/us/politics/kamala -harris-rally-2020.html.

73 "people of America": Shirley Chisholm Presidential Campaign An- nouncement Speech, January 25, 1972, https://www.c-span.org /video/?325324-2/1972-shirley-chisholm-presidential-campaign -announcement.

75 "might hurt a few others": Shirley Chisholm Presidential Campaign Announcement Speech, January 25, 1972, https://www.c-span.org /video/?325324-2/1972-shirley-chisholm-presidential-campaign-an nouncement.

75 twenty-six between both parties: "Women Elected Officials by Posi- tion," Rutgers Center for American Women and Politics, accessed March 19, 2022, https://cawpdata.rutgers.edu/women-elected-offi cials/position?current=1&position%5b%5d=US+Senator&position %5b%5d=US+Representative&race_ethnicity%5b%5d=Asian%2F Pacific+Islander&race_ethnicity%5b%5d=Black%2FAfrican+Amer ican&race_ethnicity%5b%5d=Hispanic%2FLatina&race_ethnicity %5b%5d=Middle+Eastern%2FNorth+African&race_ethnicity%5b %5d=Multiracial&race_ethnicity%5b%5d=Native+American.

76 "desegregate the schools": Ed Kilgore, "Kamala Harris' call for a re- turn to bussing is bold and politically risky," *New York Magazine Intelli- gencer,* July 1, 2019, https://nymag.com/intelligencer/2019/07/kamala -harriss-call-to-bring-back-busing-is-bold-and-risky.html.

76 "desegregating America's schools": Alexandra Jaffe and Thomas Beaumont, "Harris says busing should be considered, not mandated," Associated Press, July 3, 2019, https://apnews.com/article/california -joe-biden-iowa-sc-state-wire-des-moines-586b1e81cb684654b0cf68 9b9074c1cb.

77 "It's horrible.": Nolan McCaskill, "Trump accuses Cruz's father of helping JFK's assassin," *Politico,* May 3, 2016, https://www.politico .com/blogs/2016-gop-primary-live-updates-and-results/2016/05 /trump-ted-cruz-father-222730.

77 "the hell alone": Ted Cruz gaggle with reporters in Wisconsin, March 24, 2016, https://www.youtube.com/watch?v=FhcI_VQdFU0.

78 that state's primary: Benenson Strategy Group, "Report from South Carolina Focus Groups Among Af Am Voters," July 21, 2019, https://

www.scribd.com/document/431372932/South-Carolina-Focus
-Groups-Findings#from_embed.

78 "an inflection point": Rep. Jim Clyburn, "Joe Biden Endorsement
Speech," February 26, 2020, https://www.cnn.com/2020/02/26
/politics/jim-clyburn-endorses-joe-biden/index.html.

83 "plans to everyone": Robert Laszewski, "Kamala Harris Has Had
Some Difficulty With The Health Care Issue," *Forbes,* August 15,
2020, https://www.forbes.com/sites/robertlaszewski2/2020/08/15
/kamala-harris-has-had-some-difficulty-with-the-health-care-issue
/?sh=3de9bfbc5cce.

86 "moving to Iowa": Matt Laslo (@MattLaslo), Twitter, September 18,
2019, https://twitter.com/MattLaslo/status/1174363966614773760.

86 "describe myself": Kamala Harris Campaign Kickoff Event, Washington, January 21, 2019.

87 "what can be": Shira Tarlo, "Kamala Harris on presidential campaign: My race and gender are the 'elephant in the room,'" *salon,* October 28, 2019, https://www.salon.com/2019/10/28/kamala-harris
-on-presidential-campaign-my-race-and-gender-are-the-elephant-in
-the-room/.

87 final breaths: Jonathan Martin, Astead W. Herndon, and Alexander Burns, "How Kamala Harris's Campaign Unraveled," *New York
Times,* November 29, 2019.

88 Harris was out: Kamala Harris, "I am suspending my campaign
today," *Medium,* December 23, 2019.

89 in open races: Sarah Bryner and Grace Haley, "Race, Gender, and
Money in Politics: Campaign Finance and Federal Candidates in the
2018 Midterms," Center for Responsive Politics, March 15, 2019,
https://www.pgpf.org/sites/default/files/US-2050-Race-Gender
-and-Money-in-Politics-Campaign-Finance-and-Federal-Candi
dates-in-the-2018-Midterms.pdf.

89 the presidential race: "Unprecedented donations poured into 2020
state and federal races," OpenSecrets, November 19, 2019, https://
www.opensecrets.org/news/2020/11/2020-state-and-federal-races
-nimp.

89 female candidates: "In 2020 women ran, won and donated in record
numbers," OpenSecrets, December 21, 2020, https://www.opense
crets.org/news/2020/12/women-ran-won-donate-record-num
bers-2020-nimp/.

90 million in Q3: Shane Goldmacher, "Kamala Harris Raised $12 Million in First Quarter for 2020 Bid, Her Campaign Says," *New York Times*, April 1, 2019 https://www.nytimes.com/2019/04/01/us/politics/kamala-harris-fundraising-2020.html.

90 "donor stampede": Elena Schneider, "Harris sets off Democratic donor stampede," *Politico*, August 19, 2020, https://www.politico.com/news/2020/08/19/kamala-harris-democratic-donors-398656.

90 Responsive Politics found: Fredreka Schouten, "Exclusive: New analysis shows how women helped fuel a Biden fundraising surge," CNN, October 26, 2020, https://www.cnn.com/2020/10/26/politics/women-donors-biden-fundraising/index.html.

98 "and about our future . . .": Elizabeth Warren campaign event, September 16, 2019, New York City, New York.

98 Triangle Shirtwaist Factory: "Triangle Shirtwaist Factory Fire," History.com, December 2, 2009, https://www.history.com/topics/early-20th-century-us/triangle-shirtwaist-fire.

99 "value in real time": Jennifer Palmieri, *Dear Madam President: An Open Letter to the Women Who Will Run the World* (New York: Grand Central Publishing, 2018), 126–127.

101 "people to back her up": Elizabeth Warren campaign event, September 16, 2019, New York City, New York.

103 he told her: Roger Lau interview with MJ Lee, CNN, June 2019.

105 she once explained: Kim Norvelle, "'That's what girls do': Elizabeth Warren tells young Iowa girls why she's running for president, with a pinky promise," *Des Moines Register*, May 9, 2019, https://www.desmoinesregister.com/story/news/elections/presidential/caucus/2019/05/09/elizabeth-warren-election-2020-girls-female-candidates-pinky-promise-iowa-caucus-women/1122078001/.

105 "achieve your own dreams": Hillary Clinton presidential concession speech, November 9, 2016, New York City, New York.

107 "being honest here": Democratic primary debate, Westerville, Ohio, October, 15, 2019.

112 Marine for sex: Bridget Read, "Smear Attempt Just Makes Elizabeth Warren Seem Cool," *New York Magazine–The Cut*, October 3, 2019, https://www.thecut.com/2019/10/jacob-wohl-smear-attempt-just-makes-elizabeth-warren-seem-cool.html.

112 "middle-class tax increases": Biden campaign statement, November 1, 2019.

114 Medicare for All plan: Bernie Sanders interview with John Harwood, CNBC, October 29, 2019, https://www.cnbc.com/2019/10/28/bernie-sanders-lets-not-make-people-overly-nervous-about-socialism.html.

116 "make it happen": Elizabeth Warren, Democratic primary presidential debate, February 25, 2020, Charleston, South Carolina.

116 "I was wrong": Elizabeth Warren gaggle with reporters, March 5, 2020, Cambridge, Massachusetts.

119 as a presidential contender: Reid J. Epstein and Lisa Lehrer, "Why Pete Buttigieg Annoys His Democratic Rivals," *New York Times*, November 9, 2019, https://www.nytimes.com/2019/11/09/us/politics/pete-buttigieg-democrats.html.

121 "reading that wrong?": Amy Klobuchar interview by Jake Tapper, *State of the Union*, CNN, November 10, 2019.

122 "qualification is assumed": Barbara Lee Family Foundation, "Opportunity Knocks: Now Is the Time For Women Candidates" (October 24, 2017): 1–9, https://www.barbaraleefoundation.org/wp-content/uploads/OpportunityKnocks_10.24.17_Final.pdf.

122 sentiment toward female candidates: Nate Cohn, "One Year From Election, Trump Trails Biden but Leads Warren in Battlegrounds," *New York Times—The Upshot*, November 4, 2019, https://www.nytimes.com/2019/11/04/upshot/trump-biden-warren-polls.html?login=smartlock&auth=login-smartlock&login=smartlock&auth=login-smartlock&login=smartlock&auth=login-smartlock.

123 "difference to be decisive": Nate Cohn, "One Year From Election, Trump Trails Biden but Leads Warren in Battlegrounds," *New York Times—The Upshot*, November 4, 2019, https://www.nytimes.com/2019/11/04/upshot/trump-biden-warren-polls.html?login=smartlock&auth=login-smartlock&login=smartlock&auth=login-smartlock&login=smartlock&auth=login-smartlock.

125 conclusion of the *Times*: Amy Klobuchar campaign event, November 6, 2019, Rochester, New Hampshire.

128 "fired for being pregnant": Ali Vitali and Benjamin Pu, "Elizabeth Warren stands by account of pregnancy discrimination," NBC News, October 8, 2019, https://www.nbcnews.com/politics/2020-election/elizabeth-warren-stands-account-pregnancy-discrimination-n1063871.

128 "pure in some way": Pete Buttigieg interview by Michael Babaro, *The Daily, New York Times*, November 22, 2019, Audio, https://www .nytimes.com/2019/11/22/podcasts/the-daily/pete-buttigieg.html.

129 "frustrating for me": Daniel Strauss, "Buttigieg's Bid for DNC Chair Ended With a Thud. Will 2020 Be Different?" *Politico*, April 23, 2019, https://www.politico.com/story/2019/04/23/buttigieg-dnc-cam paign-2020-1288768.

130 "I believe that's me": Amy Klobuchar interview by Jake Tapper, *State of the Union*, CNN, November 10, 2019.

131 correct that narrative: Ryan Brooks, "Pete Buttigieg Is Not the First Openly Gay, Major Party Presidential Candidate. This Guy Was," *Buzzfeed News*, April 2, 2019, https://www.buzzfeednews.com/article /ryancbrooks/fred-karger-mayor-pete-buttigieg-gay-2020.

133 "excitement of people": Marianne Williamson, Democratic Presiden- tial Primary Debate, June 28, 2019.

135 taught many lessons: Amy Klobuchar campaign event, Atlantic, Iowa, July 1, 2019.

135 bailout spending: "Warren appointed to Congressional panel oversee- ing Treasury's economic bailout plan," *Harvard Law Today*, Novem- ber 21, 2008, https://today.law.harvard.edu/warren-appointed-to -congressional-panel-overseeing-treasurys-economic-bailout-plan/.

138 "those double standards": Barbara Lee Family Foundation, "Ready Willing & Electable: Women Running For Executive Office" (No- vember 4, 2019): 3, https://www.barbaraleefoundation.org/wp-con tent/uploads/FINAL_Ready-Willing-Electable-11.4.19.pdf.

138 first hundred days as president: Klobuchar campaign press release, "First 100 Days Plan," June 17, 2019.

140 "what did you mean by that?": Amy Klobuchar, Democratic presi- dential primary debate, November 20, 2019, Atlanta, Georgia.

147 differ from there: MJ Lee, "Bernie Sanders told Elizabeth Warren in private 2018 meeting that a woman can't win, sources say," CNN, January 13, 2020, https://www.cnn.com/2020/01/13/politics/bernie -sanders-elizabeth-warren-meeting/index.html.

148 highlighted her pitfalls: Alex Thompson, "Warren 'disappointed' Bernie 'sending his volunteers out to trash me,'" January 12, 2020, https://www.politico.com/news/2020/01/12/warren-disappointed -bernie-volunteers-097984.

149 Enlow captured it: Courtney Enlow, "An all-caps explosion of feel-ings regarding the liberal backlash against Hillary Clinton," Pajiba, May 18, 2016, https://www.pajiba.com/politics/an-allcaps-explosion -of-feelings-regarding-the-liberal-backlash-against-hillary-clinton .php.

152 "supposed to go": Ali Vitali, Shaquille Brewster, Mike Memoli, and Marianna Sotomayor, "Iowa roiled by Democratic infighting weeks before first-in-nation vote," NBC News, January 14, 2020, https:// www.nbcnews.com/politics/2020-election/live-blog/january-demo cratic-debate-live-updates-six-candidates-face-des-moines-n111 4686/ncrd1115486#liveBlogHeader.

155 Democratic primary field: Christianne Corbett, Jan G. Voelkel, Mar-ianne Cooper, and Robb Willer, "Pragmatic Bias Impedes Women's Access to Political Leadership," *Proceedings of the National Academy of Sciences* (February 1, 2022): https://doi.org//10.31219.

159 such as this: "Putting Sexism in Its Place On the Campaign Trail," Barbara Lee Family Foundation, February 2021.

169 "a desirable profession": Jennifer L. Lawless and Richard L. Fox, "Girls Just Wanna Not Run: The Gender Gap In Young Americans' Political Ambition," March 2013.

169 relatively insignificant: Jennifer L. Lawless and Richard L. Fox, *Run-ning From Office: Why Young Americans Are Turned Off to Politics* (New York: Oxford University Press, 2015), 156–157.

170 memory on Twitter: https://twitter.com/alivitali/status/1226576999 126388738?s=20

171 "the right candidate": Claire Friedman, "The Electable Female Can-didate," *The New Yorker*, December 9, 2019, https://www.newyorker .com/magazine/2019/12/16/the-electable-female-candidate.

172 "nonwhite and nonmale": Gabrielle Magni and Andrew Reynolds, "Democrats Don't Want to Nominate a Candidate Who Looks Like Bernie or Joe," *Politico*, May 24, 2019, https://www.politico.com/maga zine/story/2019/05/24/democrats-dont-want-to-nominate-another -white-man-for-president-226977/.

175 "Ghosts of Hillary": Natasha Korecki, "Warren Battles the Ghosts of Hillary," *Politico*, December 31, 2018, https://www.politico.com /story/2018/12/31/elizabeth-warren-hillary-clinton-1077008.

177 team rolled out: "Amy's Plan to Build America's Infrastructure," Amy Klobuchar campaign release, March 29, 2019.

186 "left on the floor": Shahien Nasiripour, "Fight For the CFPA Is 'A Dispute Between Families And Banks,' Says Elizabeth Warren," *The Huffington Post*, May 3, 2010, https://www.huffpost.com/entry/fight -for-the-cfpa-is-a-d_n_483707.

187 could take place: Jane Mayer, "The Case of Al Franken," *The New Yorker*, July 22, 2019, https://www.newyorker.com/magazine /2019/07/29/the-case-of-al-franken.

192 "IQ test, or run": Dan Mangan, "'You're a damn liar, man!' – Joe Biden blasts Iowa voter, calls him 'fat' after man repeats Ukraine smear," CNBC, December 5, 2019, https://www.cnbc.com/2019/12/05 /biden-calls-iowa-voter-damn-liar-and-fat-after-ukraine-accusation .html.

193 by the second: Jake Lahut, "Joe Biden gets away with yelling at voters, and may even benefit from it," *Business Insider*, March 10, 2020, https://www.businessinsider.com/joe-biden-gets-away-yelling-at -voters-benefit-from-it-2020-3.

205 Bernie Sanders's VP: Chris Cillizza, "What is Elizabeth Warren's endgame?" CNN, February 24, 2020, https://www.cnn.com /2020/02/24/politics/elizabeth-warren-2020-bernie-sanders-mi chael-bloomberg/index.html.

236 "the eventual reckoning": Jonathan Martin, Matt Flegenheimer, and Alexander Burns, "Ted Cruz Names Carly Fiorina as His Running Mate, Seeking a Jolt," *The New York Times*, April 28, 2016, https:// www.nytimes.com/2016/04/28/us/politics/ted-cruz-carly-fiorina .html.

237 "commander-in-chief": James Hohman, "Warren met with Clinton this morning, fueling VP speculation," *The Washington Post*, June 10, 2016, https://www.washingtonpost.com/news/powerpost/wp/2016/06 /10/warren-to-meet-with-clinton-this-morning-fueling-vp-specula tion/.

237 "if you think you could be": https://www.youtube.com/watch?v= SS5bNpyOsaE

238 tapped by Mondale: Lila Thulin, "The Woman Who Paved the Way," *Smithsonian Magazine*, August 10, 2020, https://www.smithsonian mag.com/history/geraldine-ferraro-unprecedented-1984-campaign -vice-president-180975491/.

238 an adrenaline shot: https://www.realclearpolitics.com/epolls/2008 /president/us/general_election_mccain_vs_obama-225.html.

240 "dull" and unexciting: Bernard Weinraub, "How Mondale Faltered," *The New York Times*, March 8, 1984, https://www.nytimes.com/1984/03/08/us/how-mondale-faltered.html.

240 "with the Republicans": Larry J. Sabato, Kyle Kondik, and J. Miles Coleman, "Partisan Gender Gap Not Just About Women," University of Virginia: Center For Politics, April 26, 2012, https://centerforpolitics.org/crystalball/articles/partisan-gender-gap-not-just-about-women/.

241 "to lead it": Roger Rosenblatt, "Mondale: 'This Is An Exciting Choice,'" *TIME*, July 23, 1984, Vol. 124, No. 4, p. 10-11. https://time.com/vault/issue/1984-07-23/page/18/.

242 for the job: George J. Church and Ed Magnuson, "A Break With Tradition: In need of a political lift, Mondale picks a woman running mate," *TIME*, July 23, 1984, Vol. 124, No. 4, p. 12-16. https://time.com/vault/issue/1984-07-23/page/18/.

243 "our own decisions": Jane Perlez, "Ferraro Is Making Appeal to Women," *The New York Times*, November 3, 1984, https://www.nytimes.com/1984/11/03/us/ferraro-is-making-appeal-to-women.html.

244 "women, more votes": Roger Rosenblatt, "Mondale: 'This Is An Exciting Choice,'" *TIME*, July 23, 1984, Vol. 124, No. 4, p. 10-11. https://time.com/vault/issue/1984-07-23/page/18/.

245 election cycle before: *New York Times* exit polling, 1984, https://www.nytimes.com/elections/2008/results/president/national-exit-polls.html.

246 "a historic milestone": Adam Nagourney, Jim Rutenberg, and Jeff Zeleny, "Surprise running mate brings re-evaluation from both parties," *The New York Times*, August 31, 2008, https://www.nytimes.com/2008/08/31/world/americas/31iht-campaign.1.15758519.html.

246 "anything about her?": Hillary Rodham Clinton, *Hard Choices: A Memoir* (New York: Simon & Schuster, 2014).

246 doing just that: David Plouffe, *The Audacity to Win: The inside story and lessons of Barack Obama's historic victory* (Viking, 2009) p. 309-310.

247 "theme of experience": Laura Meckler, Elizabeth Holmes, and Jim Carlton, "McCain's Surprise VP Choice," *The Wall Street Journal*, August 30, 2008, https://www.wsj.com/articles/SB121993453813079803.

247 "Republican presidential ticket": Michael Cooper and Elisabeth Bumiller, "Alaskan is McCain's Choice: First Woman on GOP Ticket," *The New York Times*, August 30, 2008, https://www.nytimes.com/2008/08/30/us/politics/29palin.html.

248 of Black women: National exit polls, 2008.

248 2.1 million votes lost: Roy Elis, D. Sunshine Hillygus, Norman Nie, "The dynamics of candidate evaluations and vote choice in 2008: Looking to the past or future?" *Electoral Studies* 29, no. 4 (December 2010): 582–593.

249 "you a flake?": Michele Bachmann interview by Chris Wallace, *Fox News Sunday*, June 26, 2011.

251 was in 2016: Ruth Igielnik, Scott Keeter, and Hannah Hartig, "Behind Biden's 2020 Victory," Pew Research Center, June 30, 2021, https://www.pewresearch.org/politics/2021/06/30/behind-bidens -2020-victory/.

251 for Bill Clinton: Kelly Ditmar, "Revisiting the gender gap in 2020: Race and the gender gap," Center For American Women and Politics, October 8, 2020, https://cawp.rutgers.edu/blog/revisiting-gen der-gap-2020-race-and-gender-gap.

256 "That's politics.": Natasha Korecki, Christopher Cadelago, and Marc Caputo, " 'She had no remorse:' Why Kamala Harris Isn't a Lock for VP," *Politico*, July 27, 2020, https://www.politico.com/news /2020/07/27/kamala-harris-biden-vp-381829.

256 "and very opportunistic": Brian Schwartz, "Some Biden allies move to stop Kamala Harris from becoming vice president," CNBC, July 29, 2020, https://www.cnbc.com/2020/07/29/biden-allies-move -to-stop-kamala-harris-from-becoming-vice-president.html.

256 "So gimme a break": https://www.cnbc.com/2020/07/29/biden -allies-move-to-stop-kamala-harris-from-becoming-vice-president .html.

257 "with their presidents": Adam Nagourney and Jeff Zeleny, "Obama chooses running mate," *The New York Times*, August 24, 2008, https:// www.nytimes.com/2008/08/24/us/politics/24biden.html.

257 "others grab headlines": Christopher Cadelago and Natasha Korecki, "Karen Bass rises as sleeper pick to be Biden's VP pick," *Politico*, July 24, 2020, https://www.politico.com/news/2020/07/24/karen -bass-biden-vp-380583.

261 predominantly white male political space: https://drive.google.com /file/d/1VhhCN09VBbZeCvSlmwtEpxmR7dJiaPrU/view.

264 "may be different": Carol E. Lee, Hallie Jackson, Monica Alba, and Ali Vitali, "Pence and Harris prep for a debate with suddenly higher stakes," NBC News, October 5, 2020, https://www.nbcnews.com

/politics/2020-election/pence-harris-prep-debate-suddenly-higher
-stakes-n1242064

265 more female advisors: Carol E. Lee, Hallie Jackson, Monica Alba, and Ali Vitali, "Pence and Harris prep for a debate with suddenly higher stakes," NBC News, October 5, 2020, https://www.nbcnews .com/politics/2020-election/pence-harris-prep-debate-suddenly -higher-stakes-n1242064.

265 "sympathy for her": Peter Baker and Susan Glasser, *The Man Who Ran Washington: The Life and Times of James A. Baker III* (New York: Double-day, 2020), 242.

266 "a real friend": George W. Bush, *41: A Portrait Of My Father* (New York: Crown Publishers, 2014), 155.

266 born in California, USA: https://www.usatoday.com/story/news /nation-now/2015/09/10/trump-fiorina-look-face/71992454/; https: //www.businessinsider.com/donald-trump-hillary-clinton-presiden tial-look-2016-9.

269 of the campaign: Connie Bruck, "Hillary the Pol," *The New Yorker*, May 30, 1994, https://www.newyorker.com/magazine/1994/05/30 /hillary-the-pol.

271 "i.e. [Carly] Fiorina": Hui Bai, "When Racism and Sexism Benefit Black and Female Politicians: Politicians' Ideology Moderates Prej-udice's Effect More Than Politicians' Demographic Background," *Journal of Personality and Social Psychology: Interpersonal Relations and Group Processes* (2021): http://dx.doi.org/10.1037/pspi0000314.

273 at the time: "Dole announces presidential exploratory committee," CNN, March 10, 1999, https://www.cnn.com/ALLPOLITICS/sto ries/1999/03/10/president.2000/dole/.

274 "the White House": David Von Drehle, "Dole Bows Out of Presi-dential Race," *The Washington Post*, October 20, 1999, https://www .washingtonpost.com/wp-srv/politics/campaigns/wh2000/stories /pmdole102099.htm.

274 "to woo voters": Ceci Connolly, "Dole Crafts Strategy to Close Gender Gap," *The Washington Post*, April 11, 1999, https://www .washingtonpost.com/wp-srv/politics/campaigns/wh2000/stories /dole041199.htm.

275 media coverage lagged: Caroline Heldman, Susan J. Carroll, and Stephanie Olson, "Gender Differences in Print Media Coverage of Presidential Candidates: Elizabeth Dole's Bid for the Republican

Nomination," Center for American Women and Politics, August 2000, https://cawp.rutgers.edu/sites/default/files/resources/elizabeth dolebid_0.pdf.

276 "the U.S. Senate": Molly A. Mayhead and Brenda DeVore Marshall, *Women's Political Discourse* (Lanham, MD: Rowman & Littlefield Publishers, Inc., 2005), 56.

277 "a good thing": Carol Moseley Braun interview with Betty K. Koed for Women of the Senate Oral History Project, September 22, 2017, https://www.senate.gov/about/resources/pdf/moseley-braun-carol -9-22-2017.pdf.

279 " 'to be president' ": Gail Sheehy, "Hillaryland at War," *Vanity Fair*, June 30, 2008, https://www.vanityfair.com/news/2008/08/clinton 200808.

279 honest, and disarming: David Axelrod, *Believer: My 40 Years In Politics* (New York: Penguin Press, 2015), 252–253.

280 "catching my breath": Elise Hu, "Campaign Trail Tears: The Changing Politics of Crying," NPR, November 25, 2011, https://www.npr .org/2011/11/25/142599676/campaign-trail-tears-the-changing -politics-of-crying.

282 "at least theoretically": Aaron Blake, "Is Hillary Clinton 'likable enough'? And does it even matter?" *The Washington Post*, February 9, 2015, https://www.washingtonpost.com/news/the-fix/wp/2015/02 /09/is-hillary-clinton-likable-enough-and-why-does-it-even-matter/.

282 "sent out on social media . . .": https://abcnews.go.com/Politics/now -hillary-clintons-2016-campaign-announcement-2008/story?id=302 64756.

282 "sharp moral distinction": https://www.youtube.com/watch?v=i6iT uFvZntY.

284 "She's a disaster": Ali Vitali, "Trump: I want a female president, too— Just not Hillary Clinton," NBC News, July 27, 2016, https://www .nbcnews.com/politics/2016-election/trump-i-want-female-president -too-just-not-hillary-clinton-n618266.

284 the Trump era: Danielle Kurtzleben, "What we mean when we talk about 'suburban women voters,'" NPR, April 7, 2018, https:// www.npr.org/2018/04/07/599573817/what-we-mean-when-we-talk -about-suburban-women-voters.

285 for Black Americans: Michael Tesler, "Why the gender gap doomed Hillary Clinton," *The Washington Post*, November 9, 2016, https://www

.washingtonpost.com/news/monkey-cage/wp/2016/11/09/why-the-gender-gap-doomed-hillary-clinton/.

289 "to the bank": Ali Vitali, "Trump Supporters Ponder What's Next If Clinton Prevails," NBC News, October 19, 2016, https://www.nbcnews.com/politics/2016-election/trump-supporters-ponder-what-s-next-if-clinton-prevails-n668936.

291 "Biden-Cheney 2024": Thomas L. Friedman, "Biden-Cheney 2024?" *The New York Times*, January 11, 2022, https://www.nytimes.com/2022/01/11/opinion/democratic-ticket-liz-cheney-2024.html.

291 "on these issues": Kamala Harris interview with Craig Melvin for NBC News, January 13, 2022.

293 applying immigration law: Noah Bierman and Molly O'Toole, "Kamala Harris to head to the border amid GOP criticism," *The Los Angeles Times*, June 23, 2021, https://www.latimes.com/politics/story/2021-06-23/harris-set-to-make-first-trip-to-u-s-mexico-border-to-assess-situation-with-migrants.

293 living legally in the U.S.: https://www.tampabay.com/florida-politics/buzz/2019/06/26/democratic-candidates-visit-migrant-detention-center-in-south-florida/.

293 the public spotlight: Jeremy Diamond and Jasmine Wright, "'Her instinct is to dig in': Kamala Harris' struggles to answer border question seen as part of pattern," CNN, June 14, 2021, https://www.latimes.com/politics/story/2021-06-23/harris-set-to-make-first-trip-to-u-s-mexico-border-to-assess-situation-with-migrants.

294 "what she's doing": Ibid.

297 minus 12 points: "What Does America Think of Kamala Harris?" *The Los Angeles Times*, https://www.latimes.com/projects/kamala-harris-approval-rating-polls-vs-biden-other-vps/.

299 "if at all": Monica Hesse, "Kamala Harris knows things no vice president has ever known," *The Washington Post*, January 11, 2021, https://www.washingtonpost.com/lifestyle/style/kamala-harris-woman-vp/2021/01/11/54c398b2-4ea7-11eb-83e3-322644d82356_story.html.

307 replacing Democratic women: U.S. House election results, 2021.

310 gripped my attention instantly: https://www.youtube.com/watch?v=kY0KL-HFFHA.

314 policy brief stated: "COVID-19 and women's leadership: From an effective response to building back better," U.N. Women Policy Brief No. 18, 2020, 1–11, https://www.unwomen.org/sites/default/files

/Headquarters/Attachments/Sections/Library/Publications/2020
/Policy-brief-COVID-19-and-womens-leadership-en.pdf.

314 paltry 11 percent: Rachel B. Vogelstein and Alexandra Bro, "Women's Power Index," Council on Foreign Relations, March 29, 2021, https://www.cfr.org/article/womens-power-index.

315 the national legislature: Rachel B. Vogelstein and Alexandra Bro, "Women's Power Index," Council on Foreign Relations, March 29, 2021, https://www.cfr.org/article/womens-power-index.